The Fraud of the "Testament of _

Grover Furr

Based on the research of Valentin A. Sakharov

With chapters on Moshe Lewin's falsifications and
Leon Trotsky's lies

Erythros Press and Media, LLC
April 2022

The Fraud of the "Testament of Lenin"
April 2022

Published by Erythros Press and Media
PO Box 294994
Kettering, OH 45429-0994
media@erythrospress.com

© Grover Furr 2022

Published and printed with permission of the author, who assumes all responsibility for the content herein.

Locally Assigned LC-type Call Number DK254.L445 F87 2022

ISBN: 978-0-578-28499-6

319 pp. Includes index.

1. Lenin, Vladimir Il'ich 1870-1924 – Will. 2. Heads of State – Soviet Union – Biography. 3. Soviet Union – Politics and Government – 1917-1936. 4. Stalin, Joseph, 1878-1953. 5. Trotsky, Leon, 1879-1940. 6. Lewin, Moshe, 1921-2010

Table of Contents

Acknowledgements and Dedication 4
Introduction 5
Chapter 1. How Should We Reorganize the WPI? 12
Chapter 2. Letter to the Congress 19
Chapter 3. Letter to the Congress, Continued 67
Chapter 4. Letters to Trotsky and to Mdivani and Makharadze 88
Chapter 5. The Question of Nationalities 114
Chapter 6. The Ultimatum Letter 142
Chapter 7. Trotsky on the Testament 188
Chapter 8. Moshe Lewin 211
Chapter 9. Lidia Fotieva's Memoir 238
Chapter 10. The Diary of the Secretaries 247
Chapter 11. Ulyanova's statements 261
Chapter 12. Krupskaya 286
Chapter 13. Conclusion 301
Appendix: Ulyanova's letter to the Joint Plenum of the CC and the CCC, April, 1929 306
Bibliography and Illustrations 311
Index 314

Acknowledgements and Dedication

I wish to express my gratitude to Kevin Prendergast, Arthur Hudson – Arthur, may you enjoy your well-deserved retirement! -- and Siobhan McCarthy, the skilled and tireless Inter-Library Loan librarians at Harry S. Sprague Library, Montclair State University.

Without their help, my research would simply not be possible. With their continued help, I can persevere.

* * * * *

I would like to recognize Montclair State University for giving me a sabbatical leave in the fall semester of 2015, and special research travel funds in 2017, 2019, and 2020, which have been invaluable in my research on this book.

* * * * *

Dedication

I dedicate this book to my parents and grandparents: to: my father, Grover Carr Furr, Jr., my mother, Jacqueline Devine Kinney Furr, my maternal grandparents, Will Hoover Kinney and Josephine Devine Kinney, and my paternal grandparents, Grover Carr Furr, Sr., and Beulah Mae Little Furr.

Introduction

The canonical accounts of Lenin's last writings accept the version that Lenin left a "testament" that included a number of negative remarks about Joseph Stalin, and that Lenin wished to remove Stalin from the position of General Secretary of the All-Union Communist Party (bolshevik).[1] This version stems partly from Trotsky, who embraced it eagerly in his campaign to replace Stalin as Party leader; partly from Lenin's wife Nadezhda Konstantinovna Krupskaya; and partly from Nikita Khrushchev and the Khrushchev-era fifth and last edition of Lenin's works, the *Polnoe Sobranie Sochinenii* ("Complete Collection of Writings"), or PSS.

There is much confusion concerning just which of Lenin's last writings make up his "testament." As the reader of this book will discover, this is because the concept of a "testament of Lenin" was invented by others, not by Lenin, who never used the term and clearly was never aware that he left a "testament." Lenin made no "testament," as Nadezhda Krupskaya, his wife, admitted in 1925. Leon Trotsky admitted this too, although he later resurrected the claim that Lenin left a "testament" when, in exile from the Soviet Union, it seemed in his own interest to do so.

Throughout 1922 Lenin's health declined. In May 1922 he suffered his first stroke. By December 16, 1922, Lenin's muscular control was so impaired that he could no longer write. From this date until he became too ill to work at all Lenin had to dictate to a secretary – a task he found difficult.

---

[1] The official name of the Party until 1952; hereafter, "the Party" or "the Communist Party of the Soviet Union," or the CPSU. Until the formation of the Soviet Union in December, 1922, the Party's official name was the Russian Communist Party (bolshevik), or RKP(b).

As far as we can determine from the available records, Lenin never again met in person with any Party leaders after December 12, 1922. Only his wife Nadezhda Krupskaya, his sister Maria Il'inichna Ulyanova, the women in his secretariat, his doctors and his nurses visited him in person. None of the writings attributed to Lenin and dated after December 12, 1922, bear his personal, i.e. handwritten, signature or even his initials.

The Research of Valentin A. Sakharov

The present book is largely based on the research of Professor Valentin A. Sakharov of Moscow State University. His 2003 book, *Lenin's "Political Testament"*, published by Moscow State University Press,[2] is the result of years of access to and study of many of the archival copies of Lenin's works, drafts of those works, and originals of other important documents related to the question of Lenin's "testament."

Lenin's Last Writings

Because the concept of "Lenin's testament" originated after Lenin's death and was never clearly defined, there is disagreement over which documents attributed to Lenin should be considered a part of the "testament." Sakharov divides Lenin's last writings into two groups: those which are unproblematically Lenin's work, though dictated; and those that are attributed to Lenin but are of questionable authorship.

The texts whose authorship by Lenin is not doubted are:

* Notes On Gosplan: "Granting Legislative Functions To The State Planning Commission" Dated December 27, 1922 – CW 36, 598-602.

* The Beginning of the Development of the Reorganization Plan for the Central Committee and the People's Commissariat of the

---

[2] Sakharov, V.A. *"Politicheskoe zaveshchaniie" Lenina. Real'nost istorii is mify politiki.* (M: 2003).

Russian Republic (Addition to the Section on Increasing the Number of C.C. Members) December 29, 1922 – CW 36, 603-604.

* The Article "Pages From A Diary" – Title in English language edition is "On Education" – CW 33, 462-466.

* The "Article"[3] "On Cooperation" – CW 33, 467-475

* The "Article"[4] "Our Revolution (Apropos of N. Sukhanov's Notes)"– CW 33, 476-480

* The Original Version of the Article on the Reorganization of the CC of the RKP(b)

* "How We Should Reorganise the Wokers' and Peasants' Inspection" (19-23 January 1923) – CW 33, 481-486

* "Better Fewer, But Better" (end of January - beginning of March 1923) – CW 33, 487-502

The texts that raise doubts concerning Lenin's authorship are:

* "Letter to the Congress" (dictations of December 24-25, 1922) and "Addition to the Letter of December 24, 1922" dated January 4, 1923 – CW 36, 593-595; CW 36, 596.

* The Letter to Trotsky, March 5, 1923. – CW 45, 607

* The Letter to Mdivani and Makharadze, dated March 6, 1923. – CW 45, 607-8.

* The "Ultimatum Letter" to Stalin, dated March 5, 1923. CW 45, 607-8.

Sakharov discusses all these documents, including those whose authorship by Lenin is not contested. I will discuss only those documents whose authorship by Lenin is in doubt.

---

[3] Published as an article, but resembling notes.
[4] Published as an article, but resembling notes.

As a professor at Moscow State University Sakharov gained access to many – though far from all – of the originals of these primary documents from Lenin's secretariat, as well as other materials. At the time of this writing (March 2022) these documents are still not available to other researchers. Sakharov quotes extensively from many of these documents, describes others, and reproduces photographs of a few of the most important ones.

My Use of Sakharov's Book

Sakharov's book, 716 pages in length, is the basic source of the first six chapters of the present book.

In this book the numbers in parentheses after a passage in the text refer to pages of Sakharov's book. In many places I quote directly from this book. Where I have done so, the quotations are indented. In many other places I have paraphrased or summarized Sakharov's discussion. Quotations, paraphrases, and summary passages are always indicated by a page number in parentheses.

A translation into English of Sakharov's lengthy book would be a major undertaking and may never be done. Moreover, the Russian text is not organized in a way to make it easily understandable to a non-academic audience. For example, a given text may be discussed in several different parts of the book. The full impact of Sakharov's evidence and analysis is dissipated somewhat by the length and complexity of Sakharov's presentation.

In 2018 I decided to study Sakharov's book very closely. That study took me several years. It included making notes on long sections of the book and, when I felt it necessary, translating long sections word for word into English, just to make certain that I understood Sakharov's argument accurately. Once I had done all this it seemed to me to be more important than ever to write a shorter book for a broader audience – a book that would make Sakharov's excellent research widely available in a way that even a complete translation of his long and important Russian book might not.

Stephen Kotkin's Study of "The Testament of Lenin"

The present book also makes a number of references to Stephen Kotkin's book *Stalin. Paradoxes of Power, 1878-1928*. This is the first volume of Kotkin's projected three-volume biography of Stalin.[5] As I have sharply criticized Kotkin's second volume,[6] I will say a few words about this first volume.

This first volume does contain many problematic passages. For instance it contains plenty of gratuitous remarks that attest to Kotkin's anticommunism and his willingness at times to abandon any pretense at objectivity.

But Kotkin has clearly studied Sakharov's book with great care. He summarizes Sakharov's discussion well, and accepts Sakharov's conclusion that the anti-Stalin documents in Lenin's last works, the so-called "testament," are fabrications. Kotkin also makes some acute observations about Sakharov's analysis. This is why I cite Kotkin's discussion of the documents in the "testament" and their use in the political struggles of the 1920s.

However, Kotkin's remarks on the "testament" and its political use, and on Sakharov's analysis, are widely scattered throughout several hundred pages of his lengthy work. This makes any overall assessment of Sakharov's study inaccessible to any but the most dedicated and meticulous reader of Kotkin's book.

Kotkin also deploys Sakharov's conclusions – which he accepts – in order to promote his, Kotkin's, own notion that the struggle over the "testament" gave Stalin a sense of persecution and a suspiciousness that either created or at least strengthened a

---

[5] At the time I write this, July 2021, Kotkin's third volume has not yet been published

[6] Grover Furr. *Stalin. Waiting for ... the Truth. Exposing the Falsehoods in Stephen Kotkin's Stalin. Waiting for Hitler, 1929-1941*. New York: Red Star Publishers, 2019.

supposed paranoia that "explains," for Kotkin, Stalin's alleged persecution and murders of real and suspected oppositionists during the 1930s. The attempt to apply notions derived from psychoanalysis to account for the behavior of historical figures is called "psychohistory." Robert Tucker, Kotkin's mentor at Princeton University, avidly practiced this kind of pseudo-history in his own "psychohistorical" biography of Stalin.[7] Kotkin's application of this nonsense is on full display in the second volume of his Stalin biography *Stalin. Waiting for Hitler, 1929-1941* (2017). I have exposed Kotkin's falsifications in *Stalin. Waiting for ... the Truth* (2020).

So Kotkin abuses Sakharov's excellent analysis and conclusions, bending them to his own purposes. Nevertheless, Kotkin has studied Sakharov carefully and understands him well. Some of his remarks are acute and useful.

The Gorbunov-Fotieva-Glyasser "Commission"

I discuss the report of this "commission" in Chapter 4 of the present book. The archival files of this "commission" have not been published. As far as I am aware Professor Sakharov is the only person to have studied them in detail. For this reason my account of this "commission" consists largely of Sakharov's account in English translation. In his book *Stalin. Paradoxes of Power 1878-1928* Stephen Kotkin also draws his account of the "commission" from Sakharov's book.

The account of this "commission" in Vladen T. Loginov, in his book *Lenin. Sim pobedishi*, pages 465-471 (PDF edition) is taken from official sources such as the PSS and volume 12 of the multivolume *Biograficheskaia khronika* (Biographic chronicle) of Lenin's life. It contains no references to the actual documents of the "commission," and I do not cite it.

---

[7] Robert C. Tucker. *Stalin as revolutionary, 1879-1929 : a study in history and personality*. New York: W.W. Norton, 1973.

The Procedure in This Book

Page numbers in parentheses alone – e.g., (314) – are pages in Sakharov's book.

Page numbers of other works are identified by the author's last name plus the page number, all in parentheses: e.g. (Kotkin 314).

Volume and page numbers to the 5th Russian edition of Lenin's works, the *Polnoe Sobranie Sochinenii* (PSS), are identified by the volume in Roman numerals followed by the page number, all in parentheses: e.g. (XLV 344).

Volume and page numbers to the 4th English edition of Lenin's work are identified by the letters "CW", for collected works, followed by the volume in Arabic numbers and page numbers: e.g. (CW 42, 250).

The text of the Doctor's Journal – "Dnevnik dezhurnogo vracha V.I. Lenina v 1922-1923 gg." is cited by the journal and page number. E.g. *Voprosy Istorii KPSS* 9 (1991), 45; *Kentavr* Okt-Dek 1991, 112.

The English language translation of the text of the Secretaries Journal – "Journal of Lenin's Duty Secretaries November 21, 1922 – March 6, 1923" – is cited as "SJ" in the text or as "CW 42" plus a page number, in parentheses: (CW 42, 475).

The Russian text of the Secretaries Journal – "Dnevnik dezhurykh sekretarei V.I. Lenina 21 noiabria 1922 g. – 6 marta 1923 g." is abbreviated in the text as "SJ" and cited as the volume number of the PSS, in this case, XLV, plus the page number, all in parentheses: (XLV 460).

I have occasionally referred to the Secretaries Journal (SJ) as "Diary of Duty Secretaries" when the "diary format" is specifically under discussion.

Chapter 1. How Should We Reorganize the WPI?

The latest and last Soviet edition of Lenin's works is the *Polnoe Sobranie Sochinenii* (PSS). In this edition the next-to-last paragraph in the article "How We Should Reorganise the Workers' And Peasants' Inspection" of January, 1923, reads as follows:

> Our Central Committee has grown into a strictly centralised and highly authoritative group, but the conditions under which this group is working are not commensurate with its authority. The reform I recommend should help to remove this defect, and the members of the Central Control Commission, whose duty it will be to attend all meetings of the Political Bureau in a definite number, will have to form a compact group which should not allow anybody's authority without exception, **neither that of the General Secretary** [*gensec* in the Russian original] **nor of any other member of the Central Committee**, to prevent them from putting questions, verifying documents, and, in general, from keeping themselves fully informed of all things and from exercising the strictest control over the proper conduct of affairs. (XLV 387; CW 33. 485)

This "Gensec" (= General Secretary) passage highlighted above was not present in any edition of this article of Lenin's until the publication of volume XLV of the PSS in 1970. What is going on here?

The article was printed in *Pravda* on January 25, 1923. Presumably, therefore, Lenin completed work on it in the 45-minute long dictation mentioned in the Doctors Journal for January 23:

Chapter One. How Should We Reorganize the WPI?

> 23 января. Спал Владимир Ильич после 2-х таблеток сомиацетина с 11 до 4-х часов. Проснулся, снова принял 2 таблетки, почти тотчас же заснул и спал до 9 часов с четвертью. Проснулся в хорошем настроении. Было сделано обтирание. Завтракал с аппетитом. Утром диктовал 45 мин. стенографистке(50) и читал. Врачи видели Владимира Ильича в половине второго. Настроение хорошее, голова свежая и не болит. После обеда Владимир Ильич спал 1 час. Чувствовал себя удовлетворительно. Читал.[1]

> [translated]

> January 23. Vladimir Ilyich slept after 2 tablets of somiacetin from 11 to 4 o'clock. He woke up, took 2 pills again, fell asleep almost immediately and slept until a quarter past 9 o'clock. He woke up in a good mood. His rubdown was done. He ate breakfast with gusto. In the morning he dictated for 45 minutes to a stenographer (50) and read. The doctors saw Vladimir Ilyich at half past one. His mood was good, his head fresh and did not ache. After lunch, Vladimir Ilyich slept for 1 hour. He felt satisfactory. He read.

Sakharov has inspected the archival copies of this article.

> The final version of the article was represented by four typewritten copies. All of them are dated January 23, 1923. The date is typewritten, executed simultaneously with the text of the article. One of them was registered when it arrived at the Lenin archive on March 10, 1923 (delo 42, b/No.) [960]. On each of them, before the text of the article, is printed: "Published in Pravda on 25.1.23, in No. 16."

---

[1] *Voprosy Istorii KPSS* 9, 1991, p. 50

There is good evidence that Lenin read this article as printed.

> One of them (the second) has holes in the upper margin, made by a hole punch, thanks to which the sheets were affixed to a special folder to make it easier for Lenin to work with. This indicates that this copy was printed before the article was sent by Lenin for publication, and that he was acquainted with this text. This is confirmed by the note stored with this article, which Volodicheva wrote for M.I. Ulyanova: "Please alert Vladimir Il'ich that the entire article is attached to one folder from beginning to end."
>
> There are also two copies of the pages of this article and two copies of newspaper clippings (Pravda, January 25, 1923) with the article "How to reorganize the WPI" (strips of newspaper sheets with text pasted on sheets of paper). One newspaper version of the article also has holes in the upper margin from the punch, which suggests that Lenin read them. (299)

This seems to clinch the issue. Lenin either did read the printed version of his article, or, in any case, there was a presumption that he would read it. If Lenin had inserted the passage about the General Secretary and then had seen that it had been taken out, he would surely have complained, and some record of his complaint would remain.

If Stalin – for the absence of this passage in earlier editions was conveniently and without any evidence whatsoever blamed on Stalin – had arranged this, he would have taken a terrible chance. But there is no evidence that Stalin interfered in any way with the publication of this or of any of Lenin's articles.

On January 10, 1924, in the transcript of a Party conference near Moscow, Timofei V. Sapronov, a Left Oppositionist who until recently had been a C.C. member, testified that this article of Lenin's had been "printed without changes" and stated that "the Politburo did not change anything."

> САПРОНОВ: Я, товарищи, не понимаю этого вопроса.
>
> * Статья была напечатана без изменения?
>
> САПРОНОВ: Да, без изменения. Политбюро не изменило ничего. (Izv TsK 11, 1989, p. 186)

[translated]

> SAPRONOV: Comrades, I do not understand this question.
>
> * Was the article printed unchanged?
>
> SAPRONOV: Yes, without change. The Politburo changed nothing.

Sakharov has also discovered the source of the version of Lenin's article with the "gensec" passage.

> In addition to the archive file (No. 23543), in which the texts of the article discussed above are stored, it turns out that there is another one (No. 24821), in which are stored three texts of the article "How to reorganize Rabkrin." All of them differ from the variants of the article in file No. 23543 in that they do contain the thesis about the General Secretary. At the same time, they differ, firstly, in the dating and, secondly, in a different way of including the thesis of the General Secretary in the text. Two (l. 1-5, 5-10) are dated January 22, the third (l. 11-15) - January 23. This last one has a typewritten mark on the first page about the publication of an article in *Pravda* on January 25 and is not fundamentally different from texts dated January 23 stored in file No. 23543. Therefore, we can talk about the existence of two versions of the text of the article containing the thesis about the General Secretary.

In the texts dated January 22, the words about the General Secretary are typewritten, i.e. are an integral part of the article. They are not there in the text dated January 23. However there is a handwritten insert in it: after the words "no one's authority" above the line there is, in clear handwriting and in small letters: "neither that of the General Secretary nor of anyone," and in the margin before the beginning of the same line is the inscription, which, apparently, is a continuation of the previous one (the first part is difficult to read) and can be understood as: "of other members of the Central Committee" [abbreviated – GF]. The whole insert looks like this: "neither the General secretary, nor any of the others [other] [members] of the Central Committee."

...

Material on the history of the creation of this article captures the different stages of work on it, as well as its organic connection with Lenin's documents of the previous period. These circumstances, as well as the time of its publication — during the period when Lenin still had the ability to work — and the fact of his acquaintance with the newspaper text serve as sufficient grounds for recognizing Lenin's authorship of the version in which there is *no* warning of the danger posed to the TsKK from the General secretary of the Central Committee of the RCP(b). (301, 303-4)

Photographic copies of a page from one of the typed archival copies of the article and of the proofs of the article as published in *Pravda*, along with a reproduction of the paragraph of one of the "gensec" drafts with the handwritten "gensec" passage inserted above the typed line, are reproduced in Sakharov's book.[2]

---

[2] See illustration 4.

Chapter One. How Should We Reorganize the WPI?

Since the printed version as it appeared in *Pravda* was sent to Lenin with the expectation that he would read it, it is clear that Lenin did not write the "gensec" passage. The available evidence suggests that Maria Akimovna Volodicheva, one of Lenin's secretaries, was a participant in this forgery. She wrote the note that supports the deduction that the article as written by Lenin did not contain the "gensec" passage:

> This is confirmed by the note stored with this article, which Volodicheva wrote for M.I. Ulyanova: "Please alert Vladimir Il'ich that the entire article is attached to one folder from beginning to end." (299)

But it appears that Volodicheva was also a party to the insertion of the "gensec" passage. One of the texts that does contain the "gensec" passage,

> dated January 22, contains a handwritten note in the upper left corner of the first sheet: "Without the corrections made in the two accurate (the italicized word is read with difficulty. – V.S.) copies." The record, judging by the handwriting and characteristic signature, was made by M.V. Volodicheva. (301)

The variation in the dating of the "gensec" documents between January 22 and January 23 suggests the possibility that the January 22 date was inserted later – perhaps much later. This, however, would make little sense. Once Lenin's article was published, and, as is probable, Lenin had seen the printed version, why add the "gensec" passage to a draft and then hiding it away? Most likely, therefore, Volodicheva inserted the "gensec" passage on January 22, before the article was sent off to be printed.

But Volodicheva was not an independent political actor. She was just one of Lenin's secretaries. She could not have concocted this forgery scheme herself. Moreover, this is not the only example of falsification of Lenin's last writings. As we shall see, there are many more falsifications of important documents supposedly from Lenin.

Who had put Volodicheva up to this? Only one person in Lenin's secretariat, aside from Lenin himself, had the authority to instruct the secretaries: Lenin's wife, Nadezhda Krupskaya.

This issue – the aborted insertion of this "anti-gensec" passage into a January, 1923 article by Lenin – is important because it constitutes solid evidence that the charge that Lenin's last writings had been falsified is not just a hypothesis of Sakharov's. *Real falsification* was taking place. Moreover, it is solid evidence that the falsification was happening *in Lenin's own secretariat.*

It is important that we know that Krupskaya was responsible here. It turns out that she was the central figure in yet more, and much more significant, falsifications of Lenin's last writings.

All of the documents in Lenin's last writings that have an anti-Stalin tendency were put into circulation long after the dates on the documents. All of them were put into circulation by Krupskaya. We shall see that the explanation that Lenin had wanted to delay publication of these documents was made at a time when he was incapable of taking any action whatsoever, when he could no longer even speak.

Chapter 2. Letter to the Congress

> Few issues in soviet history involved more intrigue than Lenin's so-called testament, which is dated to December 1922-January 1923, but which, as we shall see, Lenin might not have dictated at that time—contrary to entrenched scholarship—or even dictated at all.
>
> – Stephen Kotkin, Stalin. Volume 1. *Paradoxes of Power* 1878 – 1928, 418.

The first document conventionally classified as part of the "Letter to the Congress" (L2C) is dated December 23, 1922. (XLV 343-4; CW 36, 593-4) Sakharov notes:

> The dictation on December 23 has never attracted the proper attention of traditional historiography, perhaps because the questions posed in it received more extensive development in subsequent dictations, and the history of its creation seemed very clear. It is traditionally considered that this is the first part of the "Letter to the Congress" (278)

"Traditionally" – but not originally. In fact, not until the "Khrushchev" edition in the journal *Kommunist*, no. 9, 1956, pages 16-17. Sakharov points out that

> in the Bulletin (30) of the XV Congress of the CPSU(b) the texts of the "Letter to the Congress" (also known as the "testament") – the "Characteristics" and "Addition" to them – were published without the dictation of December 23, which is now [since Khrushchev, 1956] considered to be the first part of the "Letter to the Congress." (279)

The XV Party Congress was held from December 2 – 19, 1927. The English language Wikipedia page on "Lenin's Testament" states

> The full English text of Lenin's testament was published as part of an article by Eastman that appeared in *The New York Times* in 1926.[1]

That is not true. This version, which was transmitted to the *Times* by Max Eastman, does not contain the document dated December 23, 1922. We know that Eastman obtained his text of the "testament" indirectly from Lenin's wife Nadezhda Krupskaya. Therefore, Krupskaya did not include the December 23, 1922 document as part of the "Letter to the Congress" when she passed it to the oppositionist, who then took it to France, where Eastman obtained it.

This history just serves to deepen the mystery of the document of December 23, 1922.

The Secretaries Journal (CW 42, 481; XLV 474) has an entry by Volodicheva in which she claims that Lenin had dictated to her:

> 23 декабря (запись М. А. Володичевой).
>
> В начале 9-го Владимир Ильич вызывал на квартиру. В продолжение 4-х минут диктовал. Чувствовал себя плохо. Были врачи. Перед тем, как начать диктовать, сказал: «Я хочу Вам продиктовать письмо к съезду. Запишите!». Продиктовал быстро, но болезненное состояние его чувствовалось. По окончании спросил, которое число. Почему такая бледная, почему не на съезде, пожалел, что отнимает время, которое я могла бы пробыть там. Никаких распоряжений я не получила больше. (XLV, 474)
>
> December 23 (entry by M. A. Volodicheva).
>
> A little after 8 Vladimir Ilyich called me to his flat. In the course of 4 minutes he dictated. Felt bad. Doctors

---

[1] https://en.wikipedia.org/wiki/Lenin%27s_Testament#Document_history, at note 4.

> called. Before starting to dictate, he said: "I want to dictate to you a letter to the congress. Take it down". Dictated quickly, but his sick condition was obvious. Towards the end he asked what the date was. Why was I so pale, why wasn't I at the congress, was sorry that he was taking up the time that I could have spent there. I received no more orders. (CW 42, 481)

This entry is confusing. The "congress" mentioned twice here – because Lenin (supposedly) asked Volodicheva why she was not attending it – must be the 8th All-Russian Congress of Soviets, which met in the Bolshoi Theater from December 23- 27, 1922.[2] There is no clear reference to the next *Party* Congress, the twelfth.[3]

A second problem is the date of this entry. The entry in SJ for the following day, December 24, begins this way:

> 24 декабря (запись М. А. Володичевой).
>
> На следующий день (24 декабря) ...
>
> December 24 (entry by M. A. Volodicheva).
>
> Next day (December 24) ...
>
> (XLV, 474; CW 42, 482)

The phrase "next day" means that the entry for December 23, as well as that of December 24, was not entered in real time – on that day – but at some later time. That is, this journal is no longer a "diary" of daily entries, but something else, with at least the entries like this one composed and entered later for some reason.

---

[2] See https://en.wikipedia.org/wiki/All-Russian_Congress_of_Soviets#Tenth_Congress

[3] Adding to the confusion, the Russian language has no articles – no "a / an" or "the." So *pis'mo k s"ezdu* can mean "letter to a congress" or "letter to the congress. Even if we assume that Lenin meant "the congress" the text does not tell us *which* congress.

A third problem is the following. The Doctors Journal states that on December 23, 1922, around 8:30 p.m.,

> ... Vladimir Ilyich asked permission to dictate to a stenographer for 5 minutes, as he was concerned about one question and is afraid that he will not fall asleep. This was allowed him, after which Vladimir Ilyich calmed down considerably.[4]

It is hard to imagine that a letter the length of this document – 228 words – could have been dictated by Lenin in five minutes or, as Volodicheva claimed, in *four* minutes. This is especially improbable since Lenin was not used to dictation and had trouble with it. We will discuss Lenin's problems with dictation shortly.

Sakharov has discovered that there are *two* drafts of this letter and that they differ significantly. A typed draft is initialed by Volodicheva. But a handwritten draft also exists, in the handwriting of Nadezhda S. Allilueva, one of the duty secretaries in Lenin's secretariat and Stalin's wife.[5]

Photographic reproductions of the parts of both drafts that are under discussion here are in Sakharov's book (plates between pages 352 and 353).[6]

The version of this letter in the official English translation of Lenin's works is as follows:

I

LETTER TO THE CONGRESS

> I would urge strongly that at this Congress a number of changes be made in our political structure. I want to tell

---

[4] *Voprosy Istorii KPSS* 9 (1991), 45.
[5] According to Sakharov, 278, the entry in the journal of outgoing mail is also in Allilueva's handwriting.
[6] See illustrations #1 and #1a.

you of the considerations to which I attach most importance.

At the head of the list I set an increase in the number of Central Committee members to a few dozen or even a hundred. It is my opinion that without this reform our Central Committee would be in great danger if the course of events were not quite favourable for us (and that is something we cannot count on).

Then, I intend to propose that the Congress should on certain conditions invest the decisions of the State Planning Commission with legislative force, meeting, in this respect, the wishes of Comrade Trotsky—to a certain extent and on certain conditions.

As for the first point, i.e., increasing the number of C.C. members, I think it must be done in order to raise the prestige of the Central Committee, to do a thorough job of improving our administrative machinery and to prevent conflicts between small sections of the C.C. from acquiring excessive importance for the future of the Party.

It seems to me that our Party has every right to demand from the working class 50 to 100 C.C. members, and that it could get them from it without unduly taxing the resources of that class.

Such a reform would considerably increase the stability of our Party and ease its struggle in the encirclement of hostile states, which, in my opinion, is likely to, and must, become much more acute in the next few years. I think that the stability of our Party would gain a thousandfold by such a measure.

Lenin

December 23, 1922

Taken down by M. V.[7]

According to Sakharov, who had access to the journal of outgoing mail of Lenin's secretariat,[8] Lenin's letter was registered on the same day as it was written, December 23, in Allilueva's handwriting, as follows: "Stalinu (pis'mo V.I. k s"ezdu)" – "To Stalin (letter of V.I. to a/the congress." (278) So Allilueva, or whoever made this entry, stated plainly that the letter was indeed addressed to Stalin. And *that* suggests that "k s"ezdu" means *"for a/the congress,"* "in preparation for a/the congress," rather than "to a/the congress."

The Differences in the Two Versions[9]

The manuscript version has the underlined title: "Letter to a/the Congress"[10] (*Pis'mo k s"ezdu*) and the underlined notation "Strictly secret" (*Strogo sekretno*) at the upper right. This notation is lacking in the typewritten version and in the Soviet-era publications of the letter.

Both versions use the familiar term for you – "Vy," with a capital "V" – **Вы**. This means that the letter is to an individual, not to a group, and therefore *not* "to the Congress." The contents of the letter suggest that in it Lenin is presenting suggestions to the Secretariat, whose job it was to prepare the Congress, and therefore to Stalin, who was General Secretary. This agrees with Allilueva's annotation in the journal of outgoing mail.

The fact that this letter was not intended for delegates to a party Congress but to an individual means that Volodicheva's statement in the Secretaries Journal is false.

> On the one hand, she wrote in the "Diary of the duty secretaries" that Lenin, starting the dictation, said: "I

---

[7] CW 36, 593-4; XLV 343-4.
[8] Identified by Sakharov, 272, as RGASPI F. 5 Op. 4. D. 1. (РГАСПИ. Ф. 5. Оп. 4. Д. 1.).
[9] At this point the reader should study the reproductions, which I have taken from Sakharov's book.
[10] Hereafter we will refer to the document as "Letter to the Congress" or L2C.

want to dictate to you a letter to the congress. Take it down!" But on the other hand, she seemingly did not think that she was writing a letter for the congress delegates. Otherwise, she would not have sent it to Stalin. It turns out that, on the one hand, she knew that Lenin was addressing the congress, and on the other, she did not know about this. (281)

In 1963 an aged Volodicheva told Genrikh Volkov that Lenin had not told her what to do with this "letter to the congress," so she asked Fotieva, who told her to show it to Stalin.[11] That means that Lenin did not give any instructions concerning what to do with this dictation.

And this contradicts Lidia Fotieva's letter of December 29, 1922, which we discuss below. It also fails to account for the textual issues, which show that this letter was originally *addressed* to an individual, personally. Since it was sent to Stalin, we can assume that it was meant for him, and that is confirmed by the handwritten version. This has important implications for the study of the L2C.

Recognition of the fact that this letter was not intended for delegates of a party congress, but sent to one of the leaders of the Central Committee, most likely Stalin, makes the conclusion inevitable: **Fotieva's and Volodicheva's "testimonies" are false with all the ensuing consequences for source study and historiography.** (283-4)

The change in the treatment formula from "You" singular [Вы] to "you" plural [вы] was made only when the letter was published in the Complete Works of V.I. Lenin. Formerly, in the journal *Kommunist*

---

[11] Volkov, "Stenografistka Il'icha." *Sovetskaia Kul'tura* January 21, 1989, page 3. See illustration #12.

(1956, No. 9), in volume 36 of the 4th edition of the collected works of V.I. Lenin, as well as in the transcript of the XIII Congress of the RCP(b), this fragment of the text was reproduced correctly.[12] This indicates that the "revision" of Lenin's texts was made in the period of the formation of the "Khrushchev" historiography of Lenin's testament, when the myth of Lenin's "Letter to the Congress" was introduced into historical science and public consciousness, which was supposed to serve as an important component part of the campaign of criticism of the "personality cult" of Stalin. (288)

Fotieva's Letter to Kamenev

On December 29, 1922, Fotieva wrote to Kamenev:

> 29 / XII-22. Com[rade] Stalin on Saturday 23 / XII was given a letter from Vladimir Ilyich to the Congress, written down by Volodicheva. Meanwhile, after the letter was handed over, it became clear that Vladimir Ilyich's will was that this letter be kept strictly secret in the archive, that it could be unsealed only by him or Nadezhda Konstantinovna Krupskaya, Lenin's wife, and should have been presented to anyone only after his death. Vladimir Ilyich is fully confident that he said this to Volodicheva while dictating the letter. Today, 29 / XII, Vladimir Ilyich summoned me to his place and asked if the corresponding note had been made on the letter and repeated that the letter should be read out only in case of his death. Taking into account the health of Vladimir Ilyich, I did not find it possible to tell him that a mistake had been made and reassured him that the letter was unknown to anyone and that his will had been fulfilled.

---

[12] I have verified in the version in *Kommunist* 9, 1956.

Chapter Two. Letter to the Congress

> I ask the comrades who have become aware of this letter, under no circumstances, during future meetings with Vladimir Ilyich, to reveal the mistake made, giving him no reason to assume that the letter is known, and I ask you to look at this letter as a record of the opinion of Vladimir Ilyich, which nobody would have to know.
>
> 29 / XII — 22 L. Fotieva[13]

Sakharov notes the problems, both formal and in content, with this text.

> First, if we proceed from the assumption that Lenin addressed the party congress, then the conclusion is inevitable that Lenin wanted to bring this question to the congress without any preparation during the pre-congress discussion, bypassing the party's Central Committee, and also setting himself against it. Such an assumption contradicts the tradition of congress preparation, as well as Lenin's well-known views on the role and role of the Party's Central Committee — the board of its most experienced and authoritative members, whose authority should be protected as one of the most important conditions for its success. Second, it is not clear why Lenin, having dictated a clear text, could not give more or less clear instructions as to his purpose. (281)

This letter raises other problems too:

---

[13] Izv TsK KPSS 1, 1990, 157. Sakharov's reference (696 note 16) is incorrect. This letter has been transcribed with a photographic reproduction of each page of the original, at the Russian Archive site:
http://lenin.rusarchives.ru/dokumenty/pismo-la-fotievoy-lb-kamenevu-ob-oshibochnoy-otpravke-leninskogo-pisma-k-sezdu-v

* If the December 23 letter was sent to Stalin – Fotieva says it was, and the handwritten version confirms this – why did she send this December 29 letter to Kamenev?

* The December 29 letter has a number of notes on it by the persons who saw it: by Stalin, who evidently passed it to Trotsky, who states that he "of course" did not give it to anyone else. [14]

* In his reply – not to Fotieva but to Stalin – Kamenev states that he showed Fotieva's letter only "to those members of the C.C. who had been acquainted with the contents of Vladimir Il'ich's letter," and names Trotsky, Bukharin, and Ordzhonikidze.

> «т[ов.] Л.А. Фотиева явилась ко мне сего 29/XII в 23 ч[аса] и сначала устно, а затем письменно сделала вышеизложенное заявление. Я считаю нужным познакомить с ним тех членов ЦК, которые узнали содержание письма Владимира Ильича (мне известно, что с содержанием его знакомы т.т. Троцкий, Бухарин, Орджоникидзе и ты). Я не говорил никому ни словом, ни намеком об этом письме. Полагаю, что также поступили и все вышеназванные товарищи. Если же кто-либо из них поделился с другими членами ЦК содержанием письма, то до сведения соответствующих товарищей должно быть доведено и это заявление т. Фотиевой.
>
> Л. Каменев».
>
> Помета И.В. Сталина: «Читал. Сталин. Только т. Троцкому».

---

[14] This is indicated in a note below the text of the letter (see previous footnote). A facsimile of the letter itself, with the remarks on it, is on the following page (158). A much clearer facsimile, together with a transcription, is the one at the Russian archives site (see previous footnote).

Chapter Two. Letter to the Congress

> Помета Л.Д. Троцкого: «Читал. О письме Владимира Ильича разумеется никому из цекистов не рассказывал. Л. Троцкий».

"Com. L.A. Fotieva came to me on 29/12 at 11 pm and first orally and then in writing made the above statement. I consider it necessary to show it to those members of the Central Committee who have learned the content of Vladimir Ilyich's letter (I know that Comrades Trotsky, Bukharin, Ordzhonikidze and you are familiar with its content). I did not tell anyone either a word or a hint about this letter. I believe that all the above-named comrades did the same. If any of them shared the contents of the letter with other members of the Central Committee, then this statement by Comrade Fotieva should also be brought to the attention of the respective comrades.

L. Kamenev".

Note by I.V. Stalin: "I read it. Stalin. Only to Comrade Trotsky."

Note by L. D. Trotsky: "I read it. Of course, I did not tell any of the Central Committee members about Vladimir Ilyich's letter. L. Trotsky "[15]

Who showed the letter, or summarized its contents, to Bukharin and Ordzhonikidze? *Why* did they do it? We don't know.

* Sakharov notes a number of other formal problems with this letter:

> ... why did Kamenev know about informing Bukharin and Ordzhonikidze, but Stalin and Trotsky did not? It is not clear how Kamenev had it, if Stalin assures us that he spoke of it only to Trotsky.

---

[15] Izv TsK KPSS 1 (1990) 157, 159.

> If Kamenev did receive the letter, then it means that only Volodicheva could have given him the text. Why [did she do this]?
>
> It is also noteworthy that the letter of Fotieva to Kamenev is not registered anywhere - neither as an outgoing nor as an incoming document. The original letter is an autograph. The date "23 / XII" in the first row is inserted on top. (282)[16]

These details can be seen in the Rusarchives facsimile.

> It would be possible to pass by this if it were not for the circumstances in which the letter appeared in the materials of the Secretariat of Lenin — it arrived there 19 years after the events described. On the back of it there is an inscription: "entered the Archive on October 1941." (282)

It is clear that the letter of December 23, 1922, was intended for an individual – "Vy" instead of "vy" – not for a Party Congress. That fact alone removes any possibility that it was intended to be "presented only after his death." It is apparently a number of suggestions that Lenin wanted to submit for consideration *at* the next Party Congress, but not a letter *to* the Party Congress.

But then, what's going on? Why did Fotieva write this letter to Kamenev? Whatever the reason, it must be related to the repurposing of the letter as the first part of what later came to be called the "Letter to the Congress."

In short, a conspiracy was under way to create a "letter to the congress" by Lenin composed of various elements not originally written together and – as we shall see – not all written by Lenin. This conspiracy had been set in motion by December 29, 1922, the date of Fotieva's letter to Kamenev, but had *not* been underway on

---

[16] Sakharov adds that Stalin's signature under the mark made by him looks unusual: the inscription of the letter "t" does not resemble his usual signatures.

Chapter Two. Letter to the Congress

December 23, 1922, when the first document was dictated by Lenin and sent to Stalin.

More Significant Differences between the Two Versions

In the typewritten version of Lenin's letter the fourth paragraph reads like this:

> Then, I intend to propose that the Congress should on certain conditions invest the decisions of the State Planning Commission with legislative force, meeting, in this respect, the wishes of Comrade Trotsky—*to a certain extent and on certain conditions.*

The handwritten version of the letter omits the italicized words. But there is a problem with both versions, because there is no evidence of any concession by Lenin to Trotsky. We don't even know what "meeting ... the wishes of Comrade Trotsky ..." refers to!

On December 24 and 26, Trotsky wrote two letters to the C.C. detailing his proposal, among other things, to merge the State Planning Commission and the Supreme Economic Council, and suggested himself as the person in charge.[17] Lenin politely but firmly rejected Trotsky's suggestions in his essay of December 27, "Granting Legislative Functions to the State Planning Commission."[18]

Fates or "Judges"?

In the *typewritten* version the fifth paragraph reads as follows: in Russian:

> Что касается до первого пункта, т. е. до увеличения числа членов ЦК, то я думаю, что такая вещь нужна и для поднятия авторитета ЦК,

---

[17] Sakharov publishes these two letters on pages 653-8. I have not been able to find them published anywhere else.
[18] CW 36, 598-602; XLV 340-353.

и для серьезной работы по улучшению нашего аппарата, и для предотвращения того, чтобы конфликты небольших частей ЦК могли получить слишком непомерное значение **для *всех судеб*** партии.

A literal English translation:

> As for the first point, i.e., increasing the number of C.C. members, I think it must be done in order to raise the prestige of the Central Committee, to do a thorough job of improving our administrative machinery and to prevent conflicts between small sections of the C.C. from acquiring excessive importance **for *all the fates*** of the Party.

The boldface italicized words make no more sense in Russian than they do in English. The translators of Lenin's Collected Works in English (4th edition) translate this way:

> ... from acquiring excessive importance ***for the future*** of the Party.

The translators were guessing. They too did not know what "for all the fates of the Party" means. However, the handwritten version of the Lenin letter is different:

> ... для ***всех «судей»*** партии.
>
> ... for ***all the "judges"*** of the Party.

"All the fates" is incoherent. But the meaning of "all the 'judges'" – the quotation marks are in the original (consult the plate) – is clear.

> Since the word "judges" is used in quotation marks, we are entitled to assume that Lenin used it figuratively and did not recognize the right of these people to judge the party. What are these "judges of the Party"? These are the real political forces that "judged" (i.e., condemned, criticized) the party and its

Chapter Two. Letter to the Congress 33

policies. Trotsky was the most "famous" critic who created the most problems for Lenin. There were others, lesser ones: the "Workers' Opposition," the "Decists" (Democratic Centralists), Bukharin, Preobrazhensky and many others. Of course, with respect to these critics of the party, the word "judges" could only be used in quotes, i.e. figuratively, as it is used in the text of the letter to Stalin.

Lenin fought constantly with such "judges," i.e. critics. The controversy with them is a red thread through many texts of Lenin's last letters and articles. For example, in the record of December 26, we meet the following rebuke: "That is why those "critics" who point to the defects of our administrative machinery out of mockery or malice may be calmly answered that they do not in the least understand the conditions of the revolution today."[19] In the texts about the State Planning Committee, Lenin objects to critics of the existing system of organizing the work of the State Planning Committee. He argues with the same "critics" ("party judges") - "our Sukhanovs" - in the article "On our revolution"[20]. In the article "How to reorganize The Workers and Peasants Inspectorate" he disputes those critics-judges who do not believe in the possibility and necessity of reorganizing the RKI, and in the article "Better Fewer But Better" he argues with those who do not believe in the possibility of combining study with work, and so forth.

Thus, there is no sense in the version of the text with "all the fates" of the party, but in the version with "judges" there is a clear meaning. The "'judges of the

---

[19] XLV 347; CW 36, 596.
[20] XLV 378-82; CW 33, 476-480. Lenin does use the phrase "our Sukhanovs" (XLV 381; CW 33, 480).

party" are its critics, with whom Lenin constantly fought, including in his last works. (285-6)

There is another important difference between the handwritten and the typed versions of this letter. In the second to last paragraph of the *handwritten* version we read:

> Мне думается, что 50-100 членов ЦК нашей партии вправе требовать от рабочего класса ... (XLV, 343)

> I believe that 50-100 members of the C.C. of our Party have every right to demand from the working class ...

The *typewritten* version reads differently:

> Мне думается, что 50—100 членов ЦК наша партия вправе требовать от рабочего класса ...

> It seems to me that our Party has every right to demand from the working class 50 to 100 C.C. members ... (CW 36, 593)

Either the C.C. demands the help of the Party, or the Party demands the help of the workers. But Lenin could not have been proposing non-Party workers to enter the C.C. *Therefore, only the handwritten version, not the typewritten version, makes sense.* The purpose, after all, is to

> ... и для поднятия авторитета ЦК, и для серьезной работы по улучшению нашего аппарата, и для предотвращения того, чтобы конфликты небольших частей ЦК могли получить слишком непомерное значение ...(XLV 343)

> ... raise the prestige of our Central Committee, to do a thorough job of improving our administrative machinery and to prevent conflicts between small sections of the C.C. from acquiring excessive importance ...

Chapter Two. Letter to the Congress

We have already determined that the letter cannot be an appeal to the Congress anyway, since it is address to an individual: "You" instead of "you." Moreover, the handwritten version is consistent with an appeal to an individual, probably Stalin, to present this proposal to the C.C., and for the C.C. to appeal to the Party Congress to increase the number of workers in the C.C. from among communist workers who were Party members.

The last difference between the two letters is as follows. The final sentence of the handwritten version reads "... thanks to **this** measure ..." ("... благодаря **этой** мере ..."), while the typed version says "... **such** a measure ..." ("... благодаря **такой** мере ..."). "This" is much more specific than "such;" "such" a measure could encompass things that Lenin did not intend, while "this" means "what Lenin has proposed."

From all this, Sakharov concludes (and we agree) that *the primary version of this letter is clearly the handwritten one, and it was addressed to an individual* – almost certainly to Stalin, to whom it was in fact sent. (287) But the version published during the Khrushchev period and since is the typewritten version. As we have seen, *this version also removes the heading "Strictly secret." Doing so makes it possible to claim that the letter is not for an individual but for a collective, like the Party Congress.*

By comparing the print versions of this letter Sakharov has discovered that the change from "You" to "you" (Вы – вы, singular to plural) was made only in the PSS (Complete works, also known as the 5th edition).[21] This alteration, at least, can be associated with Khrushchev's attack on the "cult of personality" of Stalin beginning with his "Secret Speech" at the XX Party Congress in February, 1956.

---

[21] PSS XLV 343-4.

Conclusion

We can't determine today what the motives were for the changes made by Volodicheva in what was clearly the original draft of this letter. The main point for our examination is that *changes were made; they were substantive, and they were made within Lenin's secretariat.*

Like the other stenographer-secretaries in the secretariat, neither Maria Volodicheva nor Lidia Fotieva had any independent political role or authority to change anything that Lenin had dictated. Aside from Lenin himself, only one person had such authority: Lenin's wife, Nadezhda Konstantinovna Krupskaya.

"Characteristics"[22]

This document, when first published, was not divided into two fragments, and was dated December 25 at the end of the text. The text in Trotsky's archive has the same date, December 25.[23]

Sakharov has noted that the remark about Zinoviev and Kamenev originally had the singular pronoun "upon him" – *ему*.

> ... октябрьский эпизод Зиновьева и Каменева, конечно, не является случайностью, но что он так же мало может быть ставим **ему** в вину лично ...

> ... the October episode with Zinoviev and Kamenev was, of course, no accident, but neither can the blame for it be laid upon **him** personally ...

Sakharov

> Prior to the publication of this document in the Complete Works, this place was accompanied by a

---

[22] See illustration #2.
[23] Fel'shtinsky, IU. Ed., *Kommunisticheskaia oppozitsiia v SSSR, 1923-1927, tom I.*(2004 [1990]), p. 44 of 168 of online edition (Hereafter Komm. Opp. 1). But Fel'shtinsky has changed "to him" – ему – to "to them" – им.

Chapter Two. Letter to the Congress

> note: "Apparently, a slip of the pen: instead of "him," it should be "them."" (314)

The text of the L2C in the first Khrushchev-era publication of these documents in *Kommunist* No. 9, 1956, does indeed read "upon him" – *ему*.[24]

Sakharov continues:

> In the Complete Works of Lenin, the word "him" was replaced by "them" without any reservations. (314)[25]

Honest editorial practice requires that the original version of the document be reproduced and any emendation be accompanied by some indication, such as the note above. But the PSS editors simply changed *"upon him"* to *"upon them"* – **ему** to **им** – without informing their readers that they had altered the text. This supports Sakharov's suspicion that the text in the PSS was altered after the XX Party Congress in February, 1956 in conformity with Nikita Khrushchev's attack on Stalin.

According to Sakharov, who cites an archival document, this same word (**ему**) occurs in three different copies of "Characteristics," that were typed at different times. This means that it is not a typists' error, which surely would have been corrected in at least one of these copies. Therefore we can conclude that it was in the original from which these copies were made.

The first mention of the document known as the "Characteristics," supposedly dictated by Lenin on December 24 or 25, 1922, was in June, 1923. It is usually assumed that Krupskaya brought it forth, along with other documents, on May 18, 1924, on the basis of this letter:

---

[24] "Neopublikovannye dokumenty V.I. Lenina." *Kommunist* No. 9 (1956), 15-26, For «ему» see the last line on page 17. Sakharov refers to volume II of the transcript of the XV Party Congress. I have not been able to obtain this volume for verification. But there is no reason to doubt Sakharov here since the 1956 *Kommunist* edition does have «ему».
[25] XLV 345

Мною переданы записи, которые Владимир Ильич диктовал во время болезни с 23 декабря по 23 января — 13 отдельных записей. В это число не входит еще запись по национальному вопросу (в данную минуту находящаяся у Марии Ильиничны).

Некоторые из этих записей уже опубликованы (о Рабкрине, о Суханове). Среди неопубликованных записей имеются записи от 24—25 декабря 1922 года и от 4 января 1923 года, которые заключают в себе личные характеристики некоторых членов Центрального Комитета. Владимир Ильич выражал твердое желание, чтобы эта его запись после его смерти была доведена до сведения очередного партийного съезда. Н. Крупская. (XLV, 594)

I have handed over the notes that Vladimir Ilyich dictated during his illness from December 23 to January 23 — 13 separate notes. This number does not yet include a note on the national question (currently in the possession of Maria Ilyinichna)

Some of these notes have already been published (about The Workers and Peasants Inspectorate, about Sukhanov). Among the unpublished notes are those dated December 24-25, 1922 and January 4, 1923, which contain personal characteristics of some members of the Central Committee. Vladimir Ilyich expressed a firm desire that after his death his note be brought to the attention of the next party congress. N. Krupskaya

Sakharov:

In this letter N.K. Krupskaya for the first time "united" two different documents which had up to this point

Chapter Two. Letter to the Congress

existed independently of one another ... (Sakharov, Opaseniia 4)

Krupskaya's claim that Lenin's "firm desire" was to bring these two documents – "Characteristics" and "Addition" – to the Party Congress "after his death" stands in contradiction to the statements that a split in the Party must be averted and removing Stalin from the post of Gensec was an urgent matter. In fact, *none* of Lenin's other "last works" mention these matters again! This makes no sense if the documents were Lenin's. But it is logical if these documents were later forgeries brought forward at a politically important moment.

The PSS quotes this letter and affirms that the documents were indeed handed over by Krupskaya on the May 1924 date. But this is incorrect. In fact, Krupskaya does not say *when* she handed over these notes, which here include the "Addition." A note sent to Kamenev "on behalf of" Valerian Kuibyshev and dated June 7, 1923, reads as follows:

> Два предложения партсъезду: 1. - Об увеличении числа членов ЦК до 50-100 чел. (как мера придания устойчивости ЦК). (Речь, очевидно, идет о письме Ленина Сталину от 23 декабря 1922 г. - В.С.). 2. - О придании законодательного характера решениям Госплана. (Вопрос уже возбуждался Троцким)». Следующий документ - «Письмо второе. 24/ХП-1922 г. Развитие первого предложения: об увеличении числа членов ЦК (характеристики)

> Two proposals to the party congress: 1. - On increasing the number of members of the Central Committee to 50-100 people (as a measure of giving stability to the Central Committee). [Obviously, this is the letter from Lenin to Stalin dated December 23, 1922 - V.S.]. 2. - On giving legislative character to decisions of the State Planning Commission. (A question that Trotsky had already raised). The next

document is "A second letter. 24 / XII-1922 Development of the first proposal: on increasing the number of members of the Central Committee (characteristics). [26]

No other document is alleged to have been dictated by Lenin on December 24, 1922 besides "Characteristics," and it is called by that name here. The "Addition" of January 4, 1923, is not mentioned.

Note that the title "Letter to the Congress" does not occur here. The copy in Trotsky's archive bears Trotsky's note that it has no title.

> « В оригинале рукопись не носит никакого заглавия, - Л. Т.»

> "In the original the manuscript [sic] has no title. L.T."[27]

We must recall that only the *first* document – the letter dated December 23, 1922, sent to Stalin and undoubtedly intended for him – carries the title "Letter to the Congress" in both the handwritten and typewritten versions.

This constitutes evidence that the "Addition" (the dictation dated January 4, 1923) had not yet been brought forth by Krupskaya by June 7, 1923. Therefore, she must have done so at a later time. And so at this time no one had yet united the "Addition" to the "Characteristics" and given them the title "Letter to the Congress." (538-9) We should recall that the only document bearing this title is the letter to Stalin dated December 23, 1922.

---

[26] Sakharov's source (p. 538 n. 107) is an article by IU. A. Buranov, in *Voprosy Istorii KPSS* (Problems of the History of the CPSU) 4 (1991), 48-9. I have verified this reference.

[27] Fel'shtinsky, Komm. Opp. I,. p. 45 of 168 in text edition available on the Internet (hereafter Komm. Op.). The word "manuscript" is obviously an error by Trotsky, since Lenin could no longer write.

Chapter Two. Letter to the Congress

As we shall see, since no one – not Krupskaya, not Trotsky, and not the Opposition – mentioned any of these documents at the XII Party Congress, which met from April 17 to April 25, 1923, we may assume that the documents dated December 24 and December 25 did not yet exist at that time. That is, "Characteristics" was fabricated – forged – between the end of the XII P.C. and June, 1923 (Kuibyshev's note to Kamenev), when Lenin could no longer dictate or even speak because of a stroke on March 10, 1923.

The fact that "Characteristics" was introduced into the political struggle in late May to June 1923[28] without the "Addition" and the fact that there was as yet no title proves that no one, neither Krupskaya nor anyone else, had yet decided to write them into one block of text and give it the title "Letter to the Congress" or to add to them the letter dated December 23, the only document that actually bears the title "Letter to a/the Congress."

"Addition" ("Dobavlenie")[29]

It is unclear when the "Addition" dated January 4, 1923, was inserted into the political struggle. It was evidently known at first as "the letter of Il'ich about the secretary." This is how Stalin refers to it when Zinoviev and Bukharin inform him of its existence, at the end of July, 1923. On August 7, 1923, Stalin wrote to Zinoviev:

> Comrade Zinoviev!
>
> I have received your letter of 31/VII. To answer your questions. 1. You write: "do not accept and do not interpret the conversation with Sergo the wrong way" I will directly say that I interpreted it "the wrong way". One of two things: either the issue is about changing the secretary now, or they want to put a special political committee over the secretary. Instead of

---

[28] In a later article Sakharov says that Krupskaya gave "Characteristics" to the Central Committee in May, 1923 and "Addition" in July, 1923. Sakharov, "Opaseniia V.I. po adresu t. Stalina ne opravdalis'" *Istoricheskii arkhiv* 1 (2005), 3.
[29] See illustrations #3 and 3a.

> stating the question clearly, you both go around and about the question, trying to get to your goal in a roundabout way and apparently counting on people's stupidity. Why are these indirect methods needed if there really is a group and if there is a minimum of trust? Why did I need references to **a letter of Ilich's about the secretary that is unknown to me** - is there really no evidence that I do not value the position and, therefore, am not afraid of letters? What is the name of the group whose members are trying to scare each other (to say the least)? I am for changing the secretary, but I am opposed to creating the institute of a political committee (there are quite a few political committees: the Organizing Bureau, the Politburo, the Plenum). (Izv TsK KPSS 4, 1991, 203)

Zinoviev and Bukharin wrote to tell Stalin about the letter – the "Addition:":

> 2) Letter from Ilyich Yes, there is **a letter from V.I. in which he advises (the XII Congress) not to choose you as secretary.** We (Bukh[arin], Kamen[ev] and I) have decided not to talk about it for the time being. For an obvious reason: You have already perceived the disagreements with V. I. too subjectively, and we did not want to annoy you. (Izv TsK KPSS 1991, 4, 205-6)

If what Zinoviev and Bukharin wrote here were true, that the "Addition" was directed to the XII Party Congress (which had ended on April 25, 1923), and if the "Characteristics" was intended for the Congress that met after Lenin's death, as Krupskaya wrote in her note of May 18, 1924,[30] this would completely disprove the story that the "Letter to the Congress" consisted of the "Characteristics" of December 24-25, 1922, and "Addition" of January 4, 1923.

---

[30] Lenin died on January 21, 1924.

Chapter Two. Letter to the Congress

Bukharin does not explain why the letter from "Lenin", which he supposes was addressed to the XII Party Congress, had not been presented at that time. Nor does he explain how he happens to have a copy when Stalin does not – a fact that Bukharin clearly knows – or who gave the copy to him. All in all, it is clear that some kind of anti-Stalin factionalizing was under way.

There is no evidence whatever of any "clashes" – political tensions and disagreements – among Politburo members until *after* the XII Party Congress. Sakharov remarks:

> Hence the conclusion that Stalin, in the position of general secretary, was considered no earlier than the end of the XII Party Congress as a factor complicating the friendly work of the Politburo and the Central Committee and threatening to split the Central Committee and the party. **Until that time no one, either in a speech at the congress or in any other document, had noted this danger.** Consequently, the "Addition" to the "Characteristics" (the dictation of January 4, 1922), which fixes this threat as emanating from Stalin, could not have appeared earlier than the end of the congress [April 25, 1923 – GF]. **In other words, it could not belong to Lenin ...** (563)

Sakharov's deduction appears to be correct. We shall see that at the XII Party Congress of April, 1923, Vladimir Kosior did speak about dangers of a split in the Party. But he did not direct those remarks against Stalin.

If he or others in the opposition had known of "Addition" they certainly could not have failed to use this weapon against Stalin. But no one mentioned it. In fact, no one even hinted that Stalin was a problem! This is further evidence that in April 1923 "Addition" did not yet exist, and therefore that Lenin did not write it.

ADDITION TO THE LETTER OF DECEMBER 24, 1922

> Stalin is too rude and this defect, although quite tolerable in our midst and in dealing among us

Communists, becomes intolerable in a Secretary-General. That is why I suggest that the comrades think about a way of removing Stalin from that post and appointing another man in his stead who in all other respects differs from Comrade Stalin in having only one advantage, namely, that of being more tolerant, more loyal, more polite and more considerate to the comrades, less capricious, etc. This circumstance may appear to be a negligible detail. But I think that from the standpoint of safeguards against a split and from the standpoint of what I wrote above about the relationship between Stalin and Trotsky it is not a [minor] detail, but it is a detail which can assume decisive importance.

Lenin

Taken down by L.F.

January 4, 1923 (CW 36, 596)[31]

There are a number of inconsistencies in this text.

" ... of which I wrote **above** ..." (in Russian, («...с точки зрения **написанного** мною **выше**...»).

By January 4, 1923, Lenin could no longer "write". He had been forced to dictate to secretaries since mid-December. Moreover, "above" does not mean "recently," i.e. in writings of previous days or weeks, but "before this, in the same text." But there is nothing about this in the same text before this passage.

Sakharov suggests that this passage indicates that this document was originally a part of a longer document, one that has been rewritten to make it look like a letter by Lenin. It is also possible that by "above" the Author of this document meant the documents

---

[31] The date of "Characteristics" is given as December 24, though we know that the date on the document itself is December 25. (XLV 344-5; CW 36, 594-5)

Chapter Two. Letter to the Congress   45

dated December 24 and 25 and published as Part Two ("II") of the "Letter to the Congress."

Lenin's Difficulty with Dictation

Sakharov notes another difficulty in accepting this document as Lenin's: its complexity.

> "Characteristics" is a complex document. It is all the more difficult for a person who dictates to a stenographer to work on if he is not accustomed to dictating texts. And Lenin, as is known, did not have such experience. The secretaries noted that he had considerable difficulties in the dictation process. (316)

Sakharov cites the following examples from the Secretaries Journal:

> January 11 ... Vladimir Ilyich called me in for half an hour between 6 and 7. He read and made corrections to his notes on Sukhanov's book on the revolution ... When dictating the sentence "Our Sukhanovs ..." he paused at the words "... never even dream ..." and while pondering the continuation, jokingly remarked: "What a memory! I have completely forgotten what I was going to say! Dash it! Extraordinary forgetfulness!"... Watching him during dictation for several days running I noticed that he did not like to be interrupted in the middle of a sentence, as he lost the thread of his thoughts.
>
> January 22 (entry by M. A. Volodicheva).
>
> Vladimir Ilyich ... Made corrections in the 2nd variant of the W.P.I. article. Finally chose this variant ... Asked me to put the article in order ...

In the entry for February 6, 1923, Lenin discussed in some detail his problems with dictation.

> February 6, evening (entry by M. A. Volodicheva).

> ... First he began to read his article "Better Fewer, But Better". The corrections, made

> in red ink, put Vladimir Ilyich in a good humour ...The article at his request had not been retyped, and the first deciphered copy had had the corrections added to it which Vladimir Ilyich had made during his reading. The corrections having been made not in proof-reader style, but in the ordinary secretarial way, Vladimir Ilyich, on second reading, found this inconvenient. He asked that the next time the whole thing should be retyped anew. Running through the article, Vladimir Ilyich made passing remarks, spoke about his old habit of writing and not dictating; that he understood now why stenographers do not satisfy him ("did not satisfy him," he said); that he was accustomed to seeing his manuscript in front of him ...

> He recollected how he tried to dictate an article of his to Trotsky's stenographer back in 1918, and how, when he felt himself getting "stuck", he "plunged" on in confusion with "incredible" speed, and how this led to his having had to burn the whole manuscript ...

Yet there are no drafts or corrections in "Characteristics."

> Initial variants of "characteristics" are lacking. Does it mean that in this case, Lenin suddenly got everything "at once," "considered," honed so much that it satisfied him completely, so that later he no longer returned to them? If we consider that the work on other texts was not easy, and was accompanied not only by serious editing, but also by thorough reworking of the texts, then such ease in working on "characteristics" would be surprising. Surprise, which gives rise to wariness. Therefore, it is difficult to admit that the well-known text of "Letter to the Congress" from which the publication was made did not have a predecessor text. But it is unknown. (316)

Chapter Two. Letter to the Congress

In fact, we know that there *were* "predecessor texts." We have seen the evidence of them: "... of which I wrote **above**..." and "upon him («ему»)."

> The existence of predecessor texts is indicated by the above-noted minor "defects" of the text, that give away the places of "stitching" the text from different blocks left after hasty editorial correction. **But they also tell us that these predecessor texts could not belong to Lenin.** (316)

In her October, 1963 interview with journalist Genrikh Volkov Fotieva recalled Lenin's difficulties with dictation:

> In general, dictation was hard for Vladimir Il'ich. Earlier he rarely resorted to the help of stenography. It was hard for him to become accustomed to this, all the more so because of his situation.

Fotieva then recounts that Lenin told Volodicheva about how dictation contradicted his normal practice of writing, rewriting, "walking about the room," even rushing outdoors to take a walk. Then Lenin told another story of how in 1918 he had tried dictation but had become bogged down. Having dictated a sentence, he would forget how it began. Finally, determining to press on, he had dictated more and more "with unimaginable speed"

> And this ended in my having to burn the manuscript. After that, I sat down and wrote everything myself from the beginning. And it came out much better.[32]

In view of all the evidence that Lenin found dictation difficult, it is hardly possible to imagine him dictating a complicated text such as "Characteristics" without any corrections.

---

[32] Genrikh Volkov, "Stenografistka Il'icha." *Sovetskaia Kul'tura*, January 21, 1989, p. 3.

There are further problems with "Characteristics":

* In March, 1922, at the XI Party Congress, Lenin had fought hard to make Stalin the General Secretary (Gensec).[33] How could he have written "Stalin has *made himself* gensec" when it was he, Lenin, who had done it?

* There is no evidence, either before the purported dates of "Characteristics" and "Addition" or after them, that Lenin was dissatisfied with Stalin's performance in that post. In fact, *no one*, either before or during the XII Party Congress, had found fault with Stalin's performance as Gensec.

* "Stalin is too rude." In order for this to be threatening a split in the party and grounds for removing Stalin from his post, this "rudeness" must have been well known, spoken or written about by a number of persons. But there is no record that *anyone*, including Lenin, had ever complained of rudeness by Stalin.

* "Addition" states that Stalin's "rudeness" was "quite tolerable" among communists, but not to non-communists. Krupskaya, however, was a Party member. There is no record of any complaint that Stalin was rude to *non*-Party members.

* Reference to "more tolerant, more loyal,[34] more polite and more considerate to the comrades, less capricious, etc.," only make sense if these traits were well known and often mentioned. But no one, including Lenin himself, had mentioned them.

* No danger of a split can be found in the writings of other Bolsheviks at this time. The relations between Stalin and Trotsky

---

[33] We discussed this point fully, with quotations from Lenin's speech in favor of Stalin at the XI Party Congress, in *Trotsky's 'Amalgams'* 19-23, and in *Trotsky's Lies*, 17-23.

[34] In a note on page 367, Sakharov notes that "loyal'nost'" in Russian does not mean what it means in English, but "maintaining oneself formally within the limits of legality, of a benevolently neutral attitude towards another person." In short, it means about the same as "tolerant," "polite," and "considerate," the other adjectives used here.

Chapter Two. Letter to the Congress

were no more stressful than other conflicts. Trotsky did not report any such danger either.

* Removing Stalin from the post of Gensec would not remove the danger of a split (assuming that there was such a danger). It would simply change the balance of forces, creating a situation more favorable for Trotsky.

* In his letter of December 23, 1922, Lenin had proposed "a number of changes be made in our political structure." (CW 36, 593) However, Lenin did not mean getting rid of Stalin as Gensec, but rather increasing the size of the Central Committee and reorganizing the Workers and Peasants Inspectorate.

* At the end of 1922 Lenin had no materials at all that might allow him to evaluate Stalin negatively. Even Trotsky never claimed that by this time his own relations with Stalin had put the Central Committee on the brink of division.

* One more indication that Lenin could not have been the author of "Characteristics" and of "Addition" is this: In all his subsequent writings, from January to March, 1923, Lenin never returned to the question raised there: the urgent need to avoid a split in the Party by finding some way to remove Stalin as Gensec. Sakharov notes:

> What kind of terrible threat is this, if five, and fifteen days later, and after twenty days, and after a month or two, Lenin did not show the slightest concern that the split could occur suddenly due to the struggle between Stalin and Trotsky and did not develop the topic of the need to "remove" Stalin from the post of General Secretary of the Central Committee of the RCP(b)? He is busy with other problems, which, for all their significance (this is how the author of the "Letter to the Congress" poses this problem), cannot be compared with the threat posed by Stalin. (436-7)

The Party was Lenin's creation and the central organ that had made possible the Revolution and victory in the Civil War. Had Lenin really believed, as these two documents attributed to him state, that the future of the Party depended on removing Stalin from his position, he would surely have returned to this question. But he never did.

> In Lenin's opinion, an increase in the size of the Central Committee, and not a change in the General Secretary, was supposed to guarantee an increase the stability and authority of the Central Committee, "seriously improve the work of our apparatus," strengthen its connection with the masses, etc. Among these goals there is nothing that would indicate a desire by Lenin to deliver a political blow against Stalin. For the Author of the "Letter to the Congress," on the contrary, the mechanism does not matter (in any case, he did not indicate his attitude towards it), the problem boils down to "personalities," to the political "liquidation" of Stalin. (438)

Trotsky was opposed to Lenin's plan to retain and reorganize the Workers and Peasants Inspectorate [35] and to enlarge the Central Committee. Lenin and the Author of the "Letter to the Congress" had very different approaches and proposed different programs of action to reduce the danger of a split. Nowhere did Lenin express doubt about the Bolshevik Old Guard, whose prestige he was anxious to maintain. In view of all that has been said, Lenin and the Author of the "Letter" are different persons. (438-442).

On January 27, 1923, the Politburo discussed Lenin's article "How to reorganize the Workers and Peasants Inspectorate." The members of the Politburo were surprised by the indication in it of the danger of a split which was formulated differently and much more calmly than in the "Letter to the Congress." The Politburo unanimously responded to this article with a special letter to regional party bodies (*gubkomam i obkomam*), in which it

---

[35] In this book we will refer to this body as "The Workers and Peasants Inspectorate" or "W.P.I." rather than as Rabkrin, the conventional Soviet and Russian abbeviation.

disavowed this specific provision of the article concerning the danger of a split.

> Некоторые товарищи обратили внимание Политбюро на то, что эта статья тов. Ленина может быть истолкована товарищами на местах в том смысле, будто внутренняя жизнь ЦЕКА за последнее время обнаружила какой-либо уклон в сторону раскола и именно этим побудила тов. Ленина выдвинуть изложенные в его статье организационные предложения ... Не вдаваясь в этом чисто информационном письме в обсуждение возможных исторических опасностей, вопрос о которых вполне своевременно поднят тов. Лениным в его статье, **члены Политбюро и Оргбюро во избежание возможных недоразумений считают необходимым с полным единодушием заявить, что во внутренней работе ЦЕКА совершенно нет таких обстоятельств, которые давали бы какие бы то ни было основания для опасений «раскола»**.[36]

> Some comrades have drawn the attention of the Politburo to the fact that this article of comrade Lenin's could be interpreted by local comrades in the sense that the inner life of the Central Executive Committee has recently revealed some kind of tendency towards a split, and that this is what prompted Comrade Lenin to put forward the organizational proposals set out in his article ... Without going in this purely informational letter into a discussion of possible historical dangers, the question of which com. Lenin appropriately raised in his article, **in order to avoid possible misunderstandings, the members of the Politburo and the Organizing**

---

[36] Izv TsK KPSS 11, 1989, 179-80.

> Bureau consider it necessary, with complete unanimity, to declare that there are absolutely no circumstances in the Central Committee's internal work that would give any grounds for fears of a "split".

The letter was signed by all the members of the Politburo. It was drafted by Trotsky himself who of course signed it, as did Stalin. So Trotsky too was surprised by Lenin's remark about the danger of a split – any split. Therefore, at this time Trotsky himself was unaware of any danger of split because of his and Stalin's relationship.

Since there was no talk of the danger of a split due to tensions between Stalin and Trotsky, or due to Stalin's personal qualities, we can conclude that "Letter to the Congress" was created *after* the XII Party Congress, which ended on April 25, 1923. Moreover, Sakharov argues convincingly that the elements of the "Letter to the Congress" are reflected in statements made by oppositionists during that Congress.

The "Letter to the Congress" – a Pro-Trotsky Document

In Trotsky's archive there is an interesting document related to the discussion in the Politburo concerning whether or not to publish "Characteristics."[37] From internal evidence Sakharov dates this exchange to the end of May 1923. (536)

> Копия. Строго секретно

---

[37] Fel'shtinsky, Komm. Opp. I, 33/168 (in the online text version). The document is called "the testament of Lenin" here. This title was clearly added later, as "Characteristics" by itself never bore this name. We recall that the copy in Trotsky's archive has no title.

СВОДКА ЗАМЕЧАНИЙ ЧЛЕНОВ ПОЛИТБЮРО И ПРЕЗИДИУМА ЦК К ПРЕДЛОЖЕНИЮ ТОВ. ЗИНОВЬЕВА

о публиковании "Завещания Ленина"

1. Я думаю, что эту статью нужно опубликовать, если нет каких-либо формальных причин, препятствующих этому.

Есть ли какая-либо разница в передаче (в условиях передачи) этой статьи и других (о кооперации, о Суханове).

Троцкий

2. Печатать нельзя: это несказанная речь на П/Бюро. Не больше.

Личная характеристика - основа и содержание статьи.

Каменев

3. Н. К. тоже держалась того мнения, что следует передать только в ЦК. О публикации я не спрашивал, ибо думал (и думаю), что это исключено. Можно этот вопрос задать. В условиях передачи разницы не было.

Только эта запись (о Госплане) передана мне позже - несколько дней тому назад.

Зиновьев

4. Полагаю, что нет необходимости печатать, тем более, что санкции на печатание от Ильича не имеется.

Сталин

5. А предложение тов Зиновьева - только ознакомить членов ЦК.

Не публиковать, ибо из широкой публики никто тут ничего не поймет.

Томский

6. Эта заметка В. И. имела в виду не широкую публику, а ЦЕКА и потому так много места уделено характеристике лиц. Ничего подобного нет в статье о кооперации. Печатать не следует.

А. Сольц

7. Тт. Бухарин, Рудзутак, Молотов и Куйбышев - за предложение тов. Зиновьева.

Словатинская [начало июня]

Копия

Copy. Top secret

SUMMARY OF COMMENTS OF MEMBERS OF THE POLITBURO AND THE PRESIDIUM OF THE CENTRAL COMMITTEE

TO THE PROPOSAL OF COM. ZINOVIEV

on the publication of "The Testament of Lenin"

1. I think that this article should be published if there are no formal reasons preventing this.

Is there any difference in the transfer (in terms of transfer) of this article and others (about cooperation, about Sukhanov).

Trotsky

2. It is impossible to print: this is an unspoken speech to the P / Bureau. Nothing more. Personal characteristics are the basis and content of the article.

Kamenev

Chapter Two. Letter to the Congress

3. NK, too, was of the opinion that it should be transferred only to the Central Committee. I did not ask about the publication, because I thought (and think) that it is excluded. You can ask this question. There was no difference in the transfer conditions.

Only this note (about the State Planning Commission) was handed over to me later - a few days ago.

Zinoviev

4. I believe that there is no need to publish, especially since there is no authorization for printing from Ilyich.

Stalin

5. And Comrade Zinoviev's proposal is only to acquaint the members of the Central Committee with it. It should not be published, because no one of the general public will understand anything in it.

Tomsky

6. This note by V. I. was not intended for the general public, but the Central Committee, and therefore so much space was devoted to the characteristics of persons. There is nothing of the kind in the article on cooperation. Do not print.

A. Solts

7. Comrades Bukharin, Rudzutak, Molotov and Kuibyshev - for the proposal of Comrade Zinoviev.

Slovatinskaya [early June]

Copy

Only Trotsky was in favor of the publication of "Characteristics." This is no surprise – Trotsky was the only one who benefitted from it and Trotsky recognized this. Later, in *My Life*, he stated that the purpose of "Characteristics" was to create favorable conditions for himself, Trotsky, to lead the Party alongside Lenin, or even in Lenin's place:

> Помимо общеполитических задач, открытая Лениным кампания имела непосредственно своей целью создать наиболее благоприятные условия для моей руководящей работы либо рядом с Лениным, если б ему удалось оправиться, либо на его месте, если б болезнь одолела его.[38]
>
> In addition to general political tasks, the campaign launched by Lenin aimed directly at creating the most favorable conditions for my work in the leadership, either next to Lenin, if he was able to recover, or in his place, if the disease overcame him.

Trotsky is lying here. There is no evidence that Lenin regarded Trotsky as his colleague in leadership of the Party, much less as his successor. But the fact that Trotsky made this claim suggests that he may have played a role in the creation of "Characteristics."

Sakharov's Analysis of the XII Party Congress

During the days before the Congress, an anonymous pamphlet appeared claiming that the Central Committee was dominated by group interests and demanding the removal of Stalin, Zinoviev, and Kamenev from the C.C. These were Lenin's staunchest supporters.[39]

> Осинский ... Позвольте еще одну вещь подчеркнуть, товарищи. Тов. Зиновьев, который усиленно старается привязать ко мне анонимную платформу, подобно тому, как озорные

---

[38] Trotsky, *Moia Zhizn'*. Moscow: Panorama, 1991, 463.
[39] Therefore it appears that the pamphlet – which has so far not been found in the former Soviet archives – served the interests of Trotsky, the only prominent oppositionist.

Chapter Two. Letter to the Congress

> мальчишки привязывают жестянку к хвосту кошке,— т. Зиновьев старается привязать меня и к неумному предложению об устранении из Центрального Комитета Зиновьева, Каменева, Сталина. (XII P.C., 133)
>
> Сорин Надо вспомнить, что в 1920 г. у нас единого ЦК не было, и нам этой ошибки надо в дальнейшем избежать. Тут т. Осинский горячо ополчился против анонимной брошюры, которая предлагает изъять из ЦК основную, всей партии известную, группу из 3 человек. (149)
>
> Osinsky: Let me stress one more thing, comrades. Comrade Zinoviev, who is trying hard to tie **an anonymous platform** to me, similar to the way mischievous boys tie a tin to a cat's tail, — Comrade Zinoviev also tries to tie me to the stupid proposal to remove Zinoviev, Kamenev, and Stalin from the Central Committee.
>
> Sorin: It must be remembered that in 1920 we did not have a united Central Committee, and we must avoid this mistake in the future. There Comrade Osinsky ardently rebelled against **an anonymous pamphlet** that proposes removing from the Central Committee the principal group of 3 people that is well-known to the party.

In his address to the XII P.C. Trotsky supporter Vladimir Kosior stated the same case as was evidently made in the anonymous pamphlet.

> I believe that a party congress has the right to ask whether within our party and in our leading party bodies all the necessary conditions for the unity of the party are actually being carried out. It seems to me, comrades, that there are no such conditions within the party at the moment, or they are not to the extent that

it is necessary for the party to truly maintain its unity. The main question, in my opinion, is that the steering group of the Central Committee [Stalin, Zinoviev and Kamenev], in its organizational policy is largely pursuing a group policy - a policy that, in my opinion, very often does not coincide with the interests of the party. This policy, comrades, is primarily manifested in the organizational form in which we select and use responsible workers for Soviet and party work. Dozens of our comrades are outside of party and Soviet work. These comrades are outside this work, not because they are poor organizers, not because they are bad communists, but solely because at different times and on various occasions they participated in this or that group, because they took part in discussions against the official line, which was conducted by the Central Committee. Comrades, if the party congress wanted to, it could appoint a sufficiently objective, sufficiently authoritative commission that could do the following work: it would personally ask a number of our comrades to report what they had done for the party within a year. And the same commission could give a fairly objective assessment of each of these comrades on the subject of what they could do under other conditions for the party. Comrades, this organizational line, in my opinion, gives rise to completely unnecessary dissatisfaction within the party, it creates the atmosphere and the soil for known groups, for petty group struggle, which is not in the interests of the party. This kind of report, comrades, could begin with Comrade Trotsky, this kind of report could be completed with Comrade Shlyapnikov and other members of the "workers' opposition." (XII P.C. 101-102)

Kosior also proposed cancelling the resolution against fractions in the Party that had been passed, with Lenin's support, at the X

Chapter Two. Letter to the Congress

Party Congress in 1921.[40] This proposal was to become a basic tenet of Trotsky and his supporters.

Kosior did refer to some recent article of Lenin's:

> Мне кажется, что настоящее единство и предохранение партии от личных трений и влияний, о которых пишет т. Ленин в своей первой статье, возможны будут только тогда, когда мы изменим систему и способ подбора руководящих органов нашей партии. (104-5)
>
> It seems to me that the real unity and protection of the party from personal friction and influences, which Comrade Lenin writes about in his first article, will be possible only when we change the system and method of selecting the governing bodies of our party.

Kosior did not specify what "first article" by Lenin he had in mind, but it must have been "How To Reorganize the Workers and Peasants Inspectorate" where, as we have seen, Lenin mentions the danger of a split. It can't be the "Letter to the Congress." Kosior refers to it as to something well known, not requiring further identification. But L2C was not known at this time. No one referred to it at the XII P.C.

Moreover, Kosior repeatedly says that this is his opinion: "it seems to me," "I believe," "in my opinion." He doesn't quote the article by Lenin, no doubt because doing so would not lend support to his, Kosior's, suggestion of changing how the Party's leading bodies were chosen. In fact, we know that Lenin intended to increase the

---

[40] Noted by the editors of the 1968 edition of the XII Congress: "Съезд единодушно отверг попытки некоторых делегатов (В. Косиор, Ю. Лутовинов и др.) отменить решения X съезда партии о запрещении фракций и группировок." (p. xx) "The Congress unanimously rejected the attempts of some delegates (V. Kosior, Yu. Lutovinov and others) to abolish the decision of the X Congress forbidding fractions and groupings."

size of the C.C., not to change its makeup, and certainly not to remove his – Lenin's – principal supporters in it.

However, though Kosior does not refer to the as yet unwritten L2C, he does appear to echo some of its statements.

* He argues that the political line pursued by the "leading group of the Central Committee" creates conditions for factions.

> Here the problem of personal friction and influence in the Central Committee is presented as the reason for the possibility of a split and as a problem that the party congress should take up. In the "Letter to the Congress," this linkage of the problem closes on the proposal to the Congress to consider the "way" to remove Stalin from the post of general secretary. V. Kosior frightens the Congress and in fact sets an ultimatum - either do as I say, or there will be an internal party struggle. In the "Letter to the Congress" this position has found a more concise and clear expression and, moreover, it is brought to a higher level of generalization. (420)

> In V. Kosior, as in the Author's "Letter to the Congress," all the reasons for a possible split worthy of attention are in the leadership of the party. Like the Author of this "Letter," he seeks to change the balance of political forces by changing the composition of the governing bodies of the Central Committee of the RCP(b). In the same way, he covers up this desire with vague discussions about the danger of the unity of the party coming from Stalin, Zinoviev and Kamenev.

> His [Kosior's] position is in logical harmony with the "Letter to the Congress" in the sense that Kosior, like the Author of the "Letter to the Congress," sees the danger for the RCP(b) in the activities of Lenin's supporters and does not associate it with the political position and activities of the opposition ... Both see

Chapter Two. Letter to the Congress

> the most effective means of fighting this threat in changing the composition of the party leadership by eliminating the most active and authoritative supporters of Lenin. (421)

Sakharov (426) notes striking similarities between statements made by oppositionists at the XII P.C., and the formulations in the L2C, which did not appear until after the Congress:

* From the authors of the anonymous pamphlet and the remark of Osinsky's about the anonymous pamphlet, there are proposals to remove Stalin, Zinoviev and Kamenev from the Central Committee, i.e. "the leading group of the Central Committee."

* From V. Kosior there come:

a. the desire to present the activity of the "leading party bodies," the "troika" and the "secretariat" (that is, Stalin) as a factor threatening to split the party;

b. focusing the attention of the congress on relations within the Central Committee between this "leading group" and its other members as a splitting factor;

c. an indication of the need to find a "method" of preventing this threat through personnel movements in the Central Committee;

d. allegations of an opposition between the interests of the "leading group of the Central Committee" and the interests of the party;

e. the need for a party congress to take on the task of preventing the threat of a split due to "the leading group of the Central Committee."

* From Zinoviev, the indirect accusation that the "left" in the Party (by implication, Trotsky) represented a new kind of Menshevism (L2C says "non-Bolshevism);

> Когда наши «оппозиционеры» дразнили тогда рабочего: «гегемон, а ходишь без сапог, партия

тебя предает», они делали дело меньшевиков. (XII P.C. 28)

Я думаю, попросту говоря, что те, которые пытаются подчеркнуть наши чрезмерные «уклоны» в сторону крестьянства, они в этом смысле отражают ту же самую старую идеологию II Интернационала или меньшевизма ... Если взять эти взгляды под лупу, то это течение, которое иногда рядится в тогу «левого», как бывшая «рабочая оппозиция»,— не что иное, как отказ от руководства крестьянством, отказ от гегемонии пролетариата, преподнесенный под соусом более или менее меньшевистским. Вот к чему дело сводится. Вот почему это есть коренной вопрос. (XII P.C. 40)

When our "oppositionists" then taunted the worker: "you're the hegemon, and yet you walk without boots – the party is betraying you," they did the Mensheviks' work. (28)

I think, simply put, that those who are trying to emphasize our excessive "deviations" towards the peasantry, in this sense, reflect the same old ideology of the Second International or Menshevism ... If you take these views under a magnifying glass, then this trend, which sometimes parades in the toga of the "left," like the former "workers' opposition," is nothing more than a rejection of [the necessity of] leading the peasantry, a rejection of the hegemony of the proletariat, presented under a more or less Menshevik sauce. That's what it comes down to. That is why this is a fundamental question.

Всякая критика с «левого» фланга становится ныне меньшевистской. Объективно это есть поддержка меньшевизма ... Этот меньшевизм не страшен, а опасна та «левая» критика, которая

Chapter Two. Letter to the Congress

> вертится около нас, путается между ног,— она опасна, и мы должны ей дать отпор. (XII P.C. 53)
>
> Any criticism from the "left" is now becoming Menshevik. Objectively, this is support of Menshevism ... This Menshevism is not frightening, but the "left" criticism, which revolves around us, gets confused between our legs — it is dangerous, and we must fight back.

* From Budu Mdivani came an indication that some party building measures tolerated by *party* members have an unacceptable negative effect on *non-party* members.

> Конечно, товарищи, я признаю партийное использование сил, переброску с одного места на другое и партийные репрессии ... Но одно дело наши личные ощущения, одно дело отношение к этим перевроскам партии и нашей организации, а другое дело отношение к этим переброскам той самой беспартийной массы ... (XII P.C., 165)
>
> Of course, comrades, I recognize the party's use of its powers, the transfer from one place to another and party repressions ... But our personal feelings are one thing, our attitude to these transfers of the party and our organization is one thing, and the attitude to these transfers of the non-party masses is another thing ...

* From Krupskaya: the accusations of Stalin's rudeness. (Letter to Kamenev, dated December 23, 1922).

Sakharov concludes:

> It seems that the Author of the "Letter to the Congress" carefully studied the transcript of the XII Party Congress concerning what could be learned from it for criticizing members of the Leninist majority in the Politburo, and outlined the content of

these speeches, interpreting them accordingly and giving them the form of Lenin's thoughts. (423)

Sakharov notes that Trotsky related several versions of his supposed conversations with Lenin in the last months of 1922 about the fight against bureaucracy. However, in January 1923 Trotsky described some discussions with Lenin about Soviet administration. In them there is nothing about any "bloc" against bureaucracy. In fact the word "bureaucracy" does not appear in them. Moreover, Trotsky makes it clear that he and Lenin held differing views on the subject.[41]

But in his October 1923 account of his alleged meeting with Lenin to conspire against the "bureaucracy" of the Orgburo – a fictitious meeting, as we shall demonstrate – Trotsky claims that he and Lenin planned to form an anti-bureaucracy commission "to be the lever for breaking up the Stalin faction."[42] (425) It is likely that Trotsky had similar intentions earlier in the year, after the close of the XII P.C.

Sakharov also discovered that the adjectives used to describe Bukharin in the "Characteristics" – *tsenneishii i krupneishii*, translated in the English language fourth edition as "most valuable and major" – are also found in an earlier letter of March 17, 1922 from Lenin to the Politburo, where Lenin applied them to Radek and Sosnovsky. (XLV, 50)

Since Khrushchev's day, this phrase has been interpreted to mean that Lenin intended it as exceptionally high praise for Bukharin. But the discovery that Lenin had used it to describe Radek and Sosnovsky shows that Lenin did not mean this at all. It also means that anyone on the Politburo, or anyone familiar with Lenin's correspondence, could have copied these phrases and used them in the fabrication of the "Characteristics."

---

[41] See Fel'shtinsky, Komm. Opp. I: "V Politbiuro TsK. 15 ianvaria [January 1923]; „Vsem chlenam i kandidatam TsK." 20 ianvaria; „Vsem chlenam TsK." 25 ianvaria. "Predpolozheniia sekretariata." 29 ianvaria.
[42] Trotsky, *My Life*, Chapter 39, various editions.

Chapter Two. Letter to the Congress 65

> Thus, the entire set of ideas, assessments and proposals that make up the content of the "Letter to the Congress" existed on the eve of the time when the "Characteristics" and soon after, the "Addition" first came to the Central Committee.
>
> It is also noteworthy that if the dictation of December 24 issued a negative recommendation[43] to Stalin, Zinoviev and Kamenev, and of all Stalin's shortcomings only one is mentioned: insufficiently careful use of the "immense power," then the dictation of 4 January 1923 is devoted to Stalin alone, and it is there that, in addition to this shortcoming, others are also indicated.
>
> It turns out that the "Characteristics" (dictations of December 24-25) more closely echos the anonymous pamphlet, the opposition's speeches at the XII Party Congress (the threat of schism, criticism of the "leading group of the Central Committee"), and also Zinoviev's statement regarding the danger posed by the Mensheviks in the leadership of the party.
>
> And the "Addition" more closely echoes the circumstances of the conflict between Stalin and Krupskaya, and the performance of Mdivani at the XII Congress. (426)

Krupskaya did not cite the L2C at the XII Party Congress or even mention it in any way. In fact, she did not speak at the Congress, She could have spoken – she was a delegate with a "consultative vote" (she did not represent a Party organization or hold any elected Party position). If she thought that *Lenin* believed there was a serious danger of a split, as "Characteristics" stated, or that

---

[43] Literally, a "volchii bilet" or "wolf ticket." In pre-Revolutionary times this was a document preventing a person from a job in government service, in an educational institution, etc.

Lenin believed that Stalin needed to be removed for the good of the Party, it was her duty to speak. But she remained silent.

> There is no reason to think that Krupskaya neglected such an opportunity and was waiting for Lenin's death, because soon after the XII Congress she passed the "Characteristics" to the Central Committee of the Party without specifying any prohibition or any desire of Lenin regarding them. The reason for her silence obviously lies elsewhere. During the days of the XII Congress of the RCP(b) the "Letter to the Congress" was not at her disposal. It was not because it did not yet exist. It appeared later. (427)

Chapter 3. Letter to the Congress, Continued

The Text of the "Letter to the Congress": Problems and Contradictions

Aside from the problems we noted in the previous chapter – problems which strongly suggest that the L2C cannot have been written by Lenin – there are many aspects of the text itself that support the contention that it cannot be Lenin's work. We will review some of them here.

The Post of General Secretary

The Author[1] of the December 25 letter states:

> Comrade Stalin, having become Secretary-General[2], has unlimited authority concentrated in his hands ... (CW 36, 594)

The Russian original reads:

> Тов. Сталин, сделавшись генсеком, сосредоточил в своих руках необъятную власть (XLV, 345)

A better translation of *сделавшись генсеком* is "having made himself Gensec." An alternative translation of *сосредоточил в своих руках необъятную власть* is "has concentrated in his hands immense power." Both of these passages stress an *active* role: Stalin "made himself" Gensec; Stalin himself "has concentrated" the "immense power." But whatever the precise translation, these claims are normally not questioned.

---

[1] We will follow Sakharov's careful practice in using this term, which may or may not indicate Lenin.
[2] This is normally translated as General Secretary; Russian abbreviation "gensec."

The Author of the L2C wants to remove Stalin as General Secretary of the Party. But Stalin had *not* "made himself" Gensec. Lenin had fought hard to make Stalin General Secretary. At the XI Party Congress in March, 1922, Lenin had said that there was no one else as qualified as Stalin.

So Stalin did *not* "make himself Gensec" – *Lenin* made him.[3] How are we to understand that, only 8 months later, he wished to remove him?

On top of that, Lenin did not suggest a candidate to replace Stalin as Gensec. Of course Lenin would want someone who would support his, Lenin's, views, which would greatly restrict the number of possible candidates. We are to believe that Lenin was concerned with the question of qualifications for this post but yet had no one to suggest!

Clearly the concern of the Author of the L2C is not to find a replacement for Stalin and improve the Party. Rather, it is to strengthen the political position of oppositionists – those opposed to his, Lenin's, own policies. This is obvious, since no one else would benefit from removing Stalin. Trotsky and his supporters were the most prominent among these.

The Author fails to confront the question of the position of General Secretary itself. However, if Stalin could, in only eight months, "concentrate unlimited authority in his hands," then another Gensec would likely be able to do so as well. Evidently the position of Gensec was so powerful that minor, even inevitable, defects in a person could become dangerous for the Party in a Gensec. What guarantee could there be that a different Gensec would not also become too powerful? This obvious problem is not only not faced – it is not even acknowledged. Therefore, according to this view,

---

[3] I have reprinted Lenin's remarks at the XI Party Congress from both the official transcript of that Congress and from Lenin's Complete Works (PSS) XLV 122, in chapter one of both *Trotsky's 'Amalgams'* and *Trotsky's Lies.*.

Lenin – uncharacteristically – was leaving this, the main problem, for others to solve.

If the problem is the position of Gensec itself, that means that the system of Party power must be changed. However, Lenin, in his last writings, did not want to change the current system. Instead, he wanted to strengthen it. He proposed an increase in the number of workers in the Central Committee and a reorganization of the Workers and Peasants Inspectorate.

In view of this, the proposal to remove Stalin as Gensec does not make sense. The Author proposes to set for the Party Congress not only a difficult task, but one that is formulated incorrectly from a political point of view. This is uncharacteristic of Lenin, who was a very acute political thinker.

"Unlimited Authority"

It is taken for granted that Stalin had this "immense power." Kotkin writes:

> ... Lenin appeared to call for Stalin's removal. Stalin's vast power fell under siege, just as he was energetically building it up. (472)

> ... with Lenin incapacitated, Trotsky recognized the sudden vastness of Stalin's power. (487)

Trotsky in particular frequently claimed that Stalin's power lay in the post of Gensec. Scholars have accepted this view. But it cannot be true.

> The power of the general secretary was not "immense" if only because it had its own restraints — above all, the will and authority of Lenin and other members of the Politburo. According to the exact meaning of this phrase in the "Letter to the Congress," **Lenin was stating that Stalin already had immense power at a time when Lenin himself still had the ability to decisively influence the solution of**

political and personnel issues. What kind of immense power of Stalin could Lenin talk about if Stalin was forced to concede in matters of the formation of the USSR and the monopoly regime of foreign trade? (363-4)

[I]n the party itself, the statement about the immense power of the General Secretary (and therefore the dangers that Stalin's presence in this position involves) elicited surprise and objections. It was openly disputed. At the XII Party Congress, for example, no one said that Stalin was a bad general secretary ...

[A]t the XIV Congress of the RCP (b) I.S. Gusev said: "Now, about the immense power of the Secretariat and the General Secretary, which was discussed here. The question is posed in the same abstract way as it was put a year or two ago, when we first heard these words about "immense power."

So, he considered the question of the power of the General Secretary to be unjustifiably abstract. We must agree with this. "We need to take experience into account ..." continued Gusev. "Were there abuses of this power or not? Show at least one fact of abuse of this power. Who brought such a fact of abuse? We, members of the Central Control Commission, attend the meetings of the Politburo systematically, we observe the work of the Politburo, the work of the Secretariat, and in particular the work of the General Secretary of the Central Committee. Do we see the abuse of this "immense" power? No, we do not see such abuses."[4] The political opponents of Stalin in

---

[4] *XIV S"ezd Vsesoiuznoi Kommunisticheskoi Partii (B). Stenograficheskii Otchet.* Moscow: Gosudarstvennoe izdatel'stvo, 1926, 601.

response did not give any examples that could call into question this statement of Gusev's. (364-5)

Stalin and Trotsky

As we saw in the last chapter, as late as January 27, 1923, *no one*, including Trotsky and Stalin, saw *any* conflict between them, much less a conflict sharp enough to threaten a split, as stated in the L2C. Even at the XII Party Congress in April, 1923 there were no signs of tension between Trotsky and Stalin. Some oppositionists, like Kosior, warned about the danger of a split, but no one attributed that danger to differences between Stalin and Trotsky. This is further strong circumstantial evidence that the L2C was composed *after* the XII Party Congress, and not in late December 1922-early January 1923.

Even if there had been tensions and political differences between Stalin and Trotsky, removing Stalin as Gensec would not stop them. It would really mean a change in the balance of forces in the inner-party struggle in favor of Trotsky and his supporters and against Stalin and *his* supporters.

> As a result, the "Letter to Congress" facilitated Trotsky's promotion to the levers of power in the party and was equivalent to weakening the political positions of Bolshevism and changing Lenin's political course to the course proposed by Trotsky, against whom Lenin had always fought. Thus, overcoming the threat of a split would have been achieved at the cost of defeating the political course that Lenin considered the only possible one for the party in the current conditions. These consequences were much more dangerous for the cause of the revolution than those negative features of Stalin that troubled the author of the "Letter to the Congress." The problem of the threat of a split was not important in and of itself, but in connection with the threat to the course that Lenin considered to be correct. The unity of the party was necessary as a condition for conducting this course.

> But if the course were wrong and led to the death of the party, then the problem of maintaining unity would lose its meaning. (409)

Unity above everything – unity for its own sake – was never Lenin's way. Lenin never failed to fight, even to split (Bolsheviks vs. Mensheviks) or to threaten a split for the sake of hewing to what he was convinced was the correct political line.

Trotsky did not share Lenin's conviction that socialism could be built in Russia. When the NEP was declared Trotsky had famously prophesied: "The cuckoo has already sounded," "the days of Soviet power are numbered."[5] In a response to Stalin dated January 20, 1923, Trotsky quotes the same phrase and does not deny it.

The L2C shows no concern about how Stalin's abilities might be used elsewhere. It is concerned only with removing Stalin, thereby in effect making way for Trotsky.

As for the L2C – we have seen that it had no title when it first appeared – in the final version of this document Krupskaya said that it was to be presented to the first congress after Lenin's death. But in late December 1922 – early January 1923, when the L2C was dated and supposedly written, Lenin was still planning to speak at the XII Party Congress in April, 1923. If Lenin had believed that the Party's future was endangered by a conflict between Stalin and Trotsky, and by Stalin's "rudeness," why would he then instruct that it *not* be presented until the first congress after his death which, as far as he or anyone knew, could be years in the future?

---

[5] Trotsky's letter of January 20, 1923: Fel'shtinsky, IU., Komm. Opp. I, (Moscow: 'Terra', 2004), pp. 6-9 of 168 in online text edition. Sakharov prints this letter on pp. 665-9. This statement is cited by Stalin in a letter dated January 17, 1923. Stalin's letter: *Stalin I.V. Sochineniia. T. 17.*(Tver' 'Severnaia korona', 2004), 160-163; also in Sakharov, 663-5.

The Danger of a Split

The L2C points to the danger of a split in the Party because of political differences between Stalin and Trotsky. But it fails to specify what those differences were. The Congress would have to guess. In fact, no one at the XII Party Congress mentioned any tensions or political differences between Stalin and Trotsky. Evidently, the delegates were unaware of any. But why would Lenin force the Congress to guess, without telling them? Why would Lenin pose this – whatever it was – as a serious political problem without explaining clearly what it was and providing a solution?

According to the L2C, the "split" caused by the "two qualities" of Stalin and Trotsky can happen "inadvertently" – *nenarokom* – "by chance," "unintended" – and ," *neozhidanno* – "unexpectedly. Apparently no one would intend a split, no one would foresee it – it would somehow just "happen." And it would occur because of the personal characteristics of Stalin and Trotsky, not from any political disagreements, since none are mentioned. In other words, it is completely unclear what kind of conflict between them would put the Party on the brink of a split. This kind of imprecision is uncharacteristic of Lenin.

The justifications of Stalin's "unsuitability" are reduced exclusively to emotions and the expression of doubts: "I am not sure," "always be capable of using ... with sufficient caution." No examples of Stalin's misuse of power are given, so no one has any idea what the Author, supposedly Lenin, is worried about. (412)

The nature of the "split" that might be caused by the disagreements between Stalin and Trotsky is also left unexplained. Under Lenin's leadership the Politburo often had split votes, normally with Trotsky in the minority and Stalin, along with others, supporting Lenin. In the preceding period, the fall of 1922, there was no conflict between Stalin and Trotsky on the leading issues of that time: the formation of the USSR and the monopoly of foreign trade. We saw above that no one in the Politburo, including

Trotsky, saw any danger of a split in mid-January, 1923. Lenin had no information about any such danger either.[6]

> It is not easy to understand the Author of the "characteristics" when he talks about the reasons for a possible split. The proposals of the Author of the "Letter" divert the attention of the congress from the sphere of principal political issues. They are mentioned, but not specified. The party congress would have to guess what they were. With such a confused reference to the main source of the danger of a split, the help from this "Letter to the congress" loses much of its value. Nor is the situation helped by the Author's indication that he intends to dwell only on the personal qualities of a number of leaders of the Central Committee of the party. There is much less clarity here than is commonly thought. And, most importantly, even in this part, the Author does not provide a solution to the problem which he was striving to solve.
>
> Speaking about the danger of a split, he compares, on the one hand, "the most serious disagreements in the party," and on the other, the relations between Stalin and Trotsky. If these reasons were simply put side by side, then the question would not have arisen. But the relationship between Stalin and Trotsky, it turns out, is more than half the danger of a split. Simply put, the relationship between Stalin and Trotsky as a factor in the split outweighs all the "most serious disagreements in the party," along with all other possible reasons (the "smaller" half) capable of creating a split.

---

[6] See the discussion in the previous chapter of the Politburo letter of January 27, 1923, published in Izv TsK 11, 1989, 179-80.

Chapter Three. Letter to the Congress, Continues

> If we seriously pose the issue of preventing the threat of a split, then we cannot pass over the problem of the "smaller" half ... But half, even the "smaller" one, is quite a lot and very serious. Without its elimination, the problem of overcoming the threat of a split is not fully resolved, since a serious reduction in the danger posed by the "greater half" immediately turns its "smaller" part into a new "greater" one. It follows that the Author of the "Letter to the Congress" either thought out the problem poorly and suggested measures to the party congress that did not give its solution, or the threat of splitting the party did not worry him. Apparently, the latter is true. The only thing that was achieved by the measures he proposed was the elimination of Stalin from the highest position in the political system. (410-1)

At the XII Party Congress of April 17-25, 1923, the opposition did raise the danger of a split. But no one attributed this danger to either the political positions or personal characteristics of Stalin or Trotsky. The opposition did not blame Stalin for lack of democracy.

Together with the evidence cited in the previous chapter, this again suggests that the L2C could not have been written until after the XII Party Congress, which means no earlier than the last week of April, 1923. But Lenin had lost all ability to work by March 10 at the latest. Therefore, the L2C cannot be by Lenin.

The Other Party Members Mentioned in the "Letter to the Congress"

Stalin and Trotsky are called "the two outstanding leaders of the present C.C." But no positive qualities of Stalin's are mentioned, while Trotsky is contrasted to him and praised highly:

> Comrade Trotsky, on the other hand, as his struggle against the C.C. on the question of the People's Commissariat for Communications has already

> proved, is distinguished not only by outstanding ability. He is personally perhaps the most capable man in the present C.C. ... (CW 36, 595)

Kamenev's and Zinoviev's temporary desertion at the time of the October revolution is brought up. Obviously, this could only serve to remind everyone of their wavering at this crucial time, while saying nothing about their support for Lenin and his policies since then. What's more, it is said that this wavering was "no accident." That implies that something like it might occur again at any time, that it was an essential part of their characters.

> The waverings of Zinoviev and Kamenev are a fact, but Lenin could hardly forget that in the difficult months of 1921, the "cuckoo" of Trotsky also spoke pessimistic views on the prospects for the revolution. For the RCP(b) at the turn of 1922-1923 Trotsky's doubts about the ability of the Soviet government to overcome the political crisis that erupted in 1921 were much more important than the long-ago waverings of Zinoviev and Kamenev. It was not for nothing that at that time Lenin constantly challenged the views of Trotsky and did not recall the behavior of Zinoviev and Kamenev in the October days of 1917. If Lenin was the author of the "characteristics," what gave him confidence that Trotsky would not have relapses? (372)

Then it is said that they cannot be blamed "personally" for it. This confusing remark really serves only to absolve Trotsky of his decades of bitter opposition to Lenin by saying that Trotsky too cannot be blamed "personally" for "non-Bolshevism," that is, for his decades of *opposition to* Bolshevism.

> The thesis about the non-Bolshevism of Trotsky is embedded in the text of "characteristics" very "subtly," as a political flaw, but in such a way that the mention of it rather serves not a reproach, but an indulgence to Trotsky: "but neither can the blame for it be laid upon"

him "personally." And since that is so, then, therefore, one should not blame Trotsky for his non-Bolshevism. The deliberate uncertainty, the vagueness of the term "non-Bolshevism" draws attention to itself. The author of the "Letter to the Congress" turned Trotsky's semi-Menshevik and anti-Bolshevik past into a non-Bolshevik past. This is an uncharacteristic move for Lenin, who had clearly characterized the "non-fractional" Trotsky as a representative of a political movement that was trying to occupy a position between the Mensheviks and the Bolsheviks. (369-70)

By these remarks, Kamenev and Zinoviev are disgraced. Trotsky's Menshevism is forgiven, put behind him, while Kamenev and Zinoviev may revert to their "non-accidental" wavering or desertion at any time.

Bukharin is called "a most valuable and major theorist of the Party" – and then is immediately described as not "fully Marxist." How can one be a "major theorist" of a Marxist party and yet not be a Marxist, be "scholastic," be someone who has "never fully understood" dialectics?

> If this is, in fact, Lenin's address to the party congress, then its meaning must be explained. After all, the only thing that remains valuable to Bukharin is transient youth. It turns out that he is considered "the Party's favorite" by a misunderstanding. This is like a frank mockery of Bukharin. How to explain it in a letter addressed to the party congress? Moreover, the author addresses this dubious compliment to the party itself, which is to accept a non-Marxist and non-dialectician as a favorite and theorist.

Sakharov notes the different treatment of Bukharin and Trotsky by the Author of the L2C, which Lenin did not share.

> In the article "Once again on trade unions," Lenin wrote that "Comrade Bukharin's fundamental

> theoretical mistake" is "substitution of eclecticism (especially popular with the authors of diverse "fashionable" and reactionary philosophical systems) for Marxist dialectics." The assessment almost coincides with that in the "Letter to the Congress." Lenin, of course, could have dictated it. But anyone could have borrowed it from this Lenin pamphlet. **What is interesting is that, noting this flaw in the theoretician Bukharin, Lenin views it together with Trotsky's mistakes**: "Trotsky and Bukharin have produced a hodgepodge of political mistakes." Why, then, did Lenin "pardon" Trotsky and save him from such remarks? And again, we see in the Author of "Letter to the Congress" a manifestation of a partisan attitude towards Trotsky. He does not want to notice his shortcomings, which Lenin had often pointed out. (374)

Pyatakov is shunted aside with the remark that he cannot be "relied upon in a serious political matter." Clearly such a person cannot be considered for the top Party position.

> Pyatakov was recognized as a man of "outstanding will and outstanding ability," but only to immediately emphasize such an excessive fascination with his "administrativeness and administrative side of things" that he cannot "be relied upon in a serious political issue." And this is said about a man whom Lenin two days later, in the dictation about the State Planning Commission on December 27, 1922, took under his protection from Trotsky's criticism as a worthy deputy to the chairman of the State Planning Committee G. M. Krzhizhanovsky![7] It is clear that

---

[7] Lenin's endorsement of Pyatakov is as follows: "I think that the attacks which are now made against the Chairman of the State Planning Commission, Comrade Krzhizhanovsky, and Comrade Pyatakov, his deputy, and which proceed along two lines, so that, on the one hand, we hear charges of extreme leniency, lack of

> Lenin had a somewhat different opinion about Pyatakov than the Author of the "Letter to the Congress." The leadership of the State Planning Committee is serious administrative and political work. It was not without reason that Trotsky sought it. (375)

The end result is that Trotsky is the only person praised. Clearly, the "Characteristics" is designed to put Trotsky in the most positive light as the only logical successor to Lenin. But Stalin's only fault is that the Author "is not sure" that Stalin will be able to use his power "with sufficient caution." This remark is so vague that it can hardly be considered as a criticism.

Whose Political Interest Is Served by the "Letter to the Congress"?

Sakharov draws some obvious conclusions from the information presented above.

> Even a cursory acquaintance with the characteristics shows that they are given not just one after another. A certain system can be traced in them. Obviously, the Author considers in one block the characteristics of Stalin and Trotsky, and gives the "combined" characteristic of Zinoviev / Kamenev in close connection with the characteristic of Trotsky. The characteristics of Bukharin and Pyatakov are in many respects the same for both, and again, as will be shown below, it is possible that it has a certain connection with Trotsky. **It turns out that Trotsky is**

---

independent judgement and lack of backbone, and, on the other, charges of excessive coarseness, drill-sergeant methods, lack of solid scientific background, etc.—I think these attacks express two sides of the question, exaggerating them to the extreme, and that in actual fact we need a skillful combination in the State Planning Commission of two types of character, of which one may be exemplified by Comrade Pyatakov and the other by Comrade Krzhizhanovsky." CW 36, 598-9. (Russian at XLV 350)

> **the central figure of the "characteristics" complex. Is this a coincidence?** (377)

Stalin and Trotsky are presented as the leading persons in the Party leadership. But the comparison between them is always to the benefit of Trotsky.

> In the characteristic of Stalin, the assessment of "outstanding leader" associated with the recognition of the inability to carefully use the immense power, is equivalent to indicating that this leader is simply dangerous for the party. In the case of Trotsky, the situation is exactly the opposite. Minor and not very definite flaws serve only as a background against which an indication of his strengths turns into a genuine anthem: "distinguished by ... outstanding ability," "personally ... the most capable man in the present C.C.," he is at the same time "an outstanding leader of the present C.C.," in whom even his "non-Bolshevism" can scarcely be personally blamed. (377-8)

This leads logically to an inevitable conclusion in Trotsky's favor:

> All this phraseology brings the reader to the conclusion that after the removal of the "unworthy" leader, Stalin, from power, there remains one worthy person, Trotsky. (378)

The "Addition"

The "Addition," which is dated January 4, 1923 (CW 36, 596; XLV, 346) is aimed solely at specifying criticisms of Stalin that are absent in "Characteristics." But there are problems with it.

> The thesis of Stalin's rudeness is perhaps the "favorite" in traditional historiography. It is the easiest to prove, because Stalin himself admitted that he had such a flaw,[8] and, in addition, it is easily linked to the

> conflict between Stalin and Krupskaya, in which it receives solid support. If you believe the author of the "Letter to the Congress," Stalin's rudeness manifested itself in such proportions that it threatened to split the Central Committee and the party, therefore, it could not be overlooked, and information about it should have been directly recorded in certain documents or reflected in them indirectly. And again we must state that we are not aware of other texts of Lenin's in which there were indications of Stalin's rudeness as the dominant character trait determining his relations with people. Nor are we aware of any cases of written or oral complaints to Lenin about Stalin's rudeness.
>
> Even in the materials of the so-called "Lenin commission" (Fotieva, Glyasser, Gorbunov), that attempted to collect compromising materials on Stalin and Ordzhonikidze, there are no materials that speak either about rudeness as characteristic of Stalin's personality or politics, or about any manifestations of it. (365)[9]

To remove Stalin for "rudeness" implies that this quality must be well known, have been noted often, and is familiar to the Congress to which these documents are supposedly written. In fact, Stalin's "rudeness" had not been noted by anyone else. Nor was anything like this mentioned at the XII Party Congress in April, 1923.

In fact, the opposite was noted. Viktor P. Nogin, Chairman of the Central Auditing Commission (*Tsentral'naia revizionnaia komissiia*) from 1921 until his death in 1924, made the following remarks at the XII Party Congress:

---

[8] Stalin admitted that he was "grub" – rude, crude – several times. See XIV S"ezd, 499; Stalin's concluding speech to the XIV Party Congress, at http://www.hrono.ru/libris/stalin/7-1-408.php: "The Trotskyist Opposition Before and Now," October 21, 1927, at http://www.hrono.ru/libris/stalin/10-15.html; English at http://www.marx2mao.com/Stalin/TO27.html page 867.

[9] We will discuss this "commission" in future chapters.

> I deliberately sat in the reception area when not all comrades knew that I had come as a member of the auditing commission to see how the reception was taking place. I was in the reception area near comrade Stalin and comrade Syrtsov. **I must say that there was great propriety and great courtesy both toward the comrades working in the Central Committee**, so as not to burden them with unnecessary business, as well as toward those who were arriving. I must testify that **I do not know of any instance in the Central Committee in which our comrades were not treated in a communist way**.[10]

The only other time that "rudeness" is attributed to Stalin is in the letter of Krupskaya to Kamenev dated December 23, 1922. But this letter attributes a clash between Krupskaya and Stalin to the previous day, December 22. We know from other evidence – Stalin's reply of March 7, 1923, to the "ultimatum" letter dated March 5, 1923, Boris Bazhanov's reference to these events in his memoir,[11] and Maria Ulyanova's statement to the Central Committee in 1926 – that Stalin criticized Krupskaya five to six weeks *later*, at the end of January or beginning of February, 1923.

In any case, Lenin could not have had Stalin's purported "rudeness" to Krupskaya in mind on January 4, 1923 since, according to the traditionally accepted account, Lenin only learned about this incident of Stalin's "rudeness" in March, 1923. This means that a remark by Lenin on January 4, 1923 about Stalin's "rudeness" would have been completely unmotivated.

We have established: (1) that the L2C was written not in late December 1922 – early January 1923, but after the XII Party Congress; and (2) that the dispute between Stalin and Krupskaya did not take place on December 22, 1922, but four to five weeks

---

[10] *Dvenadtsatiy s"ezd RKP(b. 17-25 aprelia 1923 goda. Stenograficheskii otchet.* Moscow, 1968, 197.
[11] Discussed in Chapter 5.

Chapter Three. Letter to the Congress, Continues   83

later. Therefore it is now clear that these two documents were coordinated so that Krupskaya's letter to Kamenev calls Stalin "rude", and this accusation is echoed ten days later (see chapter 6) in the "Addition."

The Proposal to Remove Stalin from the Post of General Secretary

In expressing doubt about leaving Stalin as Gensec the Author – supposedly Lenin – presented some future Party Congress with a problem,

> ... the intractable task of finding a person who would differ from Stalin only by the absence of these negative traits but possessing all his virtues. The question immediately arises: where to find him? Speaking at the XI Congress of the RCP(b), Lenin directly said that there was no better candidate than Stalin for working in the people's commissariat of nationalities and the people's commissariat of the RKI, precisely because the necessary human and political qualities were happily combined in him. (405)

Lenin would surely want someone who would support and fight for his, Lenin's views.

> But there were very few people close to Lenin who possessed this combination of qualities. Among them Stalin was one of the most experienced, authoritative and proven in action. Furthermore, he should be an outstanding organizer who knows the cadres of the party, who has experience in solving all major issues of domestic and foreign policy, as well as party building. Here, perhaps, is the circle of the main features that Lenin appreciated in Stalin in connection with his work in the Secretariat of the Central Committee of the RCP(b). Of course, many prominent party leaders had a wealth of knowledge and

experience. But apart from Stalin, I suggest, no one met all these requirements. (405-6)

The "Addition" states:

> ... I suggest that the comrades think about a way of removing Stalin from that post and appointing another man in his stead ... (CW 36, 596)

But this was impossible, as Lenin certainly knew. The Congress could not remove a General Secretary. According to the Party rules, the current Central Committee resigns its powers before the Congress. The Congress then elects a new Central Committee and, at its first plenary, the new C.C. elects the Secretariat of the C.C., including the General Secretary. This is exactly the way Stalin had been elected. At the XI Party Congress in March, 1922, Lenin had urged that the post of General Secretary be created and that Stalin be chosen. Stalin was in fact elected on April 3, 1922, at the C.C. Plenum that followed the Congress.

This is the only way a General Secretary could be removed from office: a Party Congress could criticize the Gensec; members could recommend that he not be re-elected by the new C.C., or even recommend that he not be elected *to* the new C.C. So the election of a new Gensec could be prevented in some ways. But there was no way for a Congress to remove him. Lenin, of course, knew this. So turning to the Congress to "remove" Stalin from the post of Gensec is nonsense.

The "Letter to the Congress" – a Factional Document

It follows from the above that this document cannot be a letter addressed to the party congress. This conclusion is also supported by the fact that in the text of the "Letter to the Congress" the Author does not refer either to the Congress or to its delegates. He does refer to "comrades." But this cannot mean the delegates since the Congress could not remove the Gensec. And, as we have noted, this document was named "Letter to the Congress" later on. (416)

Chapter Three. Letter to the Congress, Continues   85

Recall that the copy of "Characteristics" in Trotsky's archive has the note "In the original the manuscript (*rukopis'*) does not carry any title. – L.T."[12]

All this means that the L2C could not have been addressed to a Party Congress. In fact, there was no way to remove a Gensec other than by failing to elect him by the C.C. But the C.C. is not mentioned. And anyway, the document is said – by Krupskaya – to be addressed not to the C.C. but to a Party Congress.

The words "comrades think[ing] about a way of removing Stalin" suggests something outside the Party rules, even conspiratorial. That means it is, or was in its origin, a *factional* document, addressed to a circle of like-minded people, outside the framework of the Party. It would make sense as a preparation for a C.C. Plenum, since only the Plenum could elect, or fail to elect, Stalin as Gensec.

> There is indeed meaning in this formulation of the question. This meaning is revealed only if it is assumed that the Author of the "Letter to the Congress" tried to use a path outside the Party rules. It is impossible not to notice that the very wording of this proposal – "discuss with comrades a method of removing" Stalin – carries in itself some element of "conspiracy." It reveals the Author's desire for a preliminary discussion of some steps or other not stipulated by the Party rules. Why? Apparently, in order to calculate in advance all the moves, think through the main arguments and thus prepare a question to be discussed. Such conspiracy excludes an official appeal to the Central Committee and the Politburo. It is possible only in addressing a circle of like-minded people outside the framework of the Central Committee and the Politburo. Thus, this formulation says that the so-called "Letter to the

---

[12] Fel'shtinsky, Komm. Opp. I, p. 45 of 168 of the online text edition.

> Congress" only makes sense as a factional document, as an appeal to one's associates with a proposal to discuss specific measures aimed at eliminating Stalin from the main party position – from the post of General Secretary of the Central Committee … In this case, the "method of removal" is a matter of tactics in a struggle for votes in the Central Committee, a discussion of measures aimed at winning the majority by attracting those who hesitate in support of their proposal, splitting the enemy's ranks, etc. .(417)

This also explains why there is no concern in L2C for Stalin's future as one of the two (aside from Lenin) most prominent Party leaders. If the Author – if Lenin – were concerned with the Party, he would present ideas about how to use Stalin's undoubted talents to benefit the Party. Instead, the Author of this document is only interested in getting Stalin out of the way. In effect that meant eliminating him as Trotsky's main political opponent. So he is indifferent to Stalin's fate.

To sum up:

* The L2C could not have been created before the XII Party Congress.

* Therefore, Lenin cannot have been the author.

* It is not an appeal to a Party Congress, or to the Central Committee, or the Politburo.

* It is a document of factional struggle originating from political circles opposed to the current Party leadership.

* The text is not a finished document. It is more like notes, sketches, a study of individual issues, partly for oneself, partly for others to read.

* Its main – really, its sole – purpose is to get rid of Stalin as Gensec.

The political interests of the document strongly suggest that it was created to help Trotsky. By whom? We can't be sure. But it was presented by Krupskaya. She must have played an important role in its creation.

At the XIII Party Congress (May 23 – May 31, 1924), after Lenin's death in January, the whole Congress voted not to publish the "Letter to the Congress." According to Sakharov, who cites an unpublished document, Stalin claimed that this vote was unanimous, that not even Trotsky voted to publish them. (590)

At the XIV Party Congress (December 18 – 31, 1925) Zinoviev and Kamenev, but other speakers too, began to use the term the "testament" of Lenin (Kuibyshev, 548). Zinoviev used the term "the political testament of Lenin" (97), "last testament." (115).[13]

---

[13] *XIV S'ezd Vsesoiuznoi Kommunisticheskoi Partii (B). Stenograficheskii Otchet.* Moscow: Gosudarstvennoe izdatel'stvo, 1926.

Chapter 4. Letters to Trotsky and to Mdivani and Makharadze

Two important letters attributed to Lenin are those to Trotsky, dated March 5, 1923, and to Budu Mdivani and Filip Makharadze, dated March 6, 1923 (LIV, 329-330; CW 45, 607-8)

There are a number of issues that cast doubt on the genuineness of these letters. We will begin with the evidence that they were not composed on the dates given in the texts. That in itself establishes that they could not be by Lenin because on March 10, 1923, Lenin had his final stroke, which not only further incapacitated him physically but also deprived him of the ability to speak. After this date Lenin could not dictate anything. His political life was over.

The Letter to Mdivani and Makharadze, dated March 6, 1923[1]

> Comrades Mdivani, Makharadze and others
>
> Copy to Comrades Trotsky and Kamenev
>
> Dear Comrades:
>
> I am following your case with all my heart [*vsei dushoi slezhu* – literally, "with all my soul"] I am indignant over Orjonikidze's rudeness and the connivance of Stalin and Dzerzhinsky. I am preparing for you notes and a speech.
>
> Respectfully yours,
>
> Lenin
>
> March 6, 1923

---

[1] See illustration #6a.

Chapter Four. Letters to Trotsky and to Mdivani and Makharadze

"I am preparing …" suggests that the notes and speech mentioned were more than just a vague idea. They imply an outline, or at least some indication for future work. But there is nothing. Dmitri Volkogonov, who had complete access to all archives, wrote in his biography of Stalin:

> К сожалению, ни записок, ни речи Ленин не приготовил.
>
> Unfortunately, Lenin did not prepare either notes or a speech.[2]

We know that this letter did exist at the time, because on March 7, 1923, Stalin wrote to Ordzhonikidze that he had learned of it from Kamenev:

> Я узнал от т. Каменева, что Ильич посылает тт. Махарадзе и другим письмецо, где он солидаризируется с уклонистами и ругает тебя, т. Дзержинского и меня.
>
> I learned from com. Kamenev that Ilyich has sent to com. Makharadze and to others a letter in which he expresses solidarity with the deviators and scolds you, com. Dzerzhinsky and me. (Izv TsK 9, 1990, 151)

Kamenev mentions that Lenin had given him the letter to Mdivani and Makharadze to transmit to them "and to others." We will discuss this in the chapter on the "ultimatum" letter. So Stalin believed that Lenin had sent this letter, though he had not seen it himself.[3]

Stalin continues:

---

[2] Volkogonov, *Stalin. Tom 1*. Moscow, 1991, p. 142. I was guided to this citation by a note in Sakharov, p. 341.
[3] Trotsky's copy is reproduced in Fel'shtinsky, Komm. Opp. I,, p. 20 of 168 in online text edition.

> Видимо имеется цель надавить на волю съезда Компартии Грузии в пользу уклонистов. Нечего и говорить, что уклонисты, получив это письмецо, используют его вовсю против Заккрайкома, особенно против тебя и т. Мясникова. (Izv TsK 9, 1990, 151-2
>
> Apparently the aim is to put pressure on the will of the Congress of the Com. Party of Georgia in favor of the deviators. Needless to say, the deviators, having received this letter, will use it with a vengeance against the Zakkraikom[4], especially against you and Comrade Myasnikov.

Curiously, this proved not to be the case. Neither Mdivani nor Makharadze made any reference to this letter from Lenin at the XII Party Congress of April 17-25, 1923.[5]

Meanwhile, Lenin's condition was poor and getting worse. Kotkin notes:

> Only a few months before, Lenin was admonishing Mdivani and Makharadze sternly. **It was not clear Lenin was in any condition to dictate letters**. (Kotkin 490)

On March 6, the Doctors Journal records this:

> When he awoke, he summoned a nurse, but he could almost not converse with her, he wanted the nurse to summon Nadezhda Konstantinovna, but he could not say her name ... Vladimir Ilich lay with a confused visage, the expression on his face was frightening, his eyes were sad, his look questioning, tears came down

---

[4] Abbreviation of "Zakavkazskii kraievoi komitet," Transcaucasus Regional Committee of the Russian Communist Party (Bolshevik), later the All-Union Communist Party (bolshevik).

[5] As far as we know today, they never mentioned it at all.

Chapter Four. Letters to Trotsky and to Mdivani and Makharadze

> from his eyes. Vladimir Ilich is agitated, he tries to speak, but cannot find the words, and he adds: 'Ah the devil, ah the devil, such an illness, this is a return to the old illness' and so on.[6]

Interviewed by Aleksandr Bek in 1963, Volodicheva said:

> ... официально стало известно, что Владимир Ильич 6 марта или даже уже 5-го был не в состоянии ни читать, ни работать, ни кого-то принимать, ни что-то предпринимать.[7]
>
> ... it became officially known that Vladimir Ilyich on March 6, or even on March 5, was unable to read, work, accept anyone, or do anything.

This interview is titled "Towards a history of the last documents of Lenin." It seems that neither Bek nor the editors of *Moskovskie Novosti* realized that *these remarks by Volodicheva undermine the validity of the letters supposedly dictated by Lenin on March 5 and 6, 1923.* As far as we know today, no one else has noticed it either.

On March 6, the Doctors Journal states:

> In the morning [after breakfast at 11 a.m.] Vladimir Il'ich called com. Fotieva and com. Volodicheva, to whom he dictated a few words, 1 ½ lines in all ... He seemed unwell, but not too bad. (*Kentavr*, Oct-Dec. 1991, 109)

The letter to Mdivani and Makharadze is more than twice as long as 1 ½ lines. Still, the doctor may not have been precise.

Lenin had suffered a seizure or similar episode. The Doctors Journal records no more dictation or reading of any kind. On

---

[6] *Kentavr* October – December 1991, 109.
[7] "K istorii poslednikh leninskikh dokumentov." *Moskovskie Novosti* April 23, 1989, p. 8.

March 10, Lenin suffered a third, terrible stroke. His days of working were over.

Mdivani spoke twice at the XII Party Congress, on April 18 (evening session) and April 23 (day session).[8] In his last remarks, he cited "The Question of Nationalities or 'Autonomization,'" a text attributed to Lenin but so inconsistent with the views Lenin had previously expressed that both Sakharov and Stephen Kotkin reject it as a fabrication.[9] Its genuineness was not questioned at the time, however. The views expressed in it, attributed to Lenin, strongly affirmed Mdivani's nationalist viewpoint.

According to the 1968 edition of the XII P.C. transcript, Mdivani cited (not with complete accuracy) this essay of "Lenin" at some length, putting special emphasis on the passages dealing with Georgia and the Caucasus. He was interrupted by the Chair, who reminded him that a decision had been made not to publish this essay yet. Mdivani replied that he was not publishing it, but only citing certain passages from it. The Chair allowed Mdivani to make references to this text, but not to summarize it, and Mdivani agreed. (XII Party Congress, 496-7)

Makharadze spoke three times at the XII P.C.: in the day session of April 19; in the evening session that same day; and in the day session on April 23, the final day of the Congress. He made one allusion to "Lenin's teaching" on the national question (ibid. 170).

At the close of his first remarks, in which he outlined the dispute concerning the national question, Georgia, and the Transcaucasus Federation, Makharadze even said that he expected that *Stalin* would present "a complete and very clear answer to these questions" which would "put an end once and for all" to what he termed "abnormal occurrences."

> Я думаю, что т. Сталин даст нам исчерпывающий и вполне ясный ответ на эти вопросы для того, чтобы

---

[8] XII P.C. transcript, 1968, pp. 164-8, 899-900.
[9] Kotkin 501, calls it "a blatant forgery."

раз навсегда изжить те ненормальные явления, которые у нас до этого имели место. (XII P.C., 174)

I think that Comrade Stalin will give us a complete and very clear answer to these questions in order to put an end once and for all those abnormal occurrences that have taken place in our country before this.

Makharadze's expression of confidence in Stalin here runs completely counter to "Lenin's" alleged conviction that Stalin was to blame (in some way which is never explained) for "Great-Russian chauvinism" and so could not be trusted on the Georgian issue. It also contradicts "Lenin's" remark in the purported letter to Mdivani and Makharadze about "the connivance of Stalin." If Makharadze had in fact received this "Lenin" letter, he not only chose not to mention the fact *but also went out of his way here to contradict Lenin by absolving Stalin of any blame*!

In his second remarks Makharadze presented a declaration concerning the situation in Georgia. In his third remarks (515-9) Makharadze also referred to Lenin's "The Question of Nationalities or 'Autonomization'." He specifically reminded the Congress that Lenin had written about "Great-Russian chauvinism" and had been "the first to raise the banner of struggle" against it.[10]

Neither Mdivani nor Makharadze hesitated to cite Lenin in defense of their positions.[11] Yet neither of them cited the purported letter to them of March 6, 1923. Why not? The text of that letter, which purported to be from Lenin expressing his solidarity with them and opposition to Ordzhonikidze and Stalin, might have been, in the eyes of the delegates, a strong argument in their favor.

---

[10] Note 248, on p. 880 of the 1968 edition of the Transcript of the XII P.C., confirms that these speakers meant Lenin's essay "The Question of Nationalities ..."
[11] Other speakers referred to this essay as well – for example, Avel' Enukidze (583-4).

Trotsky did not mention it either – and one might have expected Trotsky to cite this as clear evidence of Lenin's distrust of Stalin. So what Stalin had anticipated did not come to pass.

One logical conclusion might be that neither man had received that letter. But this can hardly be the case, since on April 16, 1923, Trotsky sent "The Question of Nationalities …" plus Lenin's letter to him of March 5, plus Lenin's letter to Mdivani and Makharadze of March 6, to the Central Committee (Izv TsK 1990, 9, 158).

> I have received today the attached copy of a letter from Comrade Lenin's personal secretary, Comrade L. Fotieva, to Comrade Kamenev concerning Comrade Lenin's article on the national question.
>
> Comrade Lenin's article was received by me on March 5 simultaneously with three notes of Comrade Lenin, copies of which are also attached.[12]

The following day, April 17, in another letter to the C.C. Trotsky quoted, though inaccurately, from the letter to Mdivani and Makharadze (Izv TsK 9, 1990, 160):

> 5. Какие распоряжения отданы т. Лениным относительно его статьи и других документов по грузинскому делу («готовлю речи и статьи») об этом я ничего не знал.
>
> 5. What orders were given by Comrade Lenin regarding his article and other documents on the Georgian case ("I am preparing speeches and articles"), I knew nothing about this.

What Lenin actually said was "Готовлю для вас записки и речь" – "I am preparing for you (plural) notes and a speech," not "I am

---

[12] According to the editor's note these are Fotieva's letter to Kamenev dated April 16, 1923 (TsK KPSS 9,1990, 156) and the two letters to Trotsky and to Mdivani and Makharadze.

Chapter Four. Letters to Trotsky and to Mdivani and Makharadze

preparing speeches and articles." Trotsky had the copy we have today – it was Trotsky who had sent it to the Central Committee. Why did he get this so wrong?

We cannot explain why neither of the Georgians or Trotsky referred to Lenin's very supportive letter to them during the XII Party Congress. But the main question before us remains this: Did Lenin dictate this letter, and the letter dated the previous day, March 5, to Trotsky?

From the letter to Mdivani and Makharadze:

> I am indignant over Orjonikidze's rudeness and the connivance of Stalin and Dzerzhinsky. (CW 45, 608)

What is odd about this is that Lenin had already received reports about the incident in question – Ordzhonikidze's slapping Akakii Kabakhidze, a member of the Georgian CP Central Committee – and neither of these reports blame Ordzhonikidze, Dzerzhinsky, or Stalin. Aleksei Rykov, an eyewitness to this incident, wrote the following account on February 7, 1923:

> В Тифлисе на квартире т. Орджоникидзе в моем присутствии разыгрался следующий инцидент: Для свидания со мной на квартиру т. Орджоникидзе пришел член РКП и мой товарищ по ссылке в Сибири Акакий Кабахидзе. Во время общего разговора т. Кабахидзе упрекнул Серго Орджоникидзе в том, что у него есть какая-то лошадь и что товарищи, стоящие наверху, в том числе т. Орджоникидзе, в материальном отношении обеспечены гораздо лучше, чем другие члены партии. В частности, был какой-то разговор о влиянии новой таможенной политики в Батуми на рост дороговизны. Одну из фраз, по-видимому, относительно того, что Серго Орджоникидзе на казенный счет кормит какую-то лошадь, Акакий Кабахидзе сказал Серго на ухо. Вслед за этим между ними разгорелась словесная перебранка, во

время которой т. Орджоникидзе ударил Кабахидзе. При вмешательстве моем и моей жены инцидент на этом был прекращен и т.Кабахидзе ушел с квартиры. После этого Серго Орджоникидзе пережил очень сильное нервное потрясение, кончившееся истерикой

In Tiflis, at the apartment of Comrade Ordzhonikidze in my presence, the following incident occurred:

To meet with me, at the apartment of Comrade Ordzhonikidze came member of the RCP and my friend in exile in Siberia Akaki Kabakhidze. During a general conversation, Comrade Kabakhidze rebuked Sergo Ordzhonikidze that he has some kind of horse and that comrades, standing above [in rank], including Comrade Ordzhonikidze, in material circumstances are provided much better than other party members. In particular, there's some talk about the impact of the new customs policy in Batumi on the increase in high cost. One of the phrases, apparently regarding the fact that Sergo Ordzhonikidze on state funds is feeding some horse, Akaki Kabakhidze spoke to Sergo in his ear. Following this, a verbal skirmish broke out between them, during which Comrade Ordzhonikidze struck Kabakhidze. With the intervention of myself and my wife, this incident stopped and Comrade Kabakhidze left the apartment. After that Sergo Ordzhonikidze experienced a very strong nervous shock that ended with hysterics.

Rykov concluded with this summation:

On the merits of the incident …I believe that Comrade Ordzhonikidze was right when he interpreted those reproaches made to him by com. Kabakhidze as a cruel personal insult. (250-1)

The other eyewitness, Georgii Davidovich Rtveladze, said much the same thing:

> The incident of the slap given by Comrade Ordzhonikidze to comrade Kabakhidze was a private matter, not associated with factionalism. [Kabakh]idze did not submit any written statement to the [Party] Control Commission, and this incident was not considered by the Central Committee of Georgia. (251)

Ordzhonikidze himself admitted hitting Kabakhidze while claiming that this was caused by a personal insult rather than any political disagreement.[13]

On November 25, 1922, the Politburo accepted a proposal by the Secretariat – Stalin's office – to form a commission to study the situation in Georgia, including, of course, the circumstances during which Ordzhonikidze had slapped Kabakhidze. The decision was confirmed on November 30. This means that Stalin himself had either made or approved the proposal that the Georgian incident be investigated.

This commission (Felix Dzerzhinsky, chair, Dmitri Manuil'sky and V.S. Mitskiavichius-Kapsukas, members) were to go to Tiflis, investigate, and make a report. Lenin was at work on this day, and the previous day he had received the report of the meeting of the 25th, with the proposal for the formation of the commission. Lenin was informed of this decision and of the makeup of the commission, and made no objections. (252)

The commission spent four days in Tiflis. After his return in December, 1922, Rykov spoke with Lenin by phone on December 9

---

[13] Sakharov cites Rykov's, Rtveladze's, and Ordzhonikidze's remarks from archival document. Rtveladze's and Rykov's accounts are confirmed in the recent textbook by Aleksandr Ivanovich Vdovin, *SSSR. Istoriia velikoi derzhavy 1922-1991* (Moscow: Prospekt, 2018), 30-31. While he does not accept Sakharov's contention that "The Question of Nationalities ..." is a forgery, Vdovin does confirm these two accounts..

(XLV 469; CW 42, 477) and met in person with him on December 12. (XLV 470; CW 42, 478) Presumably – assuming he really was interested enough – Lenin asked Rykov about the incident between Ordzhonikidze and Kabakhidze, and Rykov told him what he later wrote down on February 7, 1923. (254)

On the same day, December 12, Lenin met with Dzerzhinsky for 45 minutes. Dzerzhinsky must have read, or at least summarized, his report for Lenin, or why would he have met with Lenin after his return? There is no record of what Lenin thought of Dzerzhinsky's report. The Secretaries Journal does not record Lenin's mood for that evening, but for the following evening, December 13, notes that Lenin's mood was good and that he joked. (XLV, 471; CW 42, 478)

Another crucial point is this: *Stalin had nothing whatever to do with this incident in the first place!* So how could *Lenin* have written that he was "indignant … at the connivance of Stalin …"?

At the end of January, 1923, Lenin appointed a group of three to study the materials of the Dzerzhinsky commission and the Georgian affair. (346) Sakharov argues that this body was heavily biased against the results of the Dzerzhinsky commission, in favor of the "old" C.C. of the Georgian Party, against the steps taken by the Politburo, and especially against Stalin personally. The "commission," as it came to be called, was composed of N.P. Gorbunov, business manager (*upravliaiushchii delami*) of the Soviet of People's Commissars, the executive branch of the government, plus two of Lenin's secretaries, Lidia A. Fotieva and Maria I. Glyasser.

Since the documents of this "commission" have not been published I, like Kotkin, have taken the account below from Sakharov, who had access to these archival materials, specifically from Sakharov's book *Na rasput'e*, Chapter 2.3, "Use of the pseudo-Lenin texts of 'Lenin's Testament' in the power struggle within the RCP(b) and the Soviet state."

Contrary to the opinion established in historiography, no one ever gave this group ... any official status or commissioned it for any investigation into the political conflict in the Georgian Communist Party. No one ever granted its members the right to audit the work of the commission of the Central Committee of the RCP(b) which had investigated the conflict in the Communist Party of Georgia.

The members of this "commission" themselves did not claim such rights. Turning to the Politburo of the Central Committee for materials, Gorbunov, Fotieva and Glyasser stated the purpose of their work as follows: "a detailed study" of the materials. They did not call themselves a "commission."[5] Accordingly, the Politburo issued the documents of the Dzerzhinsky commission "to study them on behalf of Comrade Lenin."[6] This wording says that the materials were issued for informing Lenin, and not for independent political activity of any kind by this "commission" of technical workers of the Council of People's Commissars. In the same way Glyasser described the task of this "commission" in a letter to Bukharin on January 11, 1924: the commission was created "to **familiarize**[14] ourselves with the materials of the commission of Comrade Dzerzhinsky." To study a problem and issue a verdict on it, and to study the materials on a problem and make a report about them – these are not at all the same thing.

The name "commission" was assigned to this group later, in the process of their work ... A commission of the Council of the People's Commissars, even one created by Lenin, in the political system of that day, could not attempt to reconsider the conclusions of a

---

[14] Boldface in original.

> commission of the Central Committee of the RCP(b). In other words, the "commission" of Gorbunov, Fotieva and Glyasser was neither a Party nor a political "commission." All that remained was an auxiliary, purely technical role — to prepare material in order to bring it to the attention of Lenin in a form convenient for him.

Officially, it appears, Lenin asked it to obtain the materials of the Dzerzhinsky Commission and perhaps also to study and assess the decisions of higher state and Party organs, including the C.C., Politburo, Orgburo, and Secretariat. In reality, this group set out to prepare a political attack on Stalin.

> The surviving draft versions of the documents that it was preparing indicate that in its activity this "commission" went far beyond the boundaries of the "Georgian issue" as it was then understood, and therefore also beyond the scope of the task assigned to them by Lenin and about which the Politburo of the C.C. was informed.

> ... the materials of this "commission" contain information that, first, allows us to assert that their work was not supervised by Lenin, but by someone else and, second, that these documents were not prepared for Lenin. The latter is indicated, for example, by the following note ... "Organize the mater[ial] not so much in defense of the deviationists as in indictment of the great power chauvinists." This record is dated March 12, 1923. Therefore it could not belong to Lenin, since he had lost all power of speech by March 9-10 at the latest if not several days before that. Someone else had given these instructions to Gorbunov, Fotieva, and Glyasser. Once again we are led to wonder: For whom was this "commission" really working?

Chapter Four. Letters to Trotsky and to Mdivani and Makharadze

The materials of the "commission" also contain information indicating that it may have still been conducting its work at the end of March, 1923. This is indicated by the correspondence stored among the documents of the Lenin secretariat between M. I. Glyasser, a member of this "commission," who was also the technical secretary of the Politburo, and Trotsky at a meeting of the Politburo of the Central Committee of the RCP(b).

Glyasser's note (March 26) and Trotsky's response (March 28) are documents related to the work of the Politburo (part of a set of documents related to the meeting of the Politburo of the Central Committee on March 26, 1923). Therefore, the very fact of finding it in the materials of the secretariat of the chairman of the Council of People's Commissars of the RSFSR needs to be explained, among those documents that came into it after Lenin had lost all ability to work and, therefore, when the work of this "commission" had lost all meaning. **This note could appear among the materials of this "commission" only if it was still functioning. For whom was it working?**

Moreover, there is reason to argue that this note is not relevant to this meeting of the Politburo and was created "retroactively" – that is, that it was falsified. This, obviously, explains the mistake made by the falsifiers (Trotsky and Glyasser): **Ordzhonikidze, whose speech at the meeting of the Politburo is mentioned in a note, was not present at this meeting**. Consequently, this note is a fake, created no earlier than March 26, 1923. This fact is important because it clarifies how and by whom the fakes designed to serve the interests of those who led the fight against Stalin were introduced into the document production of Lenin's secretariat and into political life.[15]

Glyasser's Note

On January 25, 1923, the three "commission" members sent a message to Stalin asking him for all the materials of the Dzerzhinsky commission for the purpose of detailed and secret study. (347) It had no further powers.

On January 11, 1924, in a letter to Bukharin, M.I. Glyasser wrote that Lenin

> назначил к[оми]ссию (Фотиева, Горбунов и я) для ознакомления с материалами к[оми]ссии т. Дзержинского.
>
> appointed a commission (Fotieva, Gorbunov, and me) to familiarize ourselves with the materials of the commission of com. Dzerzhinsky. (Izv TsK KPSS 9, 1990, 163)

Glyasser reported that on February 5, 1923, Lenin spoke to her at 7 p.m. for 20 minutes, giving her detailed directions about the commission on the Georgian question. (348; XLV, 480-1; CW 42, 488-9). However, this is contradicted by the Doctors Journal, which clearly states that Lenin dictated in the *morning*, and to Volodicheva, not to Glyasser. After that, Lenin only napped and read after dinner.[16] There is nothing about any meeting with Glyasser or anyone else.

Evidently, therefore, this supposed meeting did not take place. Sakharov calls it "this Glyasser note, fabricated as a diary [i.e. as a journal entry]" (349) both because the Doctors Journal records no such visit with Lenin on that date, and because the Secretaries

---

[15] Sakharov, *Na rasput'e*, Ch. 2.3, pp. 137-140.

[16] *Kentavr* Oct. – Dec., 1991, 100,101,113. The editors of the Doctors Journal add, in footnote 61 to this date, that Lenin talked with Glyasser for 20 minutes at 6:15 p.m. But they admit that this information comes from Glyasser's own report in XLV 480.

Chapter Four. Letters to Trotsky and to Mdivani and Makharadze

Journal was left blank, with many entries obviously filled in later and blank spaces for entries that were never filled in..

So Glyasser lied in the Secretaries Journal! Sakharov accounts for her entry in the following way:

> This Glyasser note, fabricated as a diary [i.e. as a journal entry], is very important for understanding the history of the work of the so-called "Lenin commission." It serves as the only evidence of Lenin's aspiration to significantly expand the tasks originally assigned to the "commission," and, apparently, is intended to explain the appearance among its materials some that go far beyond the limit of the functions declared on the Politburo and fixed in its name.

Sakharov points to the importance of the discovery that Glyasser lied:

> This entry by Glyasser largely devalues her testimony about Lenin's leadership of the commission's work, contained in her letter to Bukharin of January 11, 1924, that Lenin "already had his preconceived opinion, literally guided our work and was terribly worried that we would not be able to prove in his report what he needed and that he will not have time to prepare his speech before the congress."[17] (349)

---

[17] Glyasser's words (Izv TsK KPSS 9, 1990, 163) are as follows: «Вл. Ил. свою статью по нацвопросу написал раньше, чем назначил к[оми]ссию (Фотиева, Горбунов и я) для ознакомления с материалами к[оми]ссии т. Дзержинского. Он имел уже свое предвзятое мнение, нашей работой буквально руководил и страшно волновался, что мы не сумеем доказать в своем докладе то, что ему надо и он не успеет до съезда подготовить свое выступление.» - "Vl. Il. wrote his article on the national issue before he appointed the commission (Fotieva, Gorbunov and me) to get acquainted with the materials of comrade Dzerzhinsky's commission. He already had his own preconceived opinion, literally supervised our work and was terribly worried that we would not be able to prove in our report what he needed and that he

Sakharov identifies the list of questions that, according to the editors of the PSS, Lenin gave to Fotieva on February 1, to direct the work of the "commission."

> Л. А. Фотиевой были записаны следующие указания В. И. Ленина: «1) За что старый ЦК КП Грузии обвинили в уклонизме. 2) Что им вменялось в вину, как нарушение партийной дисциплины. 3) За что обвиняют Заккрайком в подавлении ЦК КП Грузии. 4) Физические способы подавления («биомеханика»). 5) Линия ЦК (РКП(б). — Ред.) в отсутствии Владимира Ильича и при Владимире Ильиче. 6) Отношение комиссии. Рассматривала ли она только обви нения против ЦК КП Грузии или также и против Заккрайкома? Рассматривала ли она случай биомеханики? 7) Настоящее положение (выборная кампания, меньшевики, подавление, национальная рознь). (XLV, 606-7)

> Fotieva wrote down the following instructions, allegedly from Lenin: "1) Why was the old C.C. of the C.P. of Georgia accused of deviationism. 2) What breach of Party discipline were they blamed for. 3) Why is the Transcaucasian Committee accused of suppressing the C.C. of the C.P. of Georgia? 4) The physical means of suppression ('biomechanics'). 5) The line of the C.C. (of the R.C.P. (B.)— Ed.) in Vladimir Ilyich's absence and in his presence. 6) Attitude of the Commission. Did it examine only the accusations against the C.C. of the C.P. of Georgia or also against the Transcaucasian Committee? Did it examine the 'biomechanics' incident? 7) The present situation (the election campaign, the Mensheviks, suppression, national discord)" (CW 42, 620)[18]

---

would not have time to prepare his speech before the congress."

[18] For some reason the PSS editors do not give a precise archival identifier for this

Sakharov doubts that this document is genuine, i.e. that these questions come from Lenin, because the first three questions relate to facts long known to Lenin. The fourth points to an attempt to link the assault by Ordzhonikidze with the suppression of political opponents. But this

> requires an explanation, since all the eyewitness testimonies that came to Lenin, as was shown above, exclude such a connection. The sixth question is formulated as if the author had not spoken with Dzerzhinsky and Rykov about this story after their return from Georgia. Only the fifth question — about the "line" of the Central Committee under Lenin and in his absence — seems natural ... (349)

This document is not dated, not signed by Lenin, and contains questions whose answers Lenin already knew. If we accept Sakharov's analysis here, we are forced to one of two conclusions.

(1) These questions are by Lenin. In this case he has forgotten a great deal due to his illness. This can't be completely ruled out. But if it is true, then the political value of Lenin's last writings, especially "The Question of Nationalities ..." and the letters to Trotsky of March 5, 1923 and to Mdivani and Makharadze of March 6, 1923, are of no value because they reflect a significant deterioration of Lenin's mental abilities.

(2) These questions are not by Lenin. In this case Fotieva – if, as the PSS editors claim, she wrote them – is lying. This conclusion is strengthened by the note in the Doctors Journal contradicting Glyasser's claim (see above).

One might conceivably suggest that the secretaries and Krupskaya were manipulating an ill and seriously confused Lenin into "saying" what they wanted him to say. But the lucidity of many of Lenin's other last writings stands in contradiction to this

---

document in the Central Party Archives, Institute of Marxism-Leninism of the C.C., C.P.S.U.

supposition. Indeed, one argument that Glyasser was lying is the intellectual quality of those of Lenin's last writings that are undoubtedly from him, and which show no signs of mental deterioration.[19] These documents could hardly have been written by someone who was as confused as Lenin would have had to be in order to pose the questions that, according to the PSS editors, Glyasser said that he asked the commission to investigate.

An additional argument in favor of the theory that Glyasser was lying is that Krupskaya did not bring forth the L2C until well after the XII P.C. was ended, and that, as outlined in a previous chapter, the main elements of L2C were expressed during the XII P.C. This deception on Krupskaya's part could not have taken place without the knowledge of Lenin's secretaries, Fotieva, Volodicheva, and Glyasser.

Nevertheless, the "commission" found nothing to blame Stalin for. Sakharov quotes from its conclusions:

> The conclusion of the com[mission] (of Dzerzhinsky. - V.S.) was reached even before leaving Moscow. If it were not for the authority of the Central Committee, Makharadze would have a majority in the party. There is a compromise (of Zin[ov'ev] with Stalin). At their congress[20] they send two authoritative comrades. Kuibyshev and Bukharin or Kamenev. Disagree with the line of Ordzh[onikidze] Zinoviev, Trotsky, Bukharin, Kamenev (hesitates). The letter is sent with the majority abstaining.

---

[19] These are: 1. The dictation of December 23, 1923; 2."On giving legislative functions to Gosplan" (December 27 – 29, 1922); 3. "Pages from a Diary;" (end of December, 1922 – beginning of January, 1923); 4. "On Cooperation;" (unfinished article, early January, 1923); 5. "On Our Revolution (concerning notes by N. Sukhanov) (mid-January, 19223); " 6. The first draft of the article "On the reorganization of the C.C. – W.P.I" (January 9-13, 1923); 7. "How we must reorganize Rabkrin" (January 19-23, 1923); "Better Fewer, But Better" (end of January to beginning of March, 1923).

[20] A reference to the second congress of the Communist Party of Georgia.

Chapter Four. Letters to Trotsky and to Mdivani and Makharadze

> Compromise [-] return part of the deviationists.
>
> Zinoviev [thinks] - Ordzh[onikidze] must remain.
>
> Stalin - you can [send him] to Turkestan for a year. (356)

It was Stalin who had proposed the harshest penalty against Ordzhonikidze! Turkestan could be regarded as a sort of punishment, a "party exile." If the purpose of the "commission" was to find Stalin at fault, it failed to present any evidence to support that.

There is no evidence that Lenin actually saw the "commission's" report or that it was read to him. But whether he did or he didn't, how could he have dictated (he couldn't write) "I am indignant over Ordzhonikidze's rudeness and the connivance of Stalin and Dzerzhinsky" when no one, not even the "commission's" report, concluded that Stalin had done anything wrong?

Either Lenin did dictate this letter to Mdivani and Makharadze, or he did not. If he did, he had been seriously misinformed – even the "commission" had found no evidence to blame Stalin. Plus the record in the Doctors Journal was somehow incorrect in claiming that Lenin had dictated only 1 ½ lines.

Or Lenin did *not* dictate the letter to Mdivani and Makharadze, and Fotieva falsely cited the brief, 1½ line dictation mentioned by the doctor on duty in order to claim that Lenin had done so. It would have been obvious within a day or two that Lenin would never work again – in fact, he never recovered the ability to speak. At this point, March 7 or 8, it would have been safe for Krupskaya, with Fotieva's connivance, to compose the short letter to Mdivani and Makharadze and claim that this is what Lenin had dictated on March 6, his final day of work. This is consistent with the other evidence of Krupskaya's and the secretaries' falsifications, and with Volodicheva's statement to Aleksandr Beck in 1963 that Lenin was unable to do anything on March 6 or even on March 5.

Likewise, "The Question of Nationalities ..." accuses Stalin, but without citing any evidence whatever. Was Lenin informed of this? If he was, how could he write "... with the connivance of Stalin ..."? If not, suggests Sakharov, for whom was this so-called "commission" really formed, and to whom did it really report?

A final part of a report by the "commission" titled "On the conclusions of the Dzerzhinsky commission," is dated March 3, 1923 and signed by Fotieva, Gorbunov, and Glyasser,[21] Yuri. A. Buranov[22] a historian very hostile toward Stalin, concluded that Lenin was made familiar with this document. But Buranov had no evidence for this statement. There are no entries at all in the Secretaries Journal for the days between February 14 and March 5 (XLV, 485-6).

However, the account in the Doctors Journal is detailed. It does not mention any meeting by Lenin with any of the members of this commission: Gorbunov, Fotieva, or Glyasser (Kentavr, 107-112). Therefore, there is no evidence that Lenin saw this report, or even that the report was actually completed by March 3.

The letter to Mdivani and Makharadze says: "I am preparing for you notes and a speech." (*Готовлю для вас записки и речь*). Dmitri Volkogonov, who had full access to all archival materials, confirms that he could find no trace of the notes or speech. It appears clear from the Doctors Journal that Lenin was in no condition to write a speech.

* * * * *

All of this evidence – and I have greatly abbreviated Sakharov's account, for example, his detailed examination of the documents of the "commission," all of which are still unpublished – is consistent

---

[21] This note, and all of the documents of this "commission," remain unpublished. Sakharov gives the archival identifiers.

[22] "K istorii leninskogo 'politicheskogo zaveshchaniia' (1922-1923 gg)." Voprosy istorii KPSS 4 (1991), 55; Yuri Buranov, *Lenin's Will. Falsified and Forbidden.* New York: Prometheus Book, 1994, 49.

with only two possible conclusions. Either Lenin was mentally addled on the days he asked the "commission" to investigate matters that he already knew, but somehow had all his wits about him and was his usual incisive self when he composed other documents. Or the questions Lenin had supposedly given to the "commission" were not his, and the "commission" was not in fact working for Lenin at all, but for someone else.

The report of the "commission" utterly failed to find Stalin at fault in any way in the affair of the Georgian C.C. and Ordzhonikidze's slap of Kabakhidze. But this means that the letter to Mdivani and Makharadze contradicted even the results of this obviously biased "commission." In fact, the contents of the letter, insofar as they blamed Stalin, are not supported by *any* evidence – not by Rykov's and Rtveladze's eyewitness accounts, not by the Dzerzhinsky Commission, and not even by the "commission" of Gorbunov, Fotieva, and Glyasser. It is completely unmotivated.

There was no evidence – even false evidence – presented to Lenin that accused Stalin in any way. It is impossible that, if he were in full possession of his faculties, Lenin could have condemned Stalin without any evidence whatever. Yet there is none. *That means that the letter to Mdivani and Makharadze could not have been written by Lenin. It was written by someone who was an enemy of Stalin's – or on behalf of such an enemy.*

* * * * *

The Letter to Trotsky, March 5, 1923[23]

Top secret

Personal

Dear Comrade Trotsky:

---

[23] See illustration #6b.

> It is my earnest request that you should undertake the defence of the Georgian case in the Party C.C. This case is now under "persecution" by Stalin and Dzerzhinsky, and I cannot rely on their impartiality. Quite to the contrary. I would feel at ease if you agreed to undertake its defence. If you should refuse to do so for any reason, return the whole case to me. I shall consider it a sign that you do not accept.
>
> With best comradely greetings,
>
> Lenin

Dictated by phone

on March 5, 1923

(LIV, 329; CW 45, 607)

Concerning this letter to Trotsky and the letter to Mdivani and Makharadze Sakharov notes:

> Both letters (March 5 and 6, 1923) were sent by Trotsky to the Central Committee of the RCP(b) on April 17 [sic – should be April 16, G.F.], 1923, which at his request sent them to all members of the Central Committee. They were sent to Lenin too.[24] **Thus, the only trace of the passage of these letters through Lenin's secretariat is of the texts received by the Party Central Committee from Trotsky.** (344)

In fact, the provenance of these documents is even more suspicious.

> The original of the "report" by Volodicheva (typewritten text without signature) dated March 5, 1923 does not have any traces of registration (RGASPI. F. 35. Op. 2. D. 34. L. 3). Lenin's letter to

---

[24] Izv TsK KPSS 9, 1990, 158.

> Trotsky dated March 5 and the "report" to Volodicheva (addendum to this letter) were registered as a document that entered the Lenin Secretariat only on June 15, 1923 (No. 16/12) (RGASPI. F. 5. Op. 2. D 34. L. 15; Op.4 4. D. 11. L. 89). It is interesting that (with the same number) the notes "On the Question of Nationalities ..." received in the Lenin Secretariat were registered at the same time. **All these documents were received as an attachment to the letter of Trotsky dated April 16, 1923** (RGASP.F. 5. Op. 2. d. 34. ll. 7-14; Op. 4. d. 11. l, 89; Izv TsK KPSS 1990, No. I, 158)[25].

This fact is enough in itself to cast doubt on the *bona fides* of these letters – that is, whether they originated from Lenin at all.

> All of the above leads us to the conclusion that **there is no direct and reliable evidence that Lenin sent Trotsky the "articles"** – The Question of Nationalities or 'Autonomization," as well as the letters dated March 5 and 6, 1923 (to Trotsky and Mdivani). Without exception, all of the circumstantial evidence carries highly contradictory information. The circumstances of introducing these documents into politics not only do not remove doubts about Lenin's authorship, but reinforce them. (344-5)

Trotsky says nothing about when he had received these materials. On April 16, 1923, Kamenev sent a letter to Lidia Fotieva, one of Lenin's secretaries, with a copy to the Central Committee, in which he stated:

> More than a month ago com. Trotsky showed me an article by Vladimir Il'ich on the national question, with

---

[25] Sakharov, 340, note. Sakharov's last reference is incorrect. He has Izv TsK KPSS 1991 No. 9 p. 58. There is no issue No.9 of the 1991 run of this journal. I have inserted the correct reference in the quotation above.

instructions – from your words – of full and absolute secrecy ... **This was, in my opinion, already when Vladimir Il'ich had been deprived of the possibility of giving new orders.** (Izv TsK 1990, 9, 157)

There is no evidence that Trotsky received "The Question of Nationalities ..." from Lenin before Lenin was deprived of speech and could no longer work. And therefore, there is no evidence that it came from Lenin.

* The only copy of "The Question of Nationalities ..." comes not from Lenin's secretariat, but from Trotsky.

* Kamenev believes that Trotsky showed him this article after Lenin could no longer speak. This would mean after March 10, when Lenin suffered his third and final stroke, after which he could no longer work, or possibly several days earlier. Therefore, Kamenev's letter cannot provide evidence that Trotsky obtained "The Question of Nationalities ..." from Lenin.

At the XII Party Congress (April 17-25, 1923) there was indeed a lively discussion of the "Georgian question." The following delegates spoke on it: Mdivani, Makharadze, Orakelashvili, Ordzhonikidze, Stalin, Kalinin, Sturua, Ryskulov, Skrypnyk, Eliava, Rakovsky, Tsintsadze, Enukidze, Lukashin, Zinoviev, Akhundov, Bukharin, and Radek.

But Trotsky failed to do what Lenin had, supposedly, asked him to do in the letter of March 5 – to "undertake the defense of the Georgian case." In fact Trotsky failed to mention the Georgian case at all! It is true that, literally, in the March 6 letter to Trotsky Lenin is portrayed as asking Trotsky to "defend the Georgian case" in the Central Committee, and not at the Party Congress.[26] But the real

---

[26] The account of these events in Isaac Deutscher's biography, *The Prophet Unarmed*, 74-77, is extremely inaccurate. For example, Deutscher states that "Lenin's" "The Question of Nationalities ..." was not made known to the Central Committee, and not published until 1956. In fact, as we have seen, Trotsky distributed this document to the Politburo, who passed it to the Central

debate, and the Party resolution, took place at the XII P.C. Trotsky let it pass without even mentioning it.

In his inaccurate and, indeed, dishonest biography *The Prophet Unarmed* Isaac Deutscher simply repeats Trotsky's excuse that he was being "magnanimous" to Stalin. Deutscher takes all of his account of Trotsky's actions before and during the XII P.C. straight from Trotsky's own autobiography or from Trotsky's biography of Stalin. But this makes no sense. Why would Trotsky have disobeyed Lenin's last request just to be generous to Stalin?

Deutscher also repeats the story, related by Trotsky, that Krupskaya had told Kamenev that Lenin meant to "crush Stalin politically – "razgromit' Stalina politicheski."[27] But there is no evidence that Krupskaya made any such remark. Volkogonov, who had access to archival documents that no one else has even today, wrote: "I have no concrete facts about Lenin's intention to "crush" the Gensec."[28]

Committee, and both Mdivani and Makharadze referred to it directly during the XII P.C.

[27] Trotsky, *My Life*, Chapter 39, 'Lenin's Illness"; Russian edition, Moscow: Panorama, p. 461.

[28] «У меня нет конкретных данных о намерении Ленина "разгромить" генсека». *Stalin,* Russian edition, Book 1, p. 144). For some reason Volkogonov's statement is omitted in the one-volume English language edition (Boston: Grove Weidenfeld, 1988).

Chapter 5. The Question of Nationalities

"The Question of Nationalities or 'Autonomization'" is a text in three parts. The first part is dated December 30, 1922, and the last two are dated December 31, 1922. It was not sent to the Central Committee until much later, on April 17, 1923.

This is true of *all* of the "anti-Stalin" writings attributed to Lenin as part of his last works: they all appeared much later than the dates they were supposedly dictated. This in itself is suspicious. But the reasons for suspecting that this is not a genuine work by Lenin just begin here.

The Secretaries Diary has no entries for these days. It is blank between December 29, 1922, and January 5, 1923. (XLV 474; CW 42, 482). The Doctors Journal records two 15-minute dictations on December 30 and two more dictation sessions of unstated length on December 31.[1] For December 30 the Doctors Journal records that Lenin was "very satisfied" with the first dictation of 15 minutes, but not with the second. It states that on December 31 Lenin dictated twice, read what had been dictated, and was satisfied with it.

The Doctors Journal does not record what was dictated. The editors of the Doctors Journal assume it was "The Question of Nationalities ..." But their statement is based on the dates on the three parts of the article. These sessions would appear not to be enough time to dictate this article, let alone time for revisions, especially since Lenin was not accustomed to dictating.

The first documents that record the existence of this article are the letters by Lidia Fotieva of April 16, 1923: the first to Stalin, the second to Kamenev. (Izv TsK 9, 1990, 155-6) In them Fotieva says that she is enclosing a copy of Lenin's article. However, the letter

---

[1] VI KPSS 9, 1991, 46.

to Stalin is marked "Not sent, since com. Stalin said that he is not going to get involved in this."

Fotieva wrote that Lenin said to publish it "somewhat later," and then fell ill. Meanwhile, Fotieva states that she herself has been sick for two and a half weeks. Fotieva did not enclose the article with the letter to Kamenev. She did inform him that it had been "communicated" to Trotsky because Lenin had wanted Trotsky to defend his viewpoint at the Party Congress (Izv TsK 9, 1990, 156), since they were in agreement on this question. In both letters Fotieva states that Lenin dictated this article on December 31, though the first of the three parts of this article – at least as we have it today   is dated December 30.

In her January 11, 1924, letter to Bukharin Glyasser stated that Lenin "wrote" – *napisal* – the article "The Question of Nationalities ..." and Glyasser adds that Lenin also "wrote" the note to Trotsky. Evidently she meant the note dated March 5, 1923. (Izv TsK 9, 1990, 163) In his "Letter to the Bureau of Party History" of 1927 Trotsky says that Lenin "wrote" the note to Mdivani and Makharadze.[2] In his 1930 autobiography Trotsky calls the "note" – again, the letter of March 5, 1923 – that he read to Kamenev "Lenin's manuscript" (*rukopis'*) (1991, 461). But there could have been no "writing," and no "manuscript" – Lenin had not been able to write since December, 1922.

On April 16, 1923, in her unsent letter to Stalin, Fotieva asks that the article be returned to her because it was the *only* copy that there was in Lenin's archive. (Iav TsK 9, 1990, 156) In her letter to Kamenev of the same day she says that the *only* copy of the article is still in Lenin's "secret archive." Therefore, she did not send a copy to Kamenev. She does state that she "communicated" it to Trotsky but does not specify how.

In her letter to the Central Committee dated May 18, 1924, Krupskaya said that the *only* copy of Lenin's article "on the

---

[2] Berlin, Granit, 1932, p. 83.

national question" was in the possession of Maria Il'inichna, Lenin's sister. (XLV 594) In 1929 Volodicheva wrote that *five* copies were made of all the materials that Lenin dictated between December 20, 1922 and the beginning of March, 1923, after which Lenin could no longer work or speak. (XLV 592)

The copy of the article eventually printed as Lenin's "The Question of Nationalities ..." is *a copy of the copy* that Trotsky said he had made from the original that he claimed he had received from Lenin on March 5, 1923. On April 16, 1923, Trotsky forwarded to the Central Committee copies of that article, plus Lenin's March 5, 1923 letter to himself (Trotsky), and Lenin's March 6, 1923 letter to Mdivani and Makharadze. (Izv TsK 9, 1990, 158) The next day, April 17, 1923, in another letter to the Central Committee, Trotsky claimed that on March 5 Lenin, "through Fotieva," had forbidden him to communicate the article to the Politburo. (ibid. 160-1)

This means that the only extant copy of this article is, according to Trotsky, a copy of a copy that he made because he had to return the original to Lenin's secretariat on the request of Glyasser. (ibid. 160) No original of "The Question of Nationalities ..." is known today.

Sakharov has strong doubts that Lenin wrote "The Question of Nationalities ..." Stephen Kotkin notes its political bias:

> The counterdossier was blatantly tendentious. Just one example: it omitted the salient fact that Pilipe Makharadze's secret letter to the Central Committee, with Kamenev's response, had been leaked to the emigre Menshevik Socialist Herald—i.e., the Georgians had divulged state secrets. (Kotkin 489)

and rejects Lenin's authorship altogether:

> Why did Krupskaya not choose to show this document [the "Letter to the Congress"] to the 12th Party Congress? She had brought forth the "Notes on the Question of Nationalities," **a blatant forgery** that had failed to gain any attraction. (Kotkin 501)

Chapter Five. The Question of Nationalities

Kotkin elaborates, drawing upon Sakharov's analysis:

> The article, titled "Notes on the Question of Nationalities," departed significantly from Lenin's lifelong and even recent views on nationalities, advocating confederation ... Lenin's alleged "Notes" were dated December 30–31, 1922, and Fotiyeva later observed that the long article had been dictated in two fifteen-minute sessions. The typescript lacked a signature or initials. **The existing evidence strongly points to a maneuver by Krupskaya, and the staff in Lenin's secretariat**, to forge what they interpreted as Lenin's will. **They knew he was exercised over the Georgian affair; indeed, they egged him on over it.**

Kotkin then suggests that Krupskaya and the secretaries may have been in league with Trotsky:

> **Trotsky might also have been complicit by this point.** Controversy ensued over his claim that he had received Lenin's "Notes on the Question of Nationalities" before the Central Committee had—and, supposedly, before Lenin's third stroke—but had inexplicably held on to them. Lenin's purported dictation happened to dovetail with views Trotsky published in *Pravda* (March 20, 1923). Even more telling, Lenin's secretaries had kept working on the counterdossier on Georgia, for a report by Lenin to a future Party Congress, even after he had his third massive stroke and permanently lost his ability to speak ... **In fact, their counter-Dzierzynski Commission dossier reads like a first draft of the "Notes on the Question of Nationalities."** (Kotkin 494)

There is another document that casts doubt on the date of composition of "The Question of Nationalities ..." Sakharov quotes and analyzes it.

> In the "Diary" of the secretaries there is one document that indirectly indicates the date. We are talking about a piece of paper pasted in the "Diary" with typewritten text entitled "memorandum (lit. - For memory)" (RGASPI. F 5. Op. 1. D. 12. L. 34). It is published in the PSS (XLV, 592) with minor changes. Since it is of great importance for our topic, we present its text as it is stored in the archive:
>
>> Для памяти:
>>
>> В письме об увеличении числа членов Центрального Комитета пропущено об отношении членов увеличенного Центрального Комитета к Рабоче-Крестьянской инспекции.
>>
>> Намеченные темы:
>>
>> 1. О Центросоюзе и его значении с точки зрения НЭПа.
>>
>> 2. О соотношении Главпрофобра с общепросветительной работой в народе.
>>
>> 3. О национальном вопросе и об интернационализме (в связи с последним конфликтом в грузинской партии).
>>
>> 4. О новой книге статистики народного образования, вышедшей в 1922 г.
>>
>> Memorandum (lit. "For memory")
>>
>> In the letter on the increase in the number of members of the Central Committee, the relation of

the members of the enlarged Central Committee to the W.P.I. is omitted.

Intended topics [lit. "Subjects to consider"]

1. About Tsentrosoyuz [Co-operative Consumer Union] and its meaning in terms of NEP.

2. On the relationship of Glavprofobr [Course of Vocational Education] with public education work among the people.

3. On the national question and internationalism (in connection with the latest conflict in the Georgian party).

4. About the new book [on] statistics of public education, published in 1922

The document is not signed, not dated, and does not have any annotation, which makes it impossible to establish any relation between Lenin and this record. The content of the part of the note designated as "Intended topics" does not allow us to say anything definite about Lenin's authorship of this document. Such a record could be made either at Lenin's dictation or without any participation by him.

The very fact of its appearance in the "Diary" needs to be understood. The authors of the notes to the 45th volume of the Complete Works of V.I. Lenin date it to December 27 or 28, 1922. If you adhere to the traditional version of Lenin's work on the notes "On the Question of Nationalities or on 'Autonomization'" on December 30 and 31, 1922, then the time when the note "For Memory" originated should be for the period between December 26th and 29th. **However, in the Secretaries Journal (SJ) it was placed after the "journal" entry for February 10, 1923.**

Obviously, this was not accidental, as it allowed documenting Lenin's interest in national-state construction in February and supporting the falsified SJ notes related to the work of the so-called "Lenin Commission" on the materials of the conflict in the Georgian Communist Party. The falsified part of the SJ gets an opportunity to indirectly certify Lenin's authorship of the "article" on the national question, and the notes, in turn, become a witness to the authenticity of the SJ (306-7, note)

The Gorbunov-Fotieva-Glyasser "Commission"

At the end of January, 1923, Lenin appointed a body of three persons: N.P. Gorbunov, business manager of the Soviet of People's Deputies (the executive body of the USSR), and two technical secretaries from Lenin's secretariat, Lidia Fotieva, and Maria Glyasser. There is no evidence that Lenin gave this group – which did not call itself a "commission" and had no governmental or Party status – any powers.

Officially, it appears, Lenin asked it to obtain the materials of the Dzerzhinsky Commission and perhaps also to study and assess the decisions of higher state and Party organs, including the C.C., Politburo, Orgburo, and Secretariat. In reality, this group set out to prepare a political attack on Stalin.

On January 25, 1923, the commission – we will use this name for convenience – asked Stalin, and on January 27, the Secretariat, for the materials of the "Georgian Commission." In a letter to Bukharin of January 11, 1924, Glyasser described her duties as "to familiarize myself with the materials of c[omm]ission of c[omrade] Dzerzhinsky." (Izv TsK 9, 1990, 163)

There is a lengthy entry in the Secretaries Journal for February 5, 1923, in which Glyasser outlines in detail Lenin's alleged instructions to her regarding the tasks of the commission. Glyasser concludes by stating that she met with Lenin for 20 minutes.[3] (348) Glyasser says that she met with Lenin at 7 o'clock, not

---

[3] XLV 480-1; CW 42, 488.

Chapter Five. The Question of Nationalities   121

specifying morning or evening. But the Doctors Journal states that Lenin slept until 9 a.m., read and dictated – we are not told to whom or about what – and then slept and read in the evening. There is nothing about any meeting with Glyasser or anyone else.[4]

Evidently, therefore, this supposed meeting did not take place. Sakharov calls it "this Glyasser note, fabricated as a journal," (349) both because the Doctors Journal records no such visit with Lenin on that date, and because the Secretaries Journal was left blank, with many entries obviously filled in later and blank spaces for entries that were never filled in.

This fact devalues Glyasser's statement in her letter to Bukharin that Lenin "already had his preconceived opinion, literally guided our work and was terribly worried that we would not be able to prove in his report what he needed and that he will not have time to prepare his speech before the congress."

"Why Didn't Stalin React?"

In the Secretaries Journal for February 14, 1923, there is a note, written by Fotieva and supposedly dictated by Lenin.[5]

> "Vladimir Ilyich's instructions that a hint be given to Soltz (A. A. Soltz, member of the presidium of the Central Control Commission, R.C.P.(b)—Ed.) that he (Lenin) was on the side of the injured party. Someone or other of the injured party was to be given to understand he was on their side.
>
> "3 moments: 1. One should not fight. 2. Concessions should be made. 3. One cannot compare a large state with a small one.
>
> "Did Stalin know? Why didn't he react?

---

[4] Kentavr, Oct-Dec 1991, 101.
[5] XLV 607, note 293 to p. 485; CW 42, 621, note 614 to p. 493.

> "The name 'deviationist' for **a deviation towards chauvinism and Menshevism** proves the same deviation with the dominant national chauvinists.
>
> "Collect printed matter for Vladimir Ilyich."

The editors note:

> Between February 15 and March 4 no entries were made in the Journal. (ibid.)

The fact that there are no entries between February 15 and March 5 means that the note above could have been inserted there at any time.

The note is in several parts. First, the Author tries to influence Solts, obviously behind the backs of the other members of the CCC and the CC. Did Lenin really have so little confidence in the Party that he felt he had to go behind its back, so to speak, to have his views taken seriously?

A second point asks why Stalin did not react, evidently to Ordzhonikidze's slap (point 1. "One should not fight.") But Lenin knew the answer to this. He knew that the Politburo had sent the Dzerzhinsky commission to investigate the situation in the Georgian CP, including the business of Ordzhonikidze slapping Kabakhidze. In fact it was Stalin's office, the Secretariat, that had proposed to the Politburo to form such a commission.

So Lenin knew that Stalin, as a member of the Politburo, had indeed "reacted." Moreover, Lenin had heard Dzerzhinsky's report and Rykov's eyewitness account.

Sakharov quotes another note from the same archival file but as yet unpublished. This note reads: "Organize the mater[ial] not so much in defense of the deviationists as in indictment of the great power chauvinists." (351)[6] This record is dated March 12, 1923.

---

[6] See Sakharov 700 note 65 to page 351, for the archival identifiers.

Therefore it could not belong to Lenin, since he had lost the ability to speak by March 9-10 at the latest if not several days before that. *Someone else* had given these instructions to Gorbunov, Fotieva, and Glyasser.

Once again we are led to wonder: For whom was this "commission" really working? Sakharov comments:

> [I]t is clear from the text that its author was little concerned with the protection of the views of the Georgian national deviationists. He is interested in something else - how to hurt Stalin, Ordzhonikidze and other so-called "great power chauvinists," in other words, the supporters of the formation of the USSR as a federation with a strong center.
>
> This position is in harmony with the views of the author of the notes "On the Question of Nationalities or on 'Autonomization'," but does not have any basis in Lenin's writings. It is known that Lenin sharply condemned the Georgian national deviationists for the fact that after the October (1922) plenum they began to fight against the decisions of the plenum on the formation of the USSR. (351)

The document Sakharov is referring to here is a telegram from Lenin to Tsintsadze and Kavtaradze, dated October 21, 1922.[7]

TELEGRAM

TO K. M. TSINTSADZE AND S. I. KAVTARADZE

21/IX-22

---

[7] Kote Maksimovich Tsintsade was a communist and Georgian nationalist. In 1923 he joined the Left Opposition. The English language Wikipedia page takes all of its information from Simon Sebag Montefiore, a completely unreliable source. Sergei Ivanovich Kavtaradze also became a member of the Left Opposition, Imprisoned briefly during the 1930s, he was released and had a long career in the Ministry of Foreign Affairs.

Code

Tsintsadze and Kavtaradze, C.P.G. C.C., Tiflis

Copy to Orjonikidze, C.C. member and Orakhelashvili, Secretary of the Transcaucasian Territorial Committee

I am surprised at the indecent tone of the direct wire message signed by Tsintsadze and others, which was handed to me for some reason by Bukharin instead of one of the C.C. secretaries. I was sure that all the differences had been ironed out by the C.C. Plenum resolutions with my indirect participation and with the direct participation of Mdivani. That is why I resolutely condemn the abuse against Orjonikidze and insist that your conflict should be referred in a decent and loyal tone for settlement by the R.C.P. C.C. Secretariat, which has been handed your direct wire message.

Lenin[8]

It is usually assumed that the "great power chauvinist" of the Fotieva note dated February 14 was Stalin. But Stalin was not involved in the dispute in Georgia involving Ordzhonikidze. Moreover, Lenin had never accused Stalin of Menshevism. Only one person is known who did this. In "The March, 1917, Party Conference," not published until the 1930s in Trotsky's book *The Stalin School of Falsification*, Trotsky produces a text in which Stalin supposedly proposed that the Bolsheviks unite with the Mensheviks under certain conditions.[9]

Sakharov concludes:

---

[8] CW 45, 582; LIV 299-300.
[9] This text is not found anywhere else. Other accounts of the meeting in which, according to Trotsky, Stalin made this proposal, do not include this passage. Trotsky did not publish it in the early editions of his book. It first appears in the 1932 Berlin edition.

Chapter Five. The Question of Nationalities

> So the instruction, which is clearly not Lenin's, and at the same time is completely in harmony with the text of the notes on the national question, is a guideline for the members of the commission. Moreover, it says that someone directed its work to prepare the "bomb for Stalin" after Lenin had lost all ability to work. It is clear that this note is a trace of political intrigue under the cover of Lenin's name. (351)

Either "The Question of Nationalities ..." was dictated by Lenin, as Fotieva claimed, or it was not and is therefore a forgery. If it was dictated by Lenin, it contradicts Lenin's long-held and well-known views so radically that it must be due to confusion and forgetfulness because of Lenin's disease. This is in fact what speakers at the XII Party Congress assumed.

A third possibility – that Lenin's thinking had evolved, but in a logical, intelligent manner – is excluded by the nature of the statements and fact-claims in the article. Since others of Lenin's last essays do not show signs of mental deterioration, it follows that "The Question of Nationalities ..." is a forgery. Following Sakharov's sensible practice, I will refer to the author of "The Question of Nationalities ..." as "the Author," a person who may, or may not, have been Lenin.

* The Author begins by saying he was "remiss ... for not having intervened energetically and decisively enough in the notorious question of autonomization," so that "the question passed me by almost completely." He says that he "only had time for a talk with Comrade Dzerzhinsky" and to "exchange a few words with Comrade Zinoviev." But the Secretaries Journal contains no discussions between Lenin and Zinoviev, only the receipt of materials concerning other matters.

On December 12, 1922, Lenin had indeed met with Dzerzhinsky, presumably to discuss Dzerzhinsky's report on the Georgian affair. If Lenin really had been very concerned about the Georgian affair, he would certainly have discussed it with Dzerzhinsky since he was fully informed about the Dzerzhinsky commission's appointment and trip to Georgia.

As we saw in a previous chapter, Lenin spoke by phone with Rykov on December 9, 1922, and met with him on December 12, 1922. Rykov was an eye-witness to the argument between Ordzhonikidze and Kabakhidze, and witnessed the former slap the latter. Presumably, therefore, Lenin got a report from Rykov on December 12. On February 7, 1923, responding to the Gorbunov-Fotieva-Glyasser "commission" Rykov wrote the account which we have quoted in full in the previous chapter.

Both Dzerzhinsky and Rykov were clear that (a) Ordzhonikidze had been personally insulted and was only minimally to blame; and (b) the argument was over a personal matter having nothing to do with the politics of Georgia and the Caucasus.

Yet early in the article the Author of "The Question of Nationalities …" states:

> From what I was told by Comrade Dzerzhinsky, who was at the head of the commission sent by the C.C. to "investigate" the Georgian incident, I could only draw the greatest apprehensions. If matters had come to such a pass that Orjonikidze could go to the extreme of applying physical violence, as Comrade Dzerzhinsky informed me, we can imagine what a mess we have got ourselves into. Obviously the whole business of "autonomisation" was radically wrong and badly timed. (CW 36, 605)

This statement is not logical. Even if one were to incorrectly assume that the Ordzhonikidze – Kabakhidze dispute and the infamous "slap" had been about the Georgian situation, Ordzhonikidze's losing his temper would not mean that the whole policy was wrong. And in fact we know that the dispute was *not* about the Georgian affair.

Chapter Five. The Question of Nationalities   127

* If Lenin's mental abilities had sharply declined since his meetings with Dzerzhinsky and Rykov on December 12, 1922, that would remove any political significance from the article "The Question of Nationalities ..." Perhaps the person (or persons) who fabricated this article either did not know about these meetings, or did not know what was said in them. It seems most likely that he or they did not know about Lenin's meeting with Rykov, since it is not mentioned.

* The Author speaks of "the notorious [*preslovutiy*] question of autonomization." But Lenin had been very active at the X Party Congress of March, 1921, where the resolution "On the next tasks of the Party in the national question" spoke of the autonomous republics and regions.[10] Part 5 of the resolution speaks of "the experience of Russia" – that is, the RSFSR – in "confirming the expediency and flexibility of federation." The Russian Federation (RSFSR) was built on the basis of "autonomization."

The article states: "Obviously the whole business of "autonomization" was radically wrong and badly timed." But "radically wrong" and "badly timed" are mutually exclusive terms. Something basically wrong cannot be "well timed." It is impossible to attribute a formulation like this to Lenin – unless, that is, Lenin's mental faculties had been seriously depleted by his disease. (319)

Sakharov notes that towards the end of 1922 representatives of some of the autonomous republics of the RSFSR wanted their autonomous republics to be raised to the status of union republics, like the four founding republics of the USSR in December, 1922: the Russian SFSR, Transcaucasian SFSR, Ukrainian SFSR, and Byelorussian SFSR. That is, they protested "autonomization." But this policy was just as much Lenin's doing as it was Stalin's and, in fact, the policy of the Bolshevik Party.

* The Author writes that "Stalin's haste and his infatuation with pure administration, together with his spite against the notorious

---

[10] X Party Congress, 578; *KPSS v rezoliutsiakh i resheniakh I*, 553-8.

'nationalist-socialism' played a fatal role here." But where? Evidently, in the formation of the USSR, which the Author has identified as

> the notorious question of autonomization, which, it appears, is officially called the question of the union of Soviet socialist republics.

This passage blames Stalin for the founding of the USSR. But the USSR had been formed on the basis of a treaty. Lenin had certainly been involved in the discussions leading up to its signing on December 30 and 31, 1922 – just when this article was supposedly being written.

And again, the USSR was not founded on the basis of autonomization. That was the RSFSR. But the Author of this article does not say that the existence of the RSFSR is harmful, only that of the USSR. In reality "autonomization" was a question in the formation of the RSFSR, not of the USSR.[11]

* The Author writes:

> The political responsibility for all this truly Great-Russian nationalist campaign must, of course, be laid on Stalin and Dzerzhinsky.

What "truly Great Russian nationalist campaign"? Lenin had already heard from both Dzerzhinsky and Rykov that the Ordzhonkidze-Kabakhidze argument, which led to Ordzhonikidze slapping Kabakhidze, was not about the status of Georgia or the Transcaucasian Federation, much less about "autonomization," but was a purely personal affair. Stalin was not involved in this situation at all.

---

[11] In later years a number of the autonomous republics of the RSFSR were elevated to the status of union republics – in 1924, the Uzbek and Turkmen, in 1929 the Tadjik, in 1936 the Armenian, Georgian, and Azerbaijani, Kazakh and Kirgiz, and others later.

Chapter Five. The Question of Nationalities

Here is how Anastas Mikoyan described this argument years later:

> Once, one of the local deviationists, a certain Kobakhidze [sic], allowed himself a gross attack against Sergo, almost accusing him of corruption. He cited the following "fact." When Ordzhonikidze returned to the Caucasus, the Highlanders as a sign of special love for him and gratitude gave him a riding horse. According to Caucasian custom, Sergo accepted the gift, but, not counting this horse as his personal property, he put it in the stable of the Revolutionary Military Council, using it mainly for trips to ceremonial parades (in those days, not only commanders, but also members of the revolutionary military councils participated in parades. I myself well remember several cases when Sergo, on horseback, participated in such celebrations). As a member of the Revolutionary Military Council, Ordzhonikidze had every right to a state-owned horse. He considered the horse he presented to him such a state-owned horse (by the way, when Sergo left Tiflis, this horse remained at the stable of the Revolutionary Military Council). Kobakhidze distorted this whole business. To accuse Sergo, a perfectly honest man, of corruption was more than monstrous. Therefore, when he heard this, Sergo exploded, and, not restraining himself, slapped the slanderer in the face. There was an "affair." Dzerzhinsky, who, on behalf of the Central Committee of the party, took charge of this, came to the conclusion that Ordzhonikidze was not guilty.[12]

This Mikoyan memoir was published in 1971. There is no chance that he was telling a false story in order to support Stalin, for Mikoyan had long been hostile to Stalin. In fact, Mikoyan's speech to the XX Party Congress, in February, 1956, was the first official

---

[12] Anastas Mikoyan, *Dorogoi bor'by. Kniga pervaya.* M: Izd. Politicheskoi Literatury, 1971, p. 433.

statement to criticize Stalin, more than a week before Khrushchev's famous "Secret Speech."[13]

Mikoyan's statement here completely contradicts "The Question of Nationalities ..." which in Mikoyan's day was unproblematically attributed to Lenin. Lenin was still an unquestionable icon during the Brezhnev period, when Mikoyan's book was published, and writings like the "testament" that are very critical of Stalin were taken on faith as genuine and accurate. Yet Mikoyan's story implicitly gives the lie to the description of events in "The Question of Nationalities."

Mikoyan's account reflects the consensus of Party leaders in the 1920s: that this essay reflected not Lenin's real views, but the effects of his illness, plus perhaps misinformation. It was well understood – first, by Dzerzhinsky, on the basis of his commission's trip to Tbilisi, and to Rykov, an eyewitness, and then by everyone else – that Ordzhonikidze had not committed any act of "Great Russian chauvinism" in this dispute.

There is no reason to think that Lenin did not trust Dzerzhinsky's report on the findings of his commission, which almost entirely exculpated Ordzhonikidze. Nor is there any indication, aside from this essay, that Lenin had changed his opinion about Ordzhonikidze.

And what did Stalin have to do with any of this? He was not on the Dzerzhinsky commission. The Gorbunov-Fotieva-Glyasser "commission," which did not even travel to Georgia but only reviewed the documents, found nothing to blame Stalin for.

> If the members of the commission were really faced with the task of preparing a "bomb for Stalin" then they would have to admit that they were unable to fulfill this task. Its members did not find anything that

---

[13] *XX S'ezd KPSS 14-25 fevralia 1956 goda. Stenograficheskii otchet.* (Moscow, 1956) 1, 301-328. Mikoyan attacked Stalin's political line but did not mention him by name.

Chapter Five. The Question of Nationalities 131

> could compromise Stalin by presenting him as covering up or responsible for the inappropriate behavior of Ordzhonikidze. On the contrary, it turns out that it was precisely Stalin who proposed to take the strictest organizational measures against Ordzhonikidze. (355)

No documentary evidence confirms the thesis that the Dzerzhinsky commission "had a conclusion" before leaving Moscow, although its members, of course, might have had (since the conflict was long and drawn out). The thesis about Ordzhonikidze being 20% at fault also suggests that Zinoviev did not regard his guilt in this conflict as the main one.

Yet in "The Question of Nationalities ..." we read the following paragraph:

> ... exemplary punishment must be inflicted on Comrade Orjonikidze (I say this all the more regretfully as I am one of his personal friends and have worked with him abroad) and the investigation of all the material which Dzerzhinsky's commission has collected must be completed or started over again to **correct the enormous mass of wrongs and biased judgements which it doubtlessly contains**. The political responsibility for all this truly Great-Russian nationalist campaign must, of course, be laid on Stalin and Dzerzhinsky. (XLV, 361; CW 36, 610)

This paragraph contains some remarkable revelations. The Author claims that the Dzerzhinsky commission's material "doubtless contains" an "enormous mass of wrongs and biased judgments." But Lenin could not possibly have believed this, or he would have acted much sooner. He had met with Dzerzhinsky for 45 minutes upon the latter's return from Georgia, on December 12. If Lenin had been so convinced that Dzerzhinsky's report was fundamentally biased and wrong, why would he have waited 18 days before doing anything?

As for this sentence, the English translation is subtly incorrect:

> The political responsibility for all this truly Great-Russian nationalist campaign must, of course, be laid on Stalin and Dzerzhinsky.

That the Author has already made up his mind, without any further investigation, is clear from the previous sentence. But in fact, *this* sentence reads as follows:

> Политически-ответственными за всю эту поистине великорусско-националистическую кампанию **следует сделать**, конечно, Сталина и Дзержинского.
>
> Of course, Stalin and Dzerzhinsky **must be made** politically responsible for all this truly Great-Russian nationalist campaign.

If someone "must be made responsible," it follows that they are *not* responsible – or, at least, that the writer *does not care* whether they were really responsible or not. Not wishing, perhaps, to make Lenin appear unfair, the English translator has tried to soften this implication with the words "must be laid on." But the implication remains: whatever "the investigation of all the material which Dzerzhinsky's commission" may find, the Author has made up *his* mind already: Dzerzhinsky and Stalin *must be made* responsible. It is impossible to imagine a Lenin with all his faculties intact making such statements. (331-2)

Either the article "The Question of Nationalities ..." is a forgery, as both Sakharov and Kotkin conclude. Or it is evidence that Lenin, in a weakened state, his memory and reasoning powers impaired by illness, had been manipulated by others. Whichever is the case, the question remains: Why? In whose interest are these accusations against Stalin? Because only Stalin – not Dzerzhinsky, and certainly not Ordzhonikidze – was a leading political figure.

> Perhaps this note was therefore not included in the final text of the prepared documents, because it did

> not contain any serious compromising information either against Stalin or against Ordzhonikidze. In this connection, we note that in the notes "On the Question of Nationalities or on 'Autonomization'" the reproaches addressed to Stalin and Ordzhonikidze also remained unexplored and unargued. (356)

It also points to the purpose of the article: to attack Stalin. Who would want to attack Stalin, and at the same time had the confidence of persons in Lenin's secretariat? Only two persons suggest themselves: Lenin's wife, Nadezhda Krupskaya, and Leon Trotsky. Krupskaya was soon to join the "New Opposition." Trotsky was Stalin's main rival for the Party leadership

The following analysis of the "commission's" work is taken from Sakharov, *Na rasput'e,* 140-143.

> The first typewritten version of a document, supposedly prepared for Lenin (it is not dated) ends with a very interesting conclusion:
>
>> In conclusion, our commission has decided that comrades from the old composition of the Central Committee of Georgia pose the question incorrectly and weaken their position when they say that they have no fundamental disagreements with the Zakkraikom group, but only tactical ones. Since the Zakkraikom, in its desire to fight "deviation," showed a deviation towards Great Power chauvinism, which seems to us to be sufficiently clear from the materials, the disagreements are political in nature and should be put forward at the upcoming congress of the Communist Party.)
>
> We must fully appreciate this proposal of the technical workers of the Council of People's Commissars, who here assume the responsibility and courage to criticize not only the work of the commission of the Politburo

of the Central Committee of the RCP(b), but also the course towards the formation of the USSR, which Zakkraikom and the new composition of the Central Committee of the Communist Party of Georgia carried out in accordance with the decisions of the October (1922) Plenum of the Central Committee of the RCP(b), adopted in accordance with the will of Lenin himself. The Zakkraikom of the RCP(b), elected by the communist parties of Georgia, Armenia and Azerbaijan, uniting and coordinating their activities, has already, according to them, turned into a "group."

... [T]he members of the "commission" of the Council of the People's Commissars in their confrontation with the Central Committee of the RCP(b) took a much more radical and belligerent position than P. G. Mdivani, Makharadze and other Georgian "national deviators." That is the only way to understand their advice on how to develop an attack against the decisions adopted by the Central Committee of the RCP(b): to refuse formal recognition of the decisions of the October and December (1922) Plenums of the Central Committee of the RCP(b) and to openly attack them.

The technical workers of the Council of People's Commissars of the RSFSR propose starting an escalation of the political struggle not only within the Central Committee of the Party, but also in the Party. They propose that the "national deviators" now reject as harmful the disguise of their true position by talking about limiting disagreements with tactical approaches and of solving the problem, and increasing the pressure on the Central Committee and giving these disagreements a fundamental character.

This conclusion contains a number of provisions that preclude the possibility that this document was prepared for Lenin. What is the point of Lenin's blaming Lenin? Is it to urge him to approve the behavior of those forces in the Party that violated decisions in which he himself took an active part? Why should Lenin call for an escalation of the political struggle at the Party congress against the decisions with which he was satisfied? Finally, why does Lenin need to prove that the disagreements between the Central Committee of the RCP(b) and the "national deviationists" are fundamental if he, as the author of the notes "On the question of nationalities or 'autonomization'," evaluated them in this way? **What preceded what? The note on the national issue or the first typewritten version of the document of this "commission"?**

The same should be said regarding the assertion that "Zakkraikom, in its desire to fight "the deviationists" showed deviation towards great power chauvinism".[15] **It echoes the well-known provision of the notes "On the question of nationalities, or on 'autonomization'," That he who not only "dismissively throws the accusation of 'social-nationalism' (while he himself is not only a real and true 'social-nationalist', but also a rude Great Russian bully), who ... in essence violates the interests of proletarian class solidarity."[16]**

In another document, critically assessing the work of the Dzerzhinsky commission, the members of the "commission of the Council of People's Commissars" pose the task of "correcting incorrect and biased judgments."[17] **In the notes "On the question of nationalities ..." this provision also exists and looks like this: "to follow up on or investigate anew all the materials of the Dzerzhinsky commission with a view to correcting the enormous mass of errors and biased judgments that undoubtedly exist there."**

At first glance, there is nothing surprising in this: members of the commission, who knew Lenin's notes on the national question, repeated the provision formulated in them, giving them a clearer wording. The answer is simple, but the question is not simple.

Why do members of the commission inform Lenin about this as something new for him, as about a conclusion drawn precisely by them on the basis of the material studied, which Lenin knew to a large extent? It would be possible to understand if all the assessments and advice contained in these documents were addressed to anyone else, but not to Lenin. **Why do they prove to Lenin that the fighters against deviation are themselves deviators if he had long dictated this to Fotieva,[14] at whose disposal, according to legend, was the very text of these dictations?**

If we take on faith Lenin's authorship of these notes, we get a ridiculous picture: members of the commission rewrite for Lenin the provisions formulated by him, pass them off as their own, and offer them to Lenin to be guided by them. Why convince Lenin of what he himself convinces others?

If they borrowed this provision from a Lenin article, we would have the right to expect that they would somehow indicate that their conclusions confirm the conclusions made by Lenin. But in the context of the document they prepared, it is clear that the members of the commission are not *reminding* Lenin of his conclusion, they are *trying to convince* Lenin of the truthfulness of this conclusion.

---

[14] In "The Question of Nationalities or 'Autonomization'".

This means that this advice of the commission appeared before the notes "On the question of nationalities ..." were created. The materials prepared by this "commission of the Council of People's Commissars" testify, first, that work on the first version of the document prepared by it was carried out after Lenin had completely lost the ability to work and even the power of speech. **Second, work on them preceded the creation of the text of the notes "On the question of nationalities ..."** It can be assumed that the provisions formulated by the members of the commission or written down from someone else's words later took the form of "Lenin's" notes "On the question of nationalities or 'autonomization'," (and possibly the appearance of letters to Trotsky dated March 5, 1923 and Mdivani et al. dated March 6, 1923).

There is reason to affirm that the materials of this "commission" constitute tangible evidence of the history of the creation of the pseudo-Lenin text known as the articles or notes "On the question of nationalities or on 'autonomization'." They show the time and process of creating the falsification, as well as its authors and its potential customers. **The history of its introduction into political circulation** provides additional arguments in favor of this conclusion.

Sakharov, citing the unpublished text of the "commission's" report, states:

> ... the Zakkraikom, elected by the Communist Parties of Georgia, Armenia and Azerbaijan, which unites and coordinates their activities, has already become a "group" according to the members of the commission. Did they themselves think of this or did they write under someone's dictation?

> Who could have stood behind the members of this "commission"? Apparently, a significant political figure stood behind the technical workers of Lenin's secretariat. We cannot name anyone specifically now, but it is noteworthy that later, in the course of inner-party discussions, representatives of various opposition groups, including Trotsky, more than once resorted to this method – declaring the majority of the party opposing them a fraction and the party's organs under the control of the majority to be fractional bodies. (357)

The XII Party Congress, April 17 -25, 1923

Delegates to the XII Party Congress were surprised and puzzled by "The Question of Nationalities ..." It did not express what they knew of Lenin's views.

Avel' Enukidze:

> Now about the letter of Comrade Lenin. Here, Comrade Mdivani, in his speech, mentioned every second the name of Comrade Ilyich, and he wanted to create the impression that Comrade Lenin purposely wrote this letter in order to support his fellow deviators and justify their entire policy. (Bukharin: "Of course, for this purpose.") Not for this purpose, Comrade Bukharin. **Let me say here that we also know a little bit of Comrade Lenin, and we also had to meet with him on various issues, and in particular on the Georgian issue. And I affirm here, comrades, and I hope that when Comrade Lenin recovers, he will agree that many times the questions that were raised here by fellow deviators were known to him, but when they were properly covered and clarified, he agreed with politics conducted there by Comrade Ordzhonikidze. It could not be otherwise. The general policy pursued by Comrade**

Ordzhonikidze was outlined here. It was correct, and if there were complaints about the way it was conducted in Georgia, the local conditions and the chauvinistic attitude towards Russia that remained from the Mensheviks were to blame. Comrade Stalin supported in every way possible the comrades who complain of persecution here. mitigated their mistakes, instructively tried to correct them[15], and if Comrade Stalin could be blamed for anything it is only in this, that for a whole year he supported in every way a certain group of comrades, and after the policy in relation to these comrades was necessarily changed, this change, of course, seemed very sharp. Lenin really believed these comrades, supported them, and his attitude towards them is in large measure due to comrade Stalin. Most of the letter from Comrade Lenin known to you is devoted to the general questions of our national policy, and neither Comrade Stalin nor Comrade Ordzhonikidze, of course, object to these general thoughts. **As for the specific questions raised in his letter, in particular this question, it seems to me that Comrade Lenin became a victim of one-sided, incorrect information. When people come to a person who due to illness** is not able to follow the daily work, and say that such and such comrades are offended, beaten, kicked out, removed, etc., of course, he had to write a sharp letter like this. **But everything that is attributed to Comrade Ordzhonikidze in this letter, had neither the slightest relation to the national question, nor to the fellow deviators. This is a well-known fact, comrades**, and why embroil the question of Comrade Ordzhonikidze's incident with one of the comrades, who was not involved in the struggle between the

---

[15] This is consistent with Makharadze's remarks about Stalin at the XII Party Congress, quoted in an earlier chapter.

draft devotees and Zakkraikom, in questions raised by Comrade Lenin? (XII P.C., 589-90)

Stalin raised the issue in a different manner. He did not defend himself against "Lenin's" – the Author's – criticism of him. Rather, Stalin reiterated the Bolshevik and Leninist position that colonies and oppressed nations must have the freedom of political separation, while at the same time pointing out that the socialists of the oppressed nations must "uphold and enforce" organizational unity between workers of the oppressed nations with workers of the oppressing nations.

> Many here have referred to notes and articles by Vladimir Ilyich. I would not like to quote my teacher, Comrade Lenin, since he is not here, and I am afraid that maybe I will refer to him incorrectly and out of place. Nevertheless, I have to quote one axiomatic point, which does not cause any misunderstanding, so that my comrades have no doubts about the specific gravity of the national question. While analyzing Marx's letter on the national question in an article on self-determination, Comrade Lenin draws the following conclusion: "Marx had no doubt as to the subordinate position of the national question as compared with the "labour question."[16] There are only two lines, but they decide everything. This is something that some irrationally zealous comrades should have constantly before them.[17]
>
> The second question is about Great Russian chauvinism and local chauvinism ... Let me refer to Comrade Lenin here too. I wouldn't do this, but since there are many comrades at our congress who quote Comrade Lenin at random and distort him, allow me

---

[16] Quoted from section 8 of Lenin's 1914 essay "The Right of Nations to Self-Determination." CW 20, 436.
[17] Literally, "should have carved on their noses."

to read a few words from a well-known article by Comrade Lenin: "The proletariat must demand the right of political secession for the colonies and nations oppressed by "their own" nation. Otherwise the internationalism of the proletariat would be nothing but empty words; neither confidence nor class solidarity would be possible between the workers of the oppressed and the oppressor nations."[18] These are, so to speak, the obligations of the proletarians of the dominant or formerly dominant nation. Further he speaks of the duty of the proletarians or communists of nations previously oppressed:

> On the other hand, the socialists of the oppressed nations must in particular uphold and enforce the complete and unconditional, including organizational, unity of the workers of the oppressed nation with the workers of the oppressing nation. Without this, given all the sorts of tricks, betrayals and frauds of the bourgeoisie, it is impossible to defend the independent policy of the proletariat and its class solidarity with the proletariat of other countries. For the bourgeoisie of the oppressed nations constantly turns the slogans of national liberation into deception of the workers. (XII P.C., 650-1)

In the end, "The Question of Nationalities ..." had little or no effect on the delegates to the XII Party Congress. No one questioned Lenin's authorship, as far as we know. But the criticism of Ordzhonikidze and of Stalin was not used by any oppositionists for factional purposes, and no delegate suggested that the USSR, recently formed, be changed in conformity with this essay.

---

[18] Quoted from Lenin, "The Socialist Revolution and the Right of Nations to Self-Determination." CW 22, 148. There is a somewhat different translation at http://www.marx2mao.com/Lenin/SRSD16.html

Chapter 6. The Ultimatum Letter

The official, or canonical, version of Lenin's threat to break off relations with Stalin is as follows:

* On December 21, 1922, Lenin dictated to Krupskaya a letter to Trotsky concerning his desire to retain a state monopoly of foreign trade.

* On the evening of December 22 Stalin phoned Krupskaya and rudely scolded her for violating the ban on having political discussions with Lenin.

* On December 23 Krupskaya wrote a letter to Kamenev protesting Stalin's treatment of her and asking for his and Zinoviev's protection against Stalin's rudeness.

* On March 5, 1923, Lenin learned of Stalin's rudeness to Krupskaya and dictated a letter to Stalin demanding that he apologize or he, Lenin, would break off relations between them.

* On March 7, 1923, Stalin composed a note to Lenin withdrawing his remarks but expressing confusion about the whole issue. This note is not shown to Lenin.

This is the account related, with only minor variations, in Lenin biographies. But there are major problems with this version of events.

Lenin's Letter to Trotsky of December 21, 1922

TO L. D. TROTSKY

It looks as though it has been possible to take the position without a single shot, by a simple manoeuvre. I suggest that we should not stop and should continue the offensive, and for that purpose put through a motion to raise at the Party congress the question of consolidating our foreign trade, and the measures to improve its implementation. This to be announced in the group of the Congress of Soviets. I hope that you will not object to this, and will not refuse to give a report in the group.

N. Lenin

December 21, 1922

(LIV, 327-8; CW 45, 606)

There are some problems with this letter.

* Krupskaya's signature on this letter is "N.K. Ul'yanova," a version of her name that she never used before or afterwards.[1] She always signed her name either "N.K." or "N. Krupskaya." (LIV, 672)

* Lenin's signature is "N. Lenin." This had been Lenin's revolutionary pseudonym in the years before the revolution. It was the reason for the early rumor that the Bolshevik leader was "Nikolai Lenin." There was no longer any need for Lenin to use it.

Indeed he had not used for many years, except for a single letter, dated December 16, 1922, and published – for the first time – directly above the December 21, 1922, letter to Trotsky in the PSS edition. But the Secretaries Journal does not note any dictation by Lenin for December 16. (XLV, 472-3; CW 42, 480-1) The Doctors Journal records no dictation during the period December 19 – 22. So it is possible that this December 16 letter was concocted after the fact, perhaps in an attempt to legitimate Lenin's "N. Lenin" signature on the purported December 21 letter to Trotsky.[2]

---

[1] Sakharov cites examples of Krupskaya's signature on documents, of which I have verified these: XLV 594; Izv TsK KPSS 1989, No. 2, 202; 205; 208; No. 3, 178, 179, 180; No. 5, 175, 179. 180, 181,182, 183, 184, 185; No. 12, 192; 1991, No. 3, 204, 205.

[2] The entry in the Doctors Journal is ambiguous about the date of a letter Lenin had to dictate: whether the dictation was on December 16 or on the previous day. The PSS editors assume that it was on the previous day, December 15, when the

No original of this letter exists. Lenin's archive has no carbon copy ("otpusk").[3] Trotsky's archive has a copy, but with the note that this is a "copy." Moreover, the contents of this alleged letter contract the facts.

Kotkin summarizes the problem this way:

> Trotsky claimed that on December 21 Lenin dictated a warm letter to him ("with the very best comradely greetings") via Krupskaya, thanking Trotsky for winning the battle on the foreign trade monopoly. But the alleged letter in Trotsky's archive is not an original but a copy of a copy; the copy in Lenin's archive is a copy of that copy. Lenin certainly had reason to be pleased: the December 18 Central Committee plenum had voted to uphold his position on keeping the state foreign trade monopoly—the draft resolution is in Stalin's hand. The plenum had also voted for Lenin's preferred version of the new state structure, a USSR, which Stalin arranged. Finally, the plenum had rejected Trotsky's insistence on a reorganization of economic management under the state planning commission. Further doubts about the December 21 dictation are connected with Krupskaya's manufacture of an incident on December 22 whereby Stalin, having supposedly learned of Lenin's alleged congratulatory dictation for Trotsky the day before, phoned to berate her. Stalin would indeed get angry at Krupskaya, but that would take place a month later, and, as we shall see, the difference in timing is crucial. What we know for sure is that on December 22, Lenin managed to dictate a formal request (through Lidiya Fotiyeva) to Stalin for cyanide "as a humanitarian measure." Right then, Lenin's worst fears were realized: during the night of December 22–23, he

---

Secretaries Journal does note the dictation of a letter to Trotsky.
[3] Sakharov, Zagadki 22.

Chapter Six. The Ultimatum Letter

suffered his second massive stroke. "Absolutely no movement," the doctors wrote, "neither of the right arm nor of the right leg." (Kotkin 484)

The Secretaries Journal does not note any dictation by Lenin between December 16 and December 23. There is no entry for December 21. (XLV, 474).The Doctors Journal does not record any work by Lenin on this day, stating simply that he "felt a little worse," "his mood was a little worse towards evening," "headaches at times," and "poor appetite." (VI KPSS 9, 1991, 45)

As published in the volume of Trotsky's archive, the letter begins with this note allegedly by Krupskaya:

> Лев Давыдович.
>
> Проф. Ферстер разрешил сегодня Владимиру Ильичу продиктовать письмо, и он продиктовал мне следующее письмо к Вам:[4]

> Lev Davydovich.
>
> Prof. Ferster today allowed Vladimir Ilyich to dictate a letter, and he dictated to me the following letter to you:

Krupskaya justified her action here in taking dictation from Lenin by claiming that Dr. Ferster had permitted it "today", i.e. December 21. Doctors Ferster and Kramer had visited Lenin the previous day, December 20 to examine him. There is no record that any doctor saw Lenin on December 21.[5] According to a letter from Stalin to Kamenev, Dr Ferster had "absolutely forbidden" dictation by Lenin again on December 22.[6]

---

[4] Iu. Fel'shtinsky Komm. Opp. I,, online edition, p. 44 of 168.(Originally published by "Terra," Moscow, 1990).
[5] VI KPSS 9 (1991), 44-45.
[6] Izv TsK KPSS 12, 1989, 192.

On December 18, 1922, the CC Plenum had assigned Stalin "personal responsibility for isolating Vladimir Il'ich with regard to personal contacts with [Party] workers, and correspondence."

> Решение Пленума ЦК РКП(б) 18 декабря 1922 г.
>
> В случае запроса т. Ленина о решении Пленума 1 по вопросу о внешней торговле, по соглашению Сталина с врачами, сообщить ему текст резолюции с добавлением, что как резолюция, так и состав комиссии приняты единогласно.
>
> Отчет т. Ярославского 2 ни в коем случае сейчас не передавать и сохранить с тем, чтобы передать тогда, когда это разрешат врачи по соглашению с т. Сталиным.
>
> На т. Сталина возложить персональную ответственность за изоляцию Владимира Ильича как в отношении личных сношений с работниками, так и переписки.
>
> (ЦПА ИМЛ, ф. 17, оп. 2, д. 86, л. 5 и об.; автограф Л. А. Фотиевой).[7]

Decision of the Plenum of the Central Committee of the RCP(b) December 18, 1922

In the event of a request by Comrade Lenin concerning decision 1 of the Plenum on the question of foreign trade, with the agreement of Stalin and the doctors, inform him of the text of the resolution with the addition that both the resolution and the composition of the commission were adopted unanimously.

---

[7] Izv TsK KPSS 12, 1989, 189,191.

> Under no circumstances should report 2 of Comrade Yaroslavsky be transmitted now, and it should be retained in order to transmit it when the doctors permit it with comrade Stalin's agreement.
>
> Comrade Stalin is to be personally responsible for the isolation of Vladimir Ilyich, both with respect to personal relations with workers and to correspondence.
>
> (CPA IML, f. 17, op. 2, d. 86, fol. 5 and rev.; handwritten by L.A. Fotieva).

As published in Lenin's PSS the text of the December 21, 1922 letter is taken from a "typewritten copy," i.e. not the original (LIV, 328). No original exists. If it were genuine, Trotsky should have the original. Or, if he had chosen, or been requested, to return the original for Lenin's files, it should be there. In Trotsky's archive the letter is marked "kopia" (copy).[8]

Trotsky adds that the letter was written "in the hand of N.K. Ulyanova [i.e. Krupskaya]."

> (написано рукой Н. К. Ульяновой).

But the copy in Lenin's archive is typewritten. (LIV 328; CW 45, 606) Where is the handwritten original that Trotsky refers to?

According to Sakharov, the version in Lenin's archive is a copy taken from Trotsky's copy – a "copy of a copy." It's logical to think so – where else could it have been copied from?

Adding up the facts given above, *there is no evidence that this letter is genuine* – that Lenin actually dictated it – and a number of reasons to suspect that he did not.

---

[8] Fel'shtinsky, Komm. Opp. I, p. 44 of 168 in online text version.

Kotkin adds:

> The copy in Lenin's archive has a handwritten note from Krupskaya to Trotsky to answer Lenin by phone, but when that was written in remains unknown (it may have been added to explain why there was no written answer from Trotsky). (Kotkin 821 n.73)

The subject of this letter, the issue of the monopoly of foreign trade, does not come up again in any of Lenin's later writings. *There is no evidence of any "campaign" on this issue in concert with Trotsky.*

These facts are in contradiction with Lenin's supposed great concern over this issue – a concern that, allegedly, contributed to his estrangement from Stalin. Kotkin notes this:

> Scholars have perpetuated Trotsky's falsehood concerning retention of the foreign trade monopoly that only he had won the day at the plenum on Lenin's behalf ... In fact, Krupskaya, on behalf of Lenin, had also written to Yaroslavsky (a Trotsky foe), asking that he find someone to substitute for Lenin at the December 18, 1922, plenum discussion, given Lenin's turn for the worse on December 16. It is noteworthy that Trotsky was not given, nor did he request, a written-out copy of the meeting protocols on the trade monopoly. (Kotkin 821 n.74)

The Secretaries Journal records the note to Yaroslavsky on December 14. (XLV 417; CW 42, 479). Yaroslavsky himself wrote about his meeting with Lenin on the question of the monopoly of foreign trade, which may have also taken place on December 14, 1922. In this memorandum Yaroslavsky records that when he told Lenin that he, Yaroslavsky, had reminded Trotsky of his former Menshevism, Lenin had laughed out loud and said: "Trotsky will never forgive you for that."[9]

Chapter Six. The Ultimatum Letter

Я ответил тогда Троцкому, что никогда не принадлежал ни к какой другой фракции, кроме фракции большевиков, чего он, Троцкий, про себя сказать не может. (Помню, как сейчас, как перекосилось лицо Троцкого при этом, как оно менялось во время моей короткой речи).

Ильич расхохотался вдруг своим заразительным смехом.

—Повторите, Емельян,— сказал он,— как Вы ему сказали.

Я повторил, и Ильич снова заразительно рассмеялся.

—Да Вы же его меньшевиком назвали, ха-ха-ха! Этого он Вам никогда не простит! Нет, Троцкий таких вещей не забывает.

I then replied to Trotsky that I had never belonged to any other faction except the Bolshevik faction, which he, Trotsky, cannot say about himself. (I remember how now, how Trotsky's face was distorted at the same time, how it changed during my short speech).

Ilyich suddenly burst out laughing with his infectious laugh.

"Repeat it, Emelyan," he said, "just as you told him.

I repeated, and Ilyich again laughed contagiously.

- Yes, you called him a Menshevik, ha-ha-ha! He will never forgive you for this! No, Trotsky does not forget such things.

---

[9] Izv TsK KPSS 4, 1989, 187-90, at 189.

In fact, Trotsky seems to have had nothing to do with the proposal and passage of the resolution preserving the monopoly of foreign trade. The handwritten draft of the resolution passed by the CC Plenum on December 18, 1922, survives. It is in handwriting similar to Stalin's, so probably his, and signed by Stalin, Zinoviev, and Kamenev. According to the description of this document given by Sakharov, the document is in the same ink as Stalin's signature – more evidence that Stalin wrote it – while Zinoviev and Kamenev signed with different ink, and Zinoviev made corrections. (215-6)

There exists a letter from Kamenev to Stalin in which Kamenev claims that Trotsky had phoned him that same night to tell him that he had received a letter from Lenin expressing satisfaction at the resolution on foreign trade.

Л. Б. КАМЕНЕВ 8— И. В. СТАЛИНУ

[не позднее 22 декабря 1922 г.]

Иосиф,

Сегодня ночью звонил мне Тр[оцкий]. Сказал, что получил от Старика записку, в которой Ст[арик] выражая удовольствие принятой пленумом** резолюцией о Внешторге, просит, однако, Тр[оцкого] сделать по этому вопросу доклад на фракции съезда и подготовить тем почву для постановки этого вопроса на партсъезде. Смысл, видимо, в том, чтобы закрепить сию позицию. Своего мнения Тр[оцкий] не выражал, но просил передать этот вопрос в комиссию ЦК по проведению съезда. Я ему обещал передать тебе, что и делаю.

Не мог тебе дозвониться.

В моем докладе я имею в виду горячо преподнести решение пленума ЦК 10

Жму руку Л. Кам[енев].

Я имею в виду приехать завтра, ибо материалов для доклада такая куча, что я в них тону и не справляюсь.[10]

L. B. KAMENEV 8 - I. V. STALIN

[no later than December 22, 1922]

Joseph,

Tr[otsky] called me tonight. He said that he had received a note from the Old Man [in Russian, "Starik"] in which St[arik], expressing his pleasure in the resolution on Vneshtorg adopted by the plenum. However, he asks Tr[otsky] to make a report on this issue at the congress fraction and thus prepare the ground for raising this question at the party congress. The point, apparently, is to consolidate this position. Tr[otsky] did not express his opinion, but asked to refer this issue to the Central Committee commission for conducting the congress. I promised him to tell you what I am doing.

I couldn't get through to you by phone.

In my report I mean to passionately present the decision of the plenum of the Central Committee.

I shake hands L. Kam[enev].

I mean to come tomorrow, because there are so many materials for the report that I am drowning in them and cannot manage.

This would appear to confirm Lenin's letter to Trotsky of December 21. But there are problems with it. It is undated – *the editors* have inserted "[not later than December 22, 1922]". Also, Kamenev says that Trotsky told him Lenin had asked him to

---

[10] Izv TsK KPSS 12, 1989, 191.

defend the position on foreign trade by making a report "at the Congress fraction" and so prepare the ground for a discussion "at the Party Congress." The "Congress fraction" could refer to the Communist fraction of the X All-Russian Congress of Soviets, held at the Bolshoi Theater on December 22, 1922, as the purported letter of Lenin's to Trotsky says. But the XII Party Congress was held April 17 -25, 1923. Lenin was planning to attend the Congress himself.

> Judging from the letter's contents, it must refer to a commission to prepare the forthcoming XII Party Congress. But we can find no trace of the work of such a commission in the CC of the RKP(b). According to the documents, the plan for the agenda of the Congress were prepared in the Secretariat of the CC and then gone over in the Politburo. Further preparation for the Congress was conducted in the Politburo, the Secretariat, the Orgburo, and at the February and March Plenums of the CC of the RKP(b). The question of the proposal contained in the letter by Krupskaya for Trotsky was not raised at any stage of this work. (Sakharov, Zagadki 23)

In any case, the basic question is not whether the purported letter from Lenin to Trotsky of December 21, 1922 exists, but whether Lenin wrote it.

All this contradicts the tenor of the now-suspect letter of Lenin to Trotsky of December 21, 1922, the contents of which suggest some kind of alliance. If Lenin also asked a Stalin stalwart like Yaroslavsky to intervene on this question, he clearly did not foresee any opposition. And, indeed, there was none.

Therefore, the monopoly of foreign trade question cannot be seen as any kind of alliance between Lenin and Trotsky. This too argues against the *bona fides* of the letter of December 21, 1922.

Krupskaya's name does not come up in either Kamenev's undated letter to Stalin or in Stalin's reply. Therefore, there is no evidence that this letter was the cause of Stalin's supposed phone call to, and criticism of, Krupskaya.

Krupskaya's Note to Kamenev of December 23, 1922

LEV BORISOVICH!

Because of a short letter which I had written in words dictated to me by Vladimir Il'ich by permission of the doctors, Stalin allowed himself yesterday an unusually rude outburst directed at me. This is not my first day in the party. During all these 30 years I have never heard from any comrade one word of rudeness. The business of the party and of Il'ich are not less dear to me than to Stalin. I need at present the maximum of self-control. What one can and what one cannot discuss with Il'ich I know better than any doctor, because I know what makes him nervous and what does not, in any case I know better than Stalin. *I am turning to you and to Grigorii [E. Zinoviev] as much closer comrades of V. I. and I beg you to protect me from rude interference with my private life and from vile invectives and threats.* I have no doubt as to what will be the unanimous decision of the Control Commission, with which Stalin sees fit to threaten me; however, I have neither the strength nor the time to waste on this foolish quarrel. And I am a living person and my nerves are strained to the utmost.

"N. KRUPSKAYA"[11]

The text in the PSS (see footnote) gives the date of this letter as December 23, 1922. But the editors of the PSS do not include the

---

[11] Lenin, PSS LIV 674-5, at note 541. This edition omits the text that I have put in italics here. The full Russian text was first published in Izv TsK 12, 1989, 192. This letter is not in the English language 4th edition of Lenin's Collected Works.

date as part of the text. If the date is correct, Stalin spoke with Krupskaya the day before, December 22, 1922. But we can be sure that it is *not* correct. *So it was added by the editors of the PSS.* Here Krupskaya claims the right to speak to Lenin despite the resolution of the Central Committee. Sakharov notes that during the period of their opposition to Stalin in later years, neither Kamenev nor Zinoviev mentioned anything about Krupskaya's turning to them to protect her from Stalin.

As we shall see, this dispute between Stalin and Krupskaya did not in fact take place in December 1922. Only Krupskaya claims that it took place then. All other accounts of this story put it later, in late January or early February, 1923. This suggests that the letter above was written later and predated, with a view to linking this event with the letter to Trotsky.

Lenin's sister Maria Il'inichna Ulyanova, who was very close to Lenin and had witnessed the dispute between Krupskaya and Stalin, portrayed this event very differently. She wrote

> This incident took place because on the demand of the doctors the Central Committee gave Stalin the charge of keeping a watch so that no political news reached Lenin during this period of serious illness. This was done so as not to upset him and so that his condition did not deteriorate, he (Stalin) even scolded his family for conveying this type of information.[12]

So not just Krupskaya but Lenin's whole family were "scolded" by Stalin.

Ulyanova speaks of a ban on giving Lenin political news. But this ban was established only on December 24, 1922, *after* the dates that Krupskaya claimed (December 21 for the letter to Trotsky, December 22 for Stalin's criticizing her). There is nothing in the

---

[12] XLV 710; Izv TsK KPSS 12, 1989, 196. M.I. Ul'ianova's whole report of July 26, 1926, to the Joint Plenum of the Central Committee and the Central Control Committee, is on 195-6.

Chapter Six. The Ultimatum Letter

C.C. resolution of December 18, 1922 forbidding personal contacts with members of the Party leadership or with Lenin's family.

Here is the December 24, 1922 ban as quoted by Maria Il'inichna in a memoir about Lenin:

> Ввиду этого, а также считаясь с поставленным Ильичем ультиматумом, врачи (Ферстер, Крамер, Кожевников) выработали 24 декабря на совещании со Сталиным, Каменевым и Бухариным следующее постановление:
>
> «1. Владимиру Ильичу предоставляется право диктовать ежедневно 5— 10 минут, но это не должно носить характера переписки и на эти записки Владимир Ильич не должен ждать ответа. Свидания запрещаются.
>
> 2.Ни друзья, ни домашние не должны сообщать Владимиру Ильичу ничего из политической жизни, чтобы этим не давать материала для размышлений и волнений»[13].

In view of this, and also taking into account the ultimatum delivered by Il'ich, the doctors (Foerster, Kramer, Kozhevnikov) drew up the following resolution on December 24 at a meeting with Stalin, Kamenev and Bukharin:

> "1. Vladimir Ilyich is given the right to dictate 5-10 minutes daily, but this should not bear the character of a correspondence and Vladimir Ilyich should not wait for an answer to these notes. Personal meetings are prohibited.

---

[13] Izv TsK KPSS 6 (1991), 193

> 2. Neither friends nor family should communicate to Vladimir Ilyich *anything from political life*, so as not to provide material for thought and upset."

Ulyanova links this event with the "question of the Caucasus." (Izv TsK 12, 1989, 198) She also links the clash between Stalin and Krupskaya with "some conversation between N.K. [Krupskaya] and V.I. [Lenin]," not with a letter to Trotsky.

> It seems, one day coming to know about certain conversations between N.K. and V.I., Stalin called her to the telephone and spoke to her quite sharply thinking this would not reach V. Ilyich. He warned her that she should not discuss work with V.I. or this may drag her to the Central Control Commission of the party. This discussion deeply disturbed N.K. She completely lost control of herself – she sobbed and rolled on the floor. After a few days she told V.I. about this incident and added that they had already reconciled. Before this it seems Stalin had actually called her to smooth over the negative reaction his threat and warning had created upon her. She told Kamenev and Zinoviev that Stalin had shouted at her on the phone **and it seems she mentioned the Caucasus business.** (Izv TsK 12, 1989, 198)

Ulyanova does not comment on whether Krupskaya's histrionic behavior – like "rolling on the floor" – was appropriate. Kotkin suggests that Krupskaya may have been "deliberately trying to stage a memorable incident," presumably for Ulyanova's benefit. (Kotkin 488)

The main point is this: Ulyanova says Krupskaya told Lenin about this event "after a few days" and during the time that the "Caucasus business" was being discussed. These details are completely in contradiction with Krupskaya's account. When, therefore, was Krupskaya's letter to Kamenev really written?

Chapter Six. The Ultimatum Letter

In her statement of July 26, 1926, Ulyanova says that Lenin's reaction was a moderate one.

> Ilyich, who accidentally came to know about this and who was also always worried about such a strong regime of protection, in turn scolded Stalin. Stalin apologized and with this the incident was settled. (Izv TsK 12, 1989, 196)

The Russian word translated here as "scolded" – *otchital* – is somewhat vague. But there is nothing here about a threat by Lenin to break off personal relations with Stalin.

Ulyanova even suggests that Lenin's reaction was excessive:

> It goes without saying that during this period, as I have indicated, if Lenin had not been so seriously ill then he would have reacted to the incident differently.

She concludes:

> There are documents regarding this incident and on the first demand from the Central Committee I can present them.

> Thus I affirm that all the talk of the opposition about Lenin's relation towards Stalin does not correspond to reality. These relations were most intimate and friendly and remained so.

There is nothing in Ulyanova's account about any "rudeness" on Stalin's part. We have no evidence that Krupskaya, who certainly would have known about Ulyanova's statement, ever protested what Ulyanova said.

What's more, on December 22, 1922, Lenin called Fotieva to him and dictated a secret note, "outside of the diary [journal]", in which he requested cyanide "as a humanitarian measure, mentioning the example of Paul Lafargue, Marx's son-in-law." Fotieva does not state to whom the note was addressed.[14] In 1926 Maria Il'inichna, who was constantly at his side, stated that the note was to Stalin.[15] Lenin had previously, in the spring of 1922,[16] asked Stalin about obtaining cyanide for him, and Lenin did so again in March, 1923. As Maria Il'inichna noted, this argues against any estrangement between Lenin and Stalin.

In a letter to Zinoviev of March 7, 1923, Kamenev also relates this incident to Georgian affairs (the congress of the Georgian party, scheduled for March 12), stating that he and Zinoviev have received copies of Lenin's "personal letter" to Stalin.

> Узнав, что Груз[инский] съезд назначен на 12 [марта], Старик
>
> весьма взволновался, нервничал и ... послал Сталину (копия мне и тебе) персональное письмо, которое ты, наверно, уже имеешь. Сталин ответил весьма сдержанным и кислым извинением, которое вряд ли удовлетворит Старика.
>
> (Izv TsK 9, 1990, 151).
>
> When the Old Man learned that **the Georgian congress** was set for the 12th [of March], he became very excited and nervous, and ... sent Stalin (copy to me and you) a personal letter, which you, undoubtedly, already have. Stalin responded with a very restrained and sour apology, which will hardly satisfy the Old Man.

This would have made no sense in December, 1922. .Moreover, Kamenev's description doesn't sound like the "ultimatum letter," in which Stalin clearly *refuses* to apologize.

---

[14] Izv TsK KPSS 6, 1991, 191, top of left column.
[15] Izv TsK KPSS 12, 1989, 196.
[16] Maria Ul'ianova's memoir about Lenin, Izv TsK KPSS 3 (1991), 185.

Chapter Six. The Ultimatum Letter

Boris Bazhanov, Stalin's secretary, who defected to the West on January 1, 1928, wrote and rewrote memoirs which are not at all reliable in many details. But he does agree that the Krupskaya-Stalin-Lenin incident occurred in 1923, not when Krupskaya claimed.

> В январе 1923 года секретарша Ленина Фотиева запросила у него интересовавшие Ленина материалы по грузинскому вопросу. Сталин их дать отказался ("не могу без Политбюро").В начале марта он [Сталин] так обругал Крупскую, что она прибежала к Ленину в слезах, и возмущенный Ленин продиктовал письмо Сталину, что он порывает с ним всякие личные отношения.[17]

> In January 1923, Lenin's secretary Fotieva asked him **for materials on the Georgian question** that interested Lenin. Stalin refused to give them ("I can't, without the Politburo"). In early March, he [Stalin] scolded Krupskaya so much that she ran to Lenin in tears, and the indignant Lenin dictated a letter to Stalin that he would break off all personal relations with him.

Bazhanov puts Stalin's scolding Krupskaya in early March, but he mentions Lenin's request for Georgian materials and Stalin's answer, which are clearly related to January 24-29, 1923 in the Secretaries Journal.[18] This was long after the December 24, 1922, prohibition against Lenin's receiving political materials, which Stalin was appointed to oversee.

Molotov also tells about this conflict between Krupskaya and Stalin:

---

[17] Boris Bazhannov, *Vospominaniia byvshego sekretaria Stalina.* Glava 3. Sekretar' Orgbiuro. At http://www.hrono.ru/libris/lib_b/bazhan03.php Reprinted from edition by "Knigizdatel'stvo 'Vsemirnoe slovo,' Spb 1992.
[18] See "Journal of Lenin's Duty Secretaries," CW vol. 42, 484-5.

> Stalin implemented the decision of the secretariat and did not permit Zinoviev and Kamenev to visit Lenin once this was prohibited by the doctors. Zinoviev and Kamenev complained to Krupskaya. Outraged, she told off Stalin. He responded, "Lenin should not have visitors." "But Lenin himself wants it!" Stalin: "If the Central Committee says so, we might not let you see him either."[19]

If Kamenev and Zinoviev were involved in this incident from the beginning, that would help to explain why Krupskaya appealed to them in her letter to Kamenev (above)

If indeed the Stalin-Krupskaya conflict was related to the struggle in the Georgian CP concerning principled questions of nation-state building, that might help explain why in reacting to Krupskaya's position Stalin told Molotov that to be Lenin's wife "does not necessarily mean to understand Leninism!" (MR 133) The question of the monopoly of foreign trade was not a principled theoretical question but one of expediency, while the national question was central to Bolshevik theory and politics, therefore to Leninism. (Sakharov, Zagadki 28)

All accounts of the Stalin-Krupskaya conflict *except* for Krupskaya's letter to Kamenev cite the "Caucasus question" and place it at the end of January or beginning of February, 1923. This means that Krupskaya's version is a serious distortion of reality – that she was deliberately lying. Lenin showed renewed interest in the Georgian question no earlier than the end of January 1923. Fotieva, in Lenin's name, asked for the materials of the Dzerzhinsky commission on January 24. (XLV 476; CW 42, 484)

On February 1, 1923, Stalin appealed to the Politburo "to be relieved of the responsibility of monitoring the implementation of the regime established by the doctors for com. Lenin." This would

---

[19] Feliks Chuev. *Molotov Remembers. Inside Kremlin Politics* (Chicago: Dee, 1993), 132-3. Hereafter MR.

make sense if his confrontation with Krupskaya had just occurred. The Politburo turned down his request.[20] Their decision might be understood as approving Stalin's action, and thus deciding against Krupskaya's claim to be allowed to speak with Lenin whenever she wished and about whatever she wished. And that might explain why Krupskaya never referred to this incident again.

The "Ultimatum" Letter[21]

В. И. ЛЕНИН — И. В. СТАЛИНУ

5 марта 1923 г.

Строго секретно.

Лично.

Товарищу Сталину.

Копия тт. Каменеву и Зиновьеву.

Уважаемый т. Сталин! Вы имели грубость позвать мою жену к теле-

фону и обругать ее. Хотя она Вам и выразила согласие забыть сказанное, но тем не менее этот факт стал известен через нее же Зиновьеву 14 и Каменеву. Я не намерен забывать так легко то, что против меня сделано, а нечего и говорить, что сделанное против жены я считаю сделанным и против меня. Поэтому прошу Вас взвесить, согласны ли Вы взять сказанное назад и извиниться или предпочитаете порвать между нами отношения.

---

[20] "О предложении т. Сталина. Предложение т. Сталина об освобождении его от обязанностей наблюдать за исполнением режима, установленного врачами для В. И. Ленина, отклонить." Протокол заседания Политбюро #46, 1923 г. Cited in the newspaper *Kommersant-vlast'* No.3, January 27, 2003. At https://www.kommersant.ru/doc/360899
[21] See illustration #6c for two variants of this letter.

С уважением Ленин.

5-го марта 23 года

TO J. V. STALIN

Top secret

Personal

Copy to Comrades Kamenev and Zinoviev

Dear Comrade Stalin:

You have been so rude as to summon my wife to the telephone and use bad language. Although she had told you that she was prepared to forget this, the fact nevertheless became known through her to Zinoviev and Kamenev. I have no intention of forgetting so easily what has been done against me, and it goes without saying that what has been done against my wife I consider having been done against me as well. I ask you, therefore, to think it over whether you are prepared to withdraw what you have said and to make your apologies, or whether you prefer that relations between us should be broken off.

Respectfully yours,

Lenin

March 5, 1923[22]

Volkogonov ties the stress of Lenin's agitation over Stalin's alleged treatment of Krupskaya to the seizure Lenin suffered on March 6 and his final, devastating stroke of March 10. In his version Stalin ends up being guilty not just of rudeness to Lenin's wife, but of indirectly causing Lenin's final and permanent incapacitation.[23]

---

[22] Russian edition: LIV 329-30; Izv TsK 12, 1989, 192-3. English translation CW 45, 607-8.

Chapter Six. The Ultimatum Letter

According to Sakharov who, as a professor at Moscow State University, had special access to these documents during the 1990s, the archival copy is typewritten and carries the words "written down by M.V." [24] We don't know how many copies were made. Lenin's sister Maria Ulyanova later wrote that Lenin asked Volodicheva to send it to Stalin and to give her a copy in a sealed envelope.[25]

Lenin's secretaries, or perhaps just Volodicheva herself, typed a number of copies at different times. Copies were presumably sent to at least Kamenev, Zinoviev, and Trotsky. This is more evidence that an opposition conspiracy against Stalin was in progress at this time.

The Secretaries Journal, entries by M. Volodicheva, fully records the story about Lenin's letters to Stalin and Trotsky.

> March 5 (entry by M. A. Volodicheva).
>
> Vladimir Ilyich did not send for me until round about 12. Asked me to take down two letters: one to Trotsky, the other to Stalin; the first letter to be telephoned personally to Trotsky and the answer given to him as soon as possible. As to the second letter, he asked it to be put off, saying that he was not very good at it that day. He wasn't feeling too good.
>
> March 6 (entry by M. A. Volodicheva).
>
> Asked about a reply to the first letter (reply over the telephone was taken down in shorthand). Read the second letter (to Stalin) and asked it to be handed to

---

[23] Sakharov 395. See Volkogonov, *Lenin* t. 2 (Russian edition, Novosti, Moscow, 1998), 342.
[24] The published version (in Russian but not in the English translation) carries an exclamation point after the words "Dear comrade Stalin." Evidently, the Khrushchev-Brezhnev era editors wished to impart to the letter a harsher tone towards Stalin.
[25] See Chapter 10.

> him personally and receive the answer from his own hands. Dictated a letter to the Mdivani group. Felt bad. Nadezhda Konstantinovna asked that this letter to Stalin should not be sent, and it was held up throughout the 6th. On the 7th I said I had to carry out Vladimir Ilyich's instructions. She spoke to Kamenev, and the letter was handed to Stalin and Kamenev, and afterwards to Zinoviev when he got back from Petrograd. Stalin's answer was received immediately on receipt of Vladimir Ilyich's letter (the letter was handed to Stalin personally by me and his answer to Vladimir Ilyich dictated to me). The letter has not yet been handed to Vladimir Ilyich, as he has fallen ill. (XLV, 486; CW 42, 493-4)

The Doctors Journal records that Lenin did dictate two letters on March 5 to Volodicheva. But it states that

> The letters, according to Vladimir Il'ich, did not upset him in the least, since they were purely business letters, but as soon as the stenographer left, Vladimir Il'ich felt chills. (*Kentavr*, October-December, 1991, 108)

"Purely business letters" that "did not upset him in the least" does not describe the "ultimatum" letter to Stalin. This raises the question: Did Lenin dictate this letter at all?

* We know that someone in Lenin's secretariat – it could only have been Krupskaya – began to falsify Lenin's article "How Should We Reorganize the WPI?"

* We know that Krupskaya pre-dated the quarrel with Stalin, moving it from late January-early February, 1923, when the Georgian national question was in the foreground, to December 22, 1923.

* We know that Krupskaya released the "Letter to the Congress" only after the XII Party Congress, and that its contents closely reflect some of the speeches by oppositionists, and some of the discussions, at the XII P.C, and that this can hardly be accidental. Therefore, Krupskaya, perhaps in concert with others, composed the L2C *after* the XII Party Congress, which ended on April 25, 1923.

So we must pose the question: Was the "ultimatum" letter really dictated by Lenin? Or is it yet another fabrication by Krupskaya, perhaps together with other persons?

Stalin's Letter to Lenin of March 7, 1923[26]

Stalin replied to Lenin:

> Т. Ленину от Сталина.
>
> Только лично.
>
> т. Ленин!
>
> Недель пять назад я имел беседу с тов. Н. Конст., которую я считаю не только Вашей женой, но и моим старым партийным товарищем, и сказал ей (по телефону) прибл. следующее: "врачи запретили давать Ильичу полит, информацию, считая такой режим важнейшим средством вылечить его. Между тем, Вы, Н. К., оказывается, нарушаете этот режим. Нельзя играть жизнью Ильича" и пр. Я не считаю, чтобы в этих словах можно было усмотреть что- либо грубое или непозволительное, предприн. "против" Вас, ибо никаких других целей, кроме цели быстрейшего В. выздоровления, я не преследовал. Более того, я считал своим долгом смотреть за тем, чтобы режим проводился. Мои объяснения с Н. К. подтвердили, что ничего, кроме пустых недоразум., не было тут, да и не могло быть. Впрочем, если Вы считаете, что для сохранения

---

[26] See illustration #7.

"отношений" я должен "взять назад" сказанные выше слова, я их могу взять назад, отказываясь, однако, понять, в чем тут дело, где моя "вина" и чего собственно от меня хотят.

To comrade Lenin from Stalin.

Strictly personal.

Comrade Lenin!

About five weeks ago I had a talk with com. N. Konst. [Natalia Konstantinovna – Krupskaya's name and patronymic], whom I consider not only your wife, but also my old Party comrade, and told her (on the telephone) approximately the following:

'The doctors have forbidden us to give Il'ich polit. information, and consider this regimen a very important means of treating him. Meanwhile you, N.K., as it turns out, are violating this regime. We must not play with Il'ich's life," etc. I do not think that in these words it was possible to discern anything rude or impermissible, undertaken. "against" you, because I did not pursue any other goals, except for the goal of your quickest recovery. Moreover, I considered it my duty to see that the regime was carried out. My explanations with N.K. have confirmed that there is nothing in this but empty misunderstandings, and indeed there could not be. However, if you consider that I must "take back" the above words which I spoke for the sake of keeping our "relationship," I can take then back. But I do not understand what the problem here is, what my "fault" is, and what precisely is expected of me.[27]

---

[27] Not in PSS or CW. First published in Izv TsK KPSS 12, 1989, 193. Also at http://www.hrono.info/libris/stalin/16-47.php, from Volkogonov.

Chapter Six. The Ultimatum Letter

Here Stalin relates the conflict with Krupskaya to the end of January or beginning of February, 1923, "about five weeks" before his letter of March 7. This is consistent with Bazhanov's and Maria Ulyanova's accounts and contradicts Krupskaya's. By that time the issue of the conflict within the leadership of the Georgian Communist Party, not the monopoly of foreign trade, was the focus of attention.

Krupskaya's version represents only Krupskaya herself as a violator of the ban on the transfer of political information to Lenin. It is understandable why Stalin reprimanded her. But for some reason, according to Lenin's sister, he reprimanded the "family." M.I. Ulyanova was not indignant about this, perhaps because Stalin's deed was considered justified, if not in form, then in essence.

And by this she also informs us that it was not connected with the letter which Lenin allegedly dictated to Krupskaya on December 21 for Trotsky. (394) Therefore, the evidence shows that Krupskaya was lying by dating Stalin's reprimand to her – and to her alone – as having occurred on December 22, 1922, and as having to do with a purported letter from Lenin to Trotsky of December 21.

According to Maria Ulyanova, Lenin was involved in settling this issue between Krupskaya and Stalin, but it did not escalate to the point where Lenin threatened to break relations with Stalin.

> Был один инцидент между Лениным и Сталиным, о котором т. Зиновьев упомянул в своей речи и который имел место незадолго до потери Ильичём речи (март 1923 г.), но он носил <u>чисто личный характер и никакого отношения к политике не имел</u>. Это т.Зиновьев хорошо знает, и ссылаться на него было совершенно напрасно. Произошёл этот инцидент благодаря тому, что Сталин, которому по требованию врачей было поручено Пленумом ЦК следить за тем, чтобы Ильичу в этот тяжёлый период его болезни не

сообщали политических новостей, чтобы не взволновать его и не ухудшить его положения, отчитал его семейных (читай: Крупскую – Л.Б.) за передачу такого рода новостей. Ильич, который случайно узнал об этом, – а такого рода режим оберегания его вообще всегда волновал, – в свою очередь отчитал Сталина. Т. Сталин извинился, и этим инцидент был исчерпан.[28]

There was an incident between Lenin and Stalin which comrade Zinoviev mentions in his speech and which took place not long before Ilyich lost his power of speech (March, 1923) but <u>it was completely personal and had nothing to do with politics.</u> Comrade Zinoviev knew this very well and to quote it was absolutely unnecessary. This incident took place because on the demand of the doctors the Central Committee gave Stalin the charge of keeping a watch so that no political news reached Lenin during this period of serious illness. This was done so as not to upset him and so that his condition did not deteriorate, he (Stalin) even scolded his family for conveying this type of information. Ilyich, who accidentally came to know about this and who was also always worried about such a strong regime of protection, in turn scolded Stalin. Stalin apologized and with this the incident was settled. What is there to be said – during this period, as I had indicated, if Lenin had not been so seriously ill then he would have reacted to the incident differently. There are documents regarding this incident and on the first demand from the Central Committee I can present them.

This is what the evidence that we have reviewed so far shows.

---

[28] Izv TsK KPSS 12 (1989), 196.

Why did Krupskaya move this incident to December 22, 1922, instead of when it really happened, at the end of January or beginning of February, 1923? Possibly in order to link it to the "Addition" to Lenin's supposed "Letter to the Congress," where "rudeness" is said to be a characteristic of Stalin that poses a political danger on the part of the General Secretary of the Party. It was not a perfect "fit" – the L2C says that Stalin's "rudeness" is tolerable in relation to Party members but not to non-Party members, and Krupskaya was a Party member. Nevertheless, it fixed "rudeness" as an attribute of Stalin's – an attribute not alleged by anyone else.

Those able to read Russian will note that, in the version published in Izv TsK 12, 1989, 193, there is a heading: "To Comrade Lenin from Stalin. Strictly personal." But in the original, reproduced photographically in volume two of the Russian edition of Volkogonov's biography of Lenin, between pages 384 and 385, there is no heading.[29] According to Sakharov, these are the words of a note on Central Committee letterhead that is kept together with Stalin's letter. (Sakharov, Zagadki 34) There is no evidence – e.g., a date – on the note to prove that it accompanied Stalin's letter or, perhaps, has nothing to do with it. Why was it – dishonestly, of course – printed as a part of Stalin's letter? Perhaps to give the letter a great sense of authenticity?

Volodicheva claimed that she took down Stalin's reply under dictation.[30] This is the document reproduced by Volkogonov. The handwriting appears to be consistent with Volodichva's and is cursive, as would be expected if taken down by dictation. Indeed, in 1967 Volodicheva told Aleksandr Bek that she had been so upset that she herself was surprised at her "scrawl" [*karakuli*].[31] It is not signed by Stalin.[32]

---

[29] I have put it online at
https://msuweb.montclair.edu/~furrg/research/stalintolenin030723.jpg
[30] XLV 486; CW 42, 494.
[31] A. Bek. "K istorii poslednikh leninskikh dokumentov." *Moskovskie novosti* 17 (1989), 9.

But a *second* text of this letter exists, which has not been photographically reproduced. Sakharov describes this text as written "in even, calm handwriting ... signed with a signature characteristic of Stalin."³³ (399) This "Stalin version" is kept among the materials of Lenin's secretariat in an envelope together with Lenin's letter of March 5 on which is written: "Letter of V.I. of 5/III/23 (2 copies) and answer of com. St[alin], not read by V.I. Len[in]. The sole copies." (Sakharov, Zagadki, 34) How could this letter exist if Volodicheva took Stalin's answer in dictation? Its existence casts doubt on Volodicheva's account.

There are further problems with the copies of the "ultimatum" letter in Lenin's archive.

> Three copies of the letter are preserved in the archive, all with the same contents. Differences in the arrangement of the texts on the page show that they were typed at different times, as do the differences in the notation of the addressees. On one copy the notation that copies were sent to L.B. Kamenev and G.E. Zinoviev are lacking, but on two other copies this note does appear – in the upper right corner beneath the words "To com[rade] Stalin is written "Copy to c[omrades] Kamenev and Zinoviev." In addition, on one of these copies this superscription was typed at the same time as the text, while on the other it was not – the text is thicker, obviously typed with a different ribbon). So one copy of the letter was sent to Kamenev and Zinoviev. But Volodicheva stated that two different copies were send to them.

> The note about the personal nature of the letter is formulated differently ("personal"; "personal, –", as is the inscription of verification ("Written down by V.M.", "Accurate M.V.").

---

³² See illustration #11, in Volodicheva's "scrawl."
³³ Sakharov identifies this text as RGASPI. f. 2. op. 1. d. 26004. ll. 3-6.

> The notation "Accurate" on the letters means that what we have here is not the original, but a copy ... That is not surprising, but it raises some questions. When, by whom, and why was a copy made, if there were copies of the original? Why, on the originals, were the addressees typed at a different time than the text? If the letters were sent to three addressees, and one (as was the practice) remained for the archive, why are there so many texts in the secretariat? All this suggests some work by Lenin's secretaries to make multiple copies of the text of this *secret* and *personal* letter. (Sakharov, Zagadki 31-2)

According to Sakharov, who cites archival sources, neither Lenin's "ultimatum" letter nor Stalin's reply are registered in Lenin's secretariat (i.e. as they were produced) nor as entering into Lenin's archive. One logical explanation is that they were placed in Lenin's archive much later than March 1923, when the registration books were no longer in use.

Then there is the matter of the blanks, the stationery on which the two "Stalin replies" are recorded. Sakharov states that blanks like that on which the "Stalin version" is written may be found in the archives available to him, but that he has not found any blanks like the one on which Volodicheva's version is written. (Sakharov, Zagadki 36)

The contents of the letter raise questions. The "ultimatum" letter demands an apology. But in this letter Stalin only agrees – reluctantly – to "take back" what he said, but no more. Volkogonov points out that the "ultimatum" letter addresses Stalin as "respected" (*uvazhaemiy*) and ends "respectfully, Lenin" (*s uvazheniem, Lenin*), and calls Stalin's tone "disrespectful."[34]

> It turns out that in a certain sense Zinoviev and Kamenev are *central figures* in this story. This agrees

---

[34] Volkogonov, *Lenin*, t. 2, 343.

with Molotov's testimony that the conflict between Stalin and Krupskaya took place because of them. Krupskaya appealed to their protection concerning the talk with Stalin. In the "ultimatum" letter it is specifically stated that Lenin has dictated it and demands from Stalin an apology because Zinoviev and Kamenev were informed about Stalin's rudeness to Krupskaya. (Sakkharov, Zagadki 34)

Sakharov is referring to two texts. First is this passage from Krupskaya's letter to Kamenev, dated December 23, 1922:

> Я обращаюсь к Вам и к Григорию, как более близким товарищам В. И., и прошу оградить меня от грубого вмешательства в личную жизнь, недостойной брани и угроз.[35]

> I appeal to you and to Grigory [Zinoviev – GF], as the closest comrades of V.I., and ask you to protect me from rude interference in my personal life, unworthy abuse and threats.

The second text is this passage in Felix Chuev's book of interviews with Molotov:

> Stalin implemented the decision of the secretariat and did not permit Zinoviev and Kamenev to visit Lenin once this was prohibited by the doctors. Zinoviev and Kamenev complained to Krupskaya. Outraged, she told off Stalin. He responded, "Lenin should not have ·visitors." "But Lenin himself wants it!" Stalin: "If the Central Committee says so, we might not let you see him either."[36]

---

[35] "N.K. Krupskaya to L.B. Kamenev. 22 December, 1922." *Izv TsK KPSS* 12 (1989), 192. The first publication of his letter, in Lenin, PSS, LIV 674-5, omits the direct appeal to Zinoviev as well as to Kamenev.

[36] *Molotov Remembers. Conversations with Felix Chuev. Ed. and Intro. Albert Resis.* Chicago: Dee, 1993, 132-133.

Chapter Six. The Ultimatum Letter

Sakharov continues:

> Volodicheva includes among the witnesses of Lenin's work on the "ultimatum" letter M.I. Ulyanova. But Ulyanova "refuses" this "honor," and indicates that she knows about this story from Krupskaya. What's more, she doubts that Krupskaya saw this letter … (Zagadki 32)

Here too Sakharov refers to two documents. The first is to Aleksandr Bek's interview 1963 interview with Volodicheva;

> Soon a troubled Maria Il'inichna approached her [Fotieva] and said:
>
> "Vladimir Il'ich is worse. What did he dictate to you?"
>
> She took the letter from the distraught Volodicheva …[37]

The second is to Ulyanova's second document about Stalin's relationship with Lenin.

> After returning home and seeing V.I. distressed N.K. understood that something had happened. She requested Volodicheva not to send the letter. She would personally talk to Stalin and ask him to apologize. **That is what N.K. is saying now, but I feel that she did not see this letter and it was sent to Stalin as V.I. had wanted.**[38]

He also notes, correctly, that Stalin disavows what Krupskaya said. Rather than apologizing, Stalin insists that he did nothing wrong. That is, in this letter Stalin does *not* apologize on principle, clearly stating that he does not understand why he should do so.

---

[37] "Stenografistka Il'icha," *Sovetskaia Kul'tura* January 1, 1989, p. 3.
[38] Izvestiia TsK KPSS 12 (1989), 199. Russian text and English translation are an appendix to the present book.

Suppose that Stalin had received the "ultimatum" letter, but that he was puzzled, even irked, by it, because, in fact, he had *already* apologized, as Maria Ulyanova later wrote that he did.

> Ilyich, who accidentally came to know about this and who was also always worried about such a strong regime of protection, in turn scolded Stalin. **Stalin apologized and with this the incident was settled.**

Assuming that Ulyanova's account is truthful, suddenly, on March 7, 1923, Stalin received a *second* demand for an apology. That would account for the tone of this letter of March 7, and for his failure to apologize *again*.

Another possibility is that Stalin did *not* receive the "ultimatum" letter, and therefore was not responding to it.

> One cannot exclude, for example, that its appearance was inspired by rumors or stories that Lenin continued to express dissatisfaction with Stalin's conflict with Krupskaya, that Lenin had forgotten that reconciliation had already taken place, that it would be good to write him a few words about the conflict and reassure him ... In this case, the fact that Stalin's letter was written as if he knew nothing about the text of the "ultimatum" letter and did not answer it receives a natural explanation. (Sakharov 400; cf. Sakharov, Zagadki 37)

Sakharov, who had access to archival documents, questions Lenin's authorship of the "ultimatum" letter.

> There exists a "Journal of Vladimir Il'ich's directives" ("Journal of registration of outgoing mail by V.I. Lenin"), in which annotations were made from September 7, 1920, until January 16, 1924. **In it there is no information about any letters sent by Lenin on either March 5 or 6, 1923, including to Stalin.** Separate from the registration of incoming and outgoing correspondence in Lenin's secretariat there

Chapter Six. The Ultimatum Letter   175

> was conducted a registration of documents sent from the secretariat to Lenin's personal archive: "Journal No. 4 of the registration of documents of the Archive of V.I. Lenin" that was maintained from December 19, 1922 until April 16, 1923. **But here too there is no record of entry into Lenin's Archive of the "ultimatum" letter or Stalin's response to it** ... There exists still another journal of registration of documents of Lenin's Archive containing notes from January 9 to July 9, 1923. **But there too neither these letters nor the envelope are registered.** (Sakharov, Zagadki 35)

Sakharov adds further evidence that Lenin's correspondence has been tampered with.

> Meanwhile, in this journal other documents related to Lenin are mentioned. On March 5 a "note to com. Tuchkov dated March 1, 1923, concerning church collections" is registered, on March 7 – "Vl. Il. 's article 'Better Fewer But Better', ... (Sakharov 274; Sakharov, Zagadki 35-6)

The letter to Tuchkov and other documents listed by Sakharov (273) are not in Lenin's PSS. Sakharov concludes: "These facts show that we essentially know very little about Lenin's work during this final period." It appears likely that Lenin's final letters were, in reality, these as yet unpublished documents.

Sakharov plausibly explains the absence of the "ultimatum" letter from the journals of Lenin's secretariat and archive.

> How can we explain the presence of the "ultimatum" letter and Stalin's reply among the materials of Lenin's archive, and the absence of the registration of the passage of their passage through Lenin's secretariat and entry into Lenin's archive? We must assume that these letters entered Lenin's Archive *much later* than March 1923 – after the registration books had already

been removed from use and it was no longer possible to write them in "after the fact," but it was possible to add the envelope with the letters to the materials of the document collection ("fond") that was being formed. (Zagadki 36)

All of these contradictory details suggest that that Lenin did not dictate the "ultimatum" letter. On the evidence we have today, it is more likely that Krupskaya drafted this letter, perhaps with the help of Lenin's secretaries. The word "rude" in it would be echoed in Krupskaya's fabricated letter to Kamenev, post-dated to December 23, 1923, and in the "Addition," documents that were not composed until sometime after the XII Party Congress. This kind of intrigue in Lenin's Secretariat, headed by Krupskaya, would also explain why Stalin's letter was not shown to Lenin.

Twelve days later Lenin asked Stalin for poison to end his life. According to the canonical story Lenin, in the "ultimatum" letter, had threatened to break relations with Stalin, and had not seen Stalin's reply. Yet he asked Stalin the kind of favor that only one devoted friend would ask another – to help him die. This story, challenged by no one, would make sense if Lenin did not send the "ultimatum" letter.

Kamenev's Letter to Zinoviev of March 7, 1923

Совершенно] секр[етно]

7.Ш.[1]923 г. 4 часа.

Дорогой Григорий,

Уезжаю через 2 часа. Для ориентировки сообщаю тебе след[ующие] факты. Узнав, что Груз[инский] съезд назначен на 12 [марта], Старик весьма взволновался, нервничал и 1) послал Троцкому письменную просьбу «взять на себя защиту груз[инского] дела в партии: тогда я буду спокоен». Троцкий решительного ответа не дал. Вызывал вчера ночью меня для совещания, 2) написал и дал мне для передачи «Мдивани,

Мах[арадзе] и др.» (копия Троцкому и Каменеву) письмо в 2 строки фактической солидаризации с Мдивани и К ° и дезавуирования Серго, Ст[алина] и Дз[ержинского], 3) послал Сталину (копия мне и тебе) персональное письмо, которое ты, наверно, уже имеешь. Сталин ответил весьма сдержанным и кислым извинением, которое вряд ли удовлетворит Старика .

Я приложу все силы для достижения на Кавказе мира на почве решений, которые объединили бы обе группы. Полагаю, этого можно будет добиться. Боюсь, что это уже не удовлетворит Старика, который, видимо, хочет не только мира на Кавказе, но и определенных организационных выводов наверху.

Я думаю, тебе необходимо быть в Москве это время и держать связь с[о] мной в Тифлисе. Съезд отложен до 15 [апреля], и это дает возможность еще раз обсудить все возникающие из совокупности перечисленных фактов выводы. Жалею, что не могу до отъезда поговорить с тобой.

Жму руку.

Л. Каменев
Автограф[39]

Top secret

7. III.1923 4 o'clock

Dear Grigorii:

I am leaving in 2 hours. To bring you up to date I am reporting to you the following facts. Upon learning that the Georgian Congress was scheduled for 12

---

[39] Izv TsK 9, 1990, 151.

[March], the Old Man was very excited and nervous, and 1) he sent Trotsky a written request "to assume the defense of the Georgian business in the party: then I will be calm." Trotsky did not give a decisive answer. He called me yesterday night for a meeting, 2) he wrote and gave me for transmission to Mdivani, Makh[aradze] and others (a copy to Trotsky and Kamenev) a letter in 2 lines [of] actual solidarity with Mdivani and Co. and disavowing Sergo, St[alin] and Dz[erzhinsky], 3) he sent to Stalin (a copy to me and to you) a personal letter, which you probably already have. Stalin responded with a very restrained and sour apology, which is unlikely to satisfy the Old Man.

I am making every effort to achieve peace in the Caucasus on the grounds of decisions which would unite both groups. I believe that this is achievable. I am afraid that this will no longer satisfy the Old Man, who apparently wants not only peace in the Caucasus, but also certain organizational conclusions at the top.

I think that it is essential for you to be in Moscow at this time and to maintain contact with me in Tiflis. The Congress is postponed until the 15th [of April], and this makes it possible to once again discuss all conclusions arising from the totality of the facts listed [above]. I regret that I can't talk to you before you leave.

With a handshake,

L. Kamenev

Autograph[40]

This letter contains some puzzling details.

---

[40] In the author's own handwriting.

Chapter Six. The Ultimatum Letter

* Kamenev says that he has seen Stalin's reply to Lenin's letter to him. But Kamenev mentions nothing about the most important and dramatic issues in the "ultimatum" letter: Stalin's alleged rudeness to Krupskaya and Lenin's threat to break off relations with Stalin.

* Kamenev states that Stalin replied to Lenin's letter with "a very restrained and sour apology." We know that Stalin dictated his reply to Volodicheva. Therefore Volodicheva either showed Stalin's reply to Kamenev or summarized it for him.

* The published version of Stalin's letter contains the header "strictly personal." Granted, this is not on the original but on a note filed with the copies. Still, it is clearly a personal letter. Yet Kamenev either saw it, or had it read to him. Why? What was Volodicheva's motive in doing this?

We know that Krupskaya, who was in charge of Lenin's secretariat, had some kind of conspiracy under way. She had predated her argument with Stalin from later January – early February, 1923, to December 22, 1922, and must have been a party to the attempted falsification of the article about the WPI in January, 1923.

* Kamenev's letter says that Lenin "wrote and gave to me" the letters. But Lenin could neither write nor give anyone anything.

* Kamenev states in this letter that he met with Trotsky "yesterday night" – that is, March 6, 1923 – for a meeting. This is in apparent contradiction with Kamenev's letter to Fotieva of April 16, 1923.

> 16.IV.[1]923.
>
> Тов. Фотиева,
>
> Сейчас получил Вашу записку. Более месяца тому назад т. Троцкий показывал мне статью Владимира Ильича по национальному вопросу, указывая — с Ваших слов— на полную и абсолютную секретность ее и на то, что она ни в коем случае не подлежит оглашению не только

путем печати, но даже и путем устной передачи. **Было это, по-моему, уже тогда, когда Владимир Ильич был лишен возможности давать новые распоряжения.**[41]

Comrade Fotieva

I have just now received your note. More than a month ago, Comrade Trotsky showed me an article by Vladimir Ilyich on the national question, pointing out — from your own words — its complete and absolute secrecy and that it should in no way be published not only by the press, but even by oral transmission. **In my opinion, this was already when Vladimir Ilyich was deprived of the opportunity to give new orders**.

Here Kamenev is claiming that he received "The Question of Nationalities ..." from Trotsky *after* March 10, 1923. Did Kamenev meet with Trotsky another time in early March, 1923? There is no record of another meeting.

* Kamenev also writes that Lenin "apparently wants not only peace in the Caucasus, but also certain organizational conclusions at the top." (ibid.) At the top of the Georgian Communist Party? Presumably, but we can't be sure. He can't mean the removal of Stalin as Gensec since this issue is only raised in the so-called "Addition" dated January 4, 1923[42], and it was not disclosed until the summer of 1923. Nor do we know where Kamenev got this impression. The only place these claims could have originated is from the Gorbunov-Fotieva-Glyasser "Commission."

* Strong evidence that this letter could not have been written on March 7, 1923, is the fact that *Lenin had no visitors on March 6 or March 7*. The entries for those days in the Doctors Journal are

---

[41] Izv TsK KPSS 9, 1990, 157.
[42] Unless this Kamenev letter was written much later.

lengthy and detailed. None of his secretaries record passing any note from Lenin on to Kamenev or anyone else.[43]

* How could Lenin have given Kamenev the letter to Stalin "yesterday night" – the night of March 6-7 – when Kamenev's letter to Zinoviev is dated March 7, 4 p.m.? Volodicheva says that she did not give the letter to Stalin until March 7. How could Kamenev already have Stalin's reply? Volodicheva does not say that she gave it to Kamenev *before* giving it to Stalin. Again, according to Volodicheva, she gave the letter to Zinoviev "afterwards", "when he got back from Petrograd." (CW 42, 494; XLV 486) How could Kamenev have written to Zinoviev that "you probably already have" Stalin's reply, when Zinoviev is said to have gotten the letter "afterwards," i.e. after Kamenev got it?

For all these reasons Sakharov suggests that this letter by Kamenev to Zinoviev, although dated March 7, 1923, was not really written at this time. A much later date – say, around the time of the XIII Party Congress in May, 1924, or the XIV Party Congress in December, 1925 – might account for Kamenev's saying that Lenin "wrote" and "gave" the letter, when Kamenev's, and most other people's, memory of precisely when Lenin had lost the ability to write, then to dictate and finally to speak, had faded and the precise timing of all these events was no longer clear in the memories of those persons involved.

We have already noted that the letter Kamenev describes here does not sound like Lenin's "ultimatum" letter. Nor do we know why Kamenev was, evidently, privy to Stalin's reply – unless perhaps it reflects the "New Opposition" (also called the "Platform of the Four") of Zinoviev, Kamenev, Krupskaya, and Sokol'nikov against Stalin in 1925.

---

[43] *Kentavr*, Oct-Dec. 1991, 109-110.

Lenin's Request to Stalin for Poison, March 17, 1923

On March 10, 1923, the Doctors Journal notes a sharp decline in Lenin's health. His speech could not be understood. When the nurse, Ekaterina Ivanovna Fomina, came in, Lenin said to her *smertel'niy tok*, "deadly current." At first the doctors thought this meant that Lenin believed his spasm to be fatal. At one point he managed to say *nado dat'* – "you must give ..." The doctors thought he meant valerian [a sedative], and Lenin said *Da, da*.[44]

On March 17, after trying and failing to say something intelligible, somehow – Volkogonov says that it is not clear how those around Lenin figured this out – Lenin asked for potassium cyanide. Our information about this fact comes from two of Stalin's letters. The first was apparently written on March 17:

> Зин., Каменеву.
>
> Только что вызвала меня Надежда Константиновна и сообщила в секретном порядке, что Ильич в "ужасном" состоянии, с ним припадки, «не хочет, не может дольше жить и требует цианистого калия, обязательно.» Сообщила, что пробовала дать калий, но "не хватило выдержки", ввиду чего требует "поддержки Сталина".
>
> Сталин[45]

> To Zin, Kamenev:
>
> Nadezhda Konstantinovna just called me and told me in confidence that Ilyich was in a "terrible" state, he had seizures, "he doesn't want to and cannot live longer and definitely needs potassium cyanide." She said that she tried to give potassium, but "did not have

---

[44] *Kentavr*, Oct-Dec. 1991, 113.
[45] Volkogonov, *Lenin* t. 2, 346-7.

Chapter Six. The Ultimatum Letter

enough strength [*vyderzhki*, lit. "endurance"]," which is why she requires "Stalin's support."

Stalin

Zinoviev and Kamenev wrote their reactions on the letter and apparently returned it to Stalin: "This cannot be in any way. Ferster gives hope – how can you? Anything but that! Impossible, impossible, impossible!"

The second is provisionally dated March 21)[46]

Строго секретно.

Членам Пол. Бюро В субботу 17 марта т. Ульянова (Н.К.) сообщила мне в порядке архиконспиративном „просьбу Вл. Ильича Сталину" о том, чтобы я, Сталин, взял на себя обязанность достать и передать Вл. Ильичу порцию цианистого калия. В беседе со мной НК. говорила, между прочим, что „Вл. Ильич переживает неимоверные страдания", что „дальше жить так немыслимо", и упорно настаивала „не отказывать Ильичу в его просьбе". Ввиду особой настойчивости Н.К. и ввиду того, что В. Ильич требовал моего согласия (В.И. дважды вызывал к себе Н.К. во время беседы со мной и с волнением требовал "согласия Сталина"), я не счел возможным ответить отказом, заявив: „Прошу В. Ильича успокоиться и верить, что, когда нужно будет, я без колебаний исполню его требование". В. Ильич действительно успокоился.

Должен, однако, заявить, что у меня не хватит сил выполнить просьбу В. Ильича, и вынужден

---

[46] The handwritten copy is not dated. The accompanying typewritten copy is dated March 21, 1923. See
https://msuweb.montclair.edu/~furrg/research/stalinleninpoison23.pdf

отказаться от этой миссии, как бы она ни была гуманна и необходима, о чем и довожу до сведения членов П. Бюро ЦК.

И.Сталин[47]

Top secret

To the members of the Politburo.

On Saturday, March 17, Comrade Ulyanova (N.K.) informed me very secretly of Lenin's request to Stalin "that I, Stalin, take upon myself the responsibility to get and transfer to Vladimir Ilyich a dose of potassium cyanide. In an interview with me, N.K. said, among other things, that "Vl. Ilyich was experiencing incredible suffering, "that it was unthinkable to continue living like that," and stubbornly insisted "not to deny Ilyich his request." Due to N.K.'s special persistence and because Ilyich demanded my consent (V.I. twice called N.K. to himself during the conversation with me and with feeling demanded "Stalin's consent"), I did not consider it possible to refuse and said: "I ask V. Ilyich to calm down and to believe that when it is necessary I will fulfill his demand without hesitation." V. Ilyich really did become calmer.

I must, however, state that I lack the strength to fulfill V. Ilyich's request, and I am forced to abandon this mission, no matter how humane and necessary it is, and I bring it to the attention of members of the P. Bureau of the C.C.

J. Stalin

---

[47] Volkogonov, *Lenin t.2*, 346-7 (Russian edition).

Chapter Six. The Ultimatum Letter

Members of the Politburo read this letter of Stalin's. Tomsky wrote on it: "I read [it]. I believe that Stalin's "indecision" is correct. We need to discuss this strictly among the members of the Politburo. Without secretaries (tech.)." Zinoviev, Molotov, Bukharin, Trotsky and Kamenev wrote - "Read [it]"

Concerning this incident, Sakharov remarks:

> If Lenin had given Stalin an ultimatum and demanded an apology from him to Krupskaya and had not received satisfaction (and he had not received it), then he would have no reason to turn to him with such a request. The same can be said about Krupskaya, who forwarded Lenin's request to him. It is necessary to explain the behavior of Stalin too. He acted as if there was no ultimatum letter, as if he did not know about it. (404)

Lenin never did see Stalin's reply of March 7, 1923, in which he "took back" his remarks to Krupskaya. This is recorded as a footnote to Stalin's reply:

> Письмо В. И. Ленина и ответ И. В. Сталина хранились в официальном конверте Управления делами Совнаркома, на котором было помечено: «Письмо В. И. от 5/Ш—23 г. (2 экз.) **и ответ т. Ст[алина], не прочитанный В. И. Лен[иным]**. Единственные экземпляры». Ответ И. В. Сталиным был написан 7 марта тотчас после вручения ему М. А. Володичевой письма В. И. Ленина. Ред.[48]

> The letter of V.I. Lenin and the answer of I.V. Stalin were stored in an official envelope of the Office of the Sovnarkom's Affairs, on which was written: "Letter of V.I. of 5/III-23 (2 copies) and **answer by com. St[alin], not read by V. I. Len[in]**. The only copies."

---

[48] Izv TsK 12, 1989, 193, footnote.

> The answer by I.V. Stalin was written on March 7 immediately after the delivery to him by M.A. Volodicheva of the letter of V.I. Lenin. Ed.

"The only copies"? What about the copy that Maria Ulyanova says was given to her in a sealed envelope? *None* of this kind of commentary can be trusted.

> V.I. asked Volodicheva to send it to Stalin without telling N.K. about it and to give me a copy in a sealed envelope.[49]

Sakharov draws the obvious conclusion:

> Consequently, neither Lenin's ultimatum letter nor Stalin's non-response letter put an end to their relationship. Indeed, the last act of their relationship was Lenin's appeal to Stalin for poison on March 17, 1923 — an act that speaks not of a threat of breaking off their relationship from a personally offended person, but of a friend's call for help, a request to make a terrible moral sacrifice – to help his friend die. This fact is indirect evidence against the desire of Lenin to break off relations with Stalin because of the reassessment of his qualities as a person and a politician. (404)

Conclusion

On the evidence, the "Ultimatum Letter" must be a forgery. Krupskaya lied about the argument between herself and Stalin. Lenin's criticism of Stalin for scolding not just Krupskaya but Lenin's family – as stated by Ulyanova – took place about a month earlier than March 5, 1923. Stalin's March 7 reply reveals that he did not understand why he was being asked to apologize yet again. Stalin's reply was not given to Lenin because doing so would have

---

[49] This document is discussed in a separate chapter.

exposed the phony "Ultimatum Letter." Lenin's asking Stalin for poison less than two weeks later argues against any intention of Lenin's to cut off ties with Stalin.

The reason for the existence of two very different copies of Stalin's letter to Lenin remain a mystery.

Chapter 7. Trotsky on the Testament

Trotsky's booklet *On the Suppressed Testament of Lenin* is dated December, 1932. Trotsky also discussed the "testament" in his autobiography *My Life* and in *The Stalin School of Falsification*. These works were published after *On the Suppressed Testament of Lenin*, so we will use the earlier work here. Trotsky's essay, published within this booklet, is titled "On Lenin's Testament." References are to the online English language edition.[1]

This work is full of false statements. We will note them in the course of commenting on Trotsky's use of Lenin's last works.

> The first official reading of the testament in the Kremlin occurred, not at a session of the Central Committee ... but in the Council of Elders at the Thirteenth Congress of the party on May 22, 1924. It was not Stalin who read the testament, but Kamenev in his then position as permanent president of the central party bodies.

According to Trotsky, Karl Radek told Emil Ludwig that Stalin had read the "Letter to the Congress" at this Central Committee meeting. Trotsky heatedly denied this.

Trotsky also claimed:

> At that time the party apparatus was semi-officially in the hands of the troika (Zinoviev, Kamenev, Stalin) – as a matter of fact, already in the hands of Stalin. The troika decisively expressed themselves against reading the testament at the Congress ...
>
> ... The troika introduced, through one of its henchmen, a resolution previously agreed upon with the

---

[1] On line at https://www.marxists.org/archive/trotsky/1932/12/lenin.htm

> provincial leaders: the document should be read to each delegation separately in executive session; no one should dare to make notes; at the plenary session the testament must not be referred to. With the gentle insistence characteristic of her, Krupskaya argued that this was a direct violation of the will of Lenin, to whom you could not deny the right to bring his last advice to the attention of the party.

In Trotsky's version, the "troika" (as he calls, at this point in time, Zinoviev, Kamenev, and Stalin) "decisively expressed themselves against reading the testament at the Congress." But Krupskaya "insisted," and then the text was read aloud at the Council of Elders (*sovet stareishin*) by Kamenev. So Trotsky portrays Stalin (and others) as trying to avoid any reading of the L2C before the C.C. or the Congress and ignoring Lenin's wishes as expressed by Krupskaya.

Assuming that Sakharov has quoted accurately from the archival documents he cites, Trotsky's version of events is false. After Krupskaya's formal presentation of the "Letter to the Congress" to the Central Committee, the C.C. committee on the acceptance of the documents of Lenin issued this decision: "To bring these documents to the attention of the next Plenum of the C.C., with the proposal to bring them to the attention of the Party Congress." (579)

The C.C. decision was signed by Zinoviev, A. Smirnov, Kalinin, Bukharin, Stalin, and Kamenev. This means that Zinoviev, Kamenev, and Stalin were *in favor of* bringing the "testament" before the Congress *without* any reservation that the documents be read by delegation.

Trotsky:

> The mere fact that the troika was able to transgress the will of Lenin, refusing to read his letter at the Congress, sufficiently characterizes the composition of the Congress and its atmosphere.

This too is false. At the XIII Party Congress the L2C was read by delegation. At least one delegation (the Kirghiz) asked that it be read to them a second time. Kumanev and Kulikova claim that "stormy discussions of the documents in the 'testament' in some delegations (for example, the Ukrainian) were not heard by the whole Congress."[2] But in an article published subsequent to his book Sakharov publishes some texts from archival materials that contradict this.

> According to Stalin, after the reading of the "testament" "in all delegations of the Congress without exception", "the presidium of the Congress asked the Plenum of the Congress if the "testament" had been made known to all members of the Congress and whether anyone at all requests discussion of it, at which the answer of the Plenum of the Congress was: "the testament has been made known to all and there is no need to discuss it at the Congress." No protests on this account "concerning possible irregularities were stated at the Congress."

Kamenev confirms this:

> When the delegations read through this letter, I, as chairperson at the Congress at that moment, asked the Congress whether the congress wishes, in addition to a reading in the delegations, to read the "testament" in the open session of the Congress. And the Congress said that it was satisfied with the reading in the delegations and does not require a reading at the Congress." (Sakharov, Opaseniia 5-6)

In his book Sakharov wrote that there were no documents from this Congress about the discussion of the "testament" and no copy of the exact wording of the resolution taken. But in a later article

---

[2] Viktor Kumanev, Irina S. Kulikova, *Protivostoianie. Krupskaia-Stalin.* (M: Nauka, 1994), 60.

Chapter Seven. Trotsky on the Testament

Sakharov publishes the resolutions of two delegations concerning the "testament." Both state that Lenin's fears concerning Stalin had not been confirmed in practice.³ According to Stalin, all the delegations of the Congress voted that "the testament was known to all and that there was no need to discuss it."⁴ Citing an archival document, Sakharov claims that Stalin declared that all present, including Trotsky, voted not to publish the testament. (584-5)

Trotsky wrote:

> As long as there remained a glimmer of hope for Lenin's recovery, Krupskaya left the document under lock and key. After Lenin's death, not long before the Thirteenth Congress, she handed the testament to the Secretariat of the Central Committee, in order that through the party Congress it should be brought to the attention of the party for whom it was destined.
>
> ... It was here [at the Council of Elders session in May, 1924] that the oppositional members of the Central Committee first learned about the testament, I among them.

Here Trotsky is deliberately lying. In a previous chapter we showed that the "Characteristics" had been revealed to the Politburo not in May, 1924, but a year earlier, in late May or early June, 1923. The "Addition" was known to Bukharin and others in July, 1923. We should recall that n his letter of August 7, 1923, Stalin told Zinoviev that the "letter of Ilich's about the secretary ... is unknown to me." "The Question of Nationalities or on 'Autonomization'" plus the letters to Trotsky of March 5, 1923, and

---

³ Sakharov, *Opaseniia* 6-8. The delegations were (1) the Volga Region (Povolzh'e) and the Central industrial region (Kazakhstan); and (2) the united session of the Ural, Siberian, Far Eastern, Bashkir, and Viatka delegations.
⁴ Stalin, "To all members and candidate members of the Politburo and the Presidiium of the C.C.C." *Stalin. Sochineniia v 16 tomakh.* T. 16. Letter of June 17, 1925. In English translation in *Stalin's Letters to Molotov.* (Yale University Press, 1995) 78.

to Mdivani and Makharadze of March 6, 1923, were given by Trotsky to the Central Committee in April, 1923. But Trotsky's readers in 1932 would have had no way to know any of this.

Trotsky:

> Upon his first acquaintance with the document, in the Secretariat, in the circle of his closest associates, Stalin let fly a phrase which gave quite unconcealed expression to his real feelings toward the author of the testament ... Unfortunately this winged phrase cannot be quoted in print.

How would Trotsky know what Stalin had said "in the circle of Stalin's closest associates"? No source is cited, so Trotsky is lying again.

Trotsky also lies about the "ultimatum" letter:

> If Stalin actually was following Lenin up to his death, how then explain the fact that the last document dictated by Lenin, on the eve of his second stroke, was a curt letter to Stalin, a few lines in all, *breaking off all personal and comradely relations*?

This can only be a deliberate lie. The last lines of the "ultimatum" letter read:

> I ask you, therefore, to think it over whether you are prepared to withdraw what you have said and to make your apologies, or whether you prefer that relations between us should be broken off. (CW 45, 608)

We have shown in a previous chapter that there is strong evidence that this "ultimatum" letter is a fabrication. Even if it were genuine, Lenin had *not* broken off relations with Stalin in this letter. But Trotsky's readers would have had no way to know that Trotsky was lying. This means, especially, Trotsky's own followers, the only persons who believed whatever Trotsky wrote.

Trotsky goes on to claim that

> Nobody considered Stalin a theoretician, and he himself up to 1924 never made any pretense to this vocation. On the contrary, his weak theoretical grounding was too well known in a small circle.

In fact, Stalin had attracted Lenin's attention precisely because of his theoretical writing. Kotkin writes:

> Lenin considered himself one of the party's top experts on national affairs. But Jughashvili surprised him with his own work on the nationalities, prompting Lenin to write to Gorky, "We have a marvelous Georgian who has sat down to write a big article for Enlightenment, for which he has collected all the Austrian and other materials." ... the work was significant for confronting a crucial aspect of revolution in the polyglot Russian empire and largely repudiating the views of the Austro-Marxists and their Georgian Menshevik emulators. (Kotkin 103)

Trotsky knew this, of course. But probably few people outside the Bolshevik Party leadership did or could know it.

Trotsky: "Stalin is not acquainted with the West; he does not know any foreign language." But so what? Trotsky had lived long years abroad, with plenty of opportunity to study European languages. Meanwhile, Stalin had worked within Russia, mainly in clandestine work within Georgia. His native language was Georgian, which Trotsky did not know.[5]

---

[5] Stalin did study foreign languages: Latin, in school, German when he was abroad, and Esperanto. He was also well read in Marxism and European classical literature in Russian translation. B.S. Ilizarov. "Stalin. Shtriki k portretu na fone ego biblioteki i arkhiva." *Novaia i Noveishaia Istoriia* 3,4 (2000),

Stalin's life before the 1917 Revolution was spent mainly as an organizer. Trotsky states plainly that he respected Sverdlov for this very quality:

> Sverdlov was "before all and above all an organizer."

It is likely that few people outside the Bolshevik Party itself knew about Stalin's long career as an underground organizer of class struggle for the Party. Stephen Kotkin calls Stalin an organizer (Stalin vol. 1, 227)

We has already seen that Trotsky lost no opportunity to insult Stalin, even if he had to lie outright to do it. Here is another example:

> ... during the life of Sverdlov, Stalin played no leading role in the party machinery – either at the time of the October Revolution or in the period of laying the foundations and walls of the Soviet state.

In fact, just the opposite is the case. Sverdlov died on March 16, 1919. Before this:

* In 1907 Stalin was a delegate to the V Party Congress in London.

* After 1910 he was plenipotentiary ("agent") of the Central Committee for the Caucasus.

* In 1912, on Lenin's proposal, Stalin was co-opted onto the C.C. and the Russian bureau of the C.C.

* From autumn, 1912, until spring, 1913, Stalin was one of the main collaborators in *Pravda,* the first mass-circulation Bolshevik newspaper.

* Between his return to Petrograd in February, 1917, and Lenin's arrival in April, Stalin was one of the leaders of the C.C. and of the Petrograd Committee of the Bolshevik Party, and member of the editorial collective of *Pravda.*

Chapter Seven. Trotsky on the Testament

* In June, 1917, Stalin was elected as Bolshevik delegate to the First All-Russian Congress of Soviets of Workers and Soldiers Deputies, and also elected to the All-Russian Central Executive Committee and member of the Bureau of this same body.

* On August 5, 1917, he was elected member of the "narrow staff" of the Central Committee. This body later evolved into the Politburo. Trotsky was not a member.[6]

* On October 10, 1917, Stalin was elected member of the Political Bureau (Politburo), created "for political leadership in the coming period."

* On October 16, 1917, he was elected member of the Military-Revolutionary Center, which joined the Petrograd Military-Revolutionary Committee.

* On November 29, 1917, Stalin became a member of the Bureau of the C.C. of the Party, together with Lenin, Trotsky, and Sverdlov.

Trotsky must have thought that he could risk such a blatant lie because in 1932, when this pamphlet was published, few people except the elite stratum of "Old Bolsheviks" would have known about Stalin's Party career during these years.

Trotsky continues:

> Stalin was also not included in the first Secretariat which replaced Sverdlov.

This is true – but so what? Trotsky wasn't in it either. The members of the first Secretariat after Sverdlov's death were Elena Stasova and Nikolai Krestinsky, on March 25, 1919. Evgenii Preobrazhensky was added on April 5, 1920. On March 16, 1921, upon Sverdlov's death, a new secretariat was elected, whose members were Viacheslav Molotov, Vasilii Mikhailov, and

---

[6] Both Stalin and Trotsky were elected to every Politburo from October 10 (23), 1917, until Trotsky was dismissed from the Politburo on October 23, 1926.

Yemelyan Yaroslavsky. On April 3, 1922, the new C.C. elected Molotov, Valerian Kuibyshev, and Stalin to the Secretariat, with Stalin as General Secretary. Lenin had proposed Stalin and strongly supported his candidacy.

In 1932, aside from experts on Soviet affairs almost no one would know any of this. Trotsky, of course, did know it. Trotsky's evident intention was to falsely suggest that Stalin was in relative obscurity, not in the Party leadership at this time.

Trotsky Lies About Stalin's Being Chosen as General Secretary

> When at the Tenth Congress, two years after the death of Sverdlov, Zinoviev and others, not without a hidden thought of the struggle against me, supported the candidacy of Stalin for General Secretary – that is, placed him de jure in the position which Sverdlov had occupied de facto – Lenin spoke in a small circle against this plan, expressing his fear that "this cook will prepare only peppery dishes." That phrase alone, taken in connection with the character of Sverdlov, shows us the differences between the two types of organizers: the one tireless in smoothing over conflicts, easing the work of the Collegium, and the other a specialist in peppery dishes – not even afraid to spice them with actual poison. If Lenin did not in March 1921 carry his opposition to the limit – that is, did not appeal openly to the Congress against the candidacy of Stalin – it was because the post of Secretary, even though "General," had in the conditions then prevailing, with the power and influence concentrated in the Political Bureau, a strictly subordinate significance. Perhaps also Lenin, like many others, did not adequately realize the danger in time.

This is completely false. Trotsky was present at the X Party Congress, where *Lenin* proposed Stalin for the new post of General Secretary and *fought hard* to get him selected. I have documented

Chapter Seven. Trotsky on the Testament

this extensively in the Introduction to my book *Trotsky's 'Amalgams'* and in Chapter 1 of my book *Trotsky's Lies*. In the same chapters I discuss in detail how Trotsky lied frequently, over many years, about the "cook ... peppery dishes" story. Trotsky is deliberately lying here too.

Trotsky Lies About the Publication of "How To Reorganize the WPI"

> On January 23, through Krupskaya, Lenin sent for publication in *Pravda* an article on the subject of his proposed reorganization of the central institutions. Fearing at once a traitorous blow from his disease and a no less traitorous response from the Secretariat, Lenin demanded that his article be printed in *Pravda* immediately; this implied a direct appeal to the party. Stalin refused Krupskaya this request on the ground of the necessity of discussing the question in the Political Bureau. Formally this meant merely a day's postponement. But the very procedure of referring it to the Political Bureau boded no good. At Lenin's direction Krupskaya turned to me for cooperation. I demanded an immediate meeting of the Political Bureau. Lenin's fears were completely confirmed: all the members and alternates present at the meeting, Stalin, Molotov, Kuibyshev, Rykov, Kalinin and Bukharin, were not only against the reform proposed by Lenin, but also against printing his article. To console the sick man, whom any sharp emotional excitement threatened with disaster, Kuibyshev, the future head of the Central Control Commission, proposed that they print a special issue of Pravda containing Lenin's article, but consisting of only one copy.

This is a lie. According to the Secretaries Journal Lenin put the finishing touches on the article on January 23, 1922, in a 45-minute dictation.

> January 23, (entry by M. A. Volodicheva).
>
> Vladimir Ilyich sent for me between 12 and 1 o'clock. Once more glanced through the article mentioned above and made slight changes. Asked me to insert them in his copy and ours and give one to Maria Ilyinichna for Pravda. Article corrected and handed to Maria Ilyinichna before 3 o'clock. (CW 42, 484; XLV 476)

The article was in fact printed on January 25, less than two days after Lenin submitted it.

At the Unified Plenum of the C.C. and the Central Control Commission on October 26, 1923, Stalin explained the situation this way:

> 2) Why did the PB members hesitate to print Lenin's article on the WPI? ... The thing was this: in the article in 3 places there was a mention of the danger of a split. They were afraid that the party would be disoriented. And there was no shadow of disagreement in the PB. We found a way out: to send to the provincial committees at the same time as the article a notice from all members of the PB that there was no shadow of schism. (Izv TsK 10, 1990, 185)

In a question-and-answer at the Party conference of the Khamovniki raion[7] on March 4, 1924, Stalin said:

> Your first question:
>
> "Did the Politburo really not want to print an article by Ilyich and want to print a special issue of *Pravda* for Ilyich?"

---

[7] Part of the city of Moscow.

Chapter Seven. Trotsky on the Testament   199

> My answer: The Politburo unanimously decided to immediately publish Comrade Lenin's article on the WPI. Three was no talk, and moreover, no suggestions on printing a special issue of *Pravda* for Ilyich at the Politburo meeting. It is possible that in a private conversation before the Politburo meeting such conversations took place, but I have no reason to say anything definite about this.
>
> Your second question:
>
> "If that was the case, then the commission asks to indicate in detail why this question arose and whether it was at a meeting of the Politburo or in private conversation?"
>
> My answer:
>
> Since there was not and could not have been a proposal for a special issue of *Pravda* for Ilyich at the Politburo, that disposes of the second question. The question of the publication of an article by Ilyich arose at all at a meeting of the Politburo in connection with the alarm that was raised among the members of the Central Committee by the phrase in Ilyich's article about a split in the Central Committee. The members of the Politburo rightly believed that Ilyich's phrase about a split in the Central Committee might raise concern in the party for the integrity of the Central Committee, which is why it was necessary to send a special circular to local organizations along with the publication of Ilyich's article (Izv TsK 11, 1989, 190, 192)

In order to allay fears of a split that might arise from reading Lenin's article the Politburo sent a letter to all provincial and oblast' Party committees to explain that three was no threat of any split. It was drafted by Trotsky and signed by all the Politburo members. (Izv TsK 11, 1989, 179-180) But Trotsky's readers of 1932 would have had no way of knowing any of this.

Valerian Kuibyshev, who was not a Politburo member, had fleetingly made such a proposal. He explained this to the Khamovniki Party conference on February 23, 1924. Here are the relevant parts of his remarks

> I answer the questions posed by your letter of 11/II-24 on the article by Ilyich about the WPI:
>
> 1) The Politburo at a meeting where the issue of Comrade Lenin's article was discussed decided to put Comrade Lenin's article in the next issue. The article was published the next day. Thus, the question of "whether the Politburo really did not want to print an article by Ilyich" cannot be answered otherwise than categorically in the negative.

After giving some more details Kuibyshev admitted that he had indeed made such a suggestion:

> ... In this nervous atmosphere, created due to fears for Ilyich's health, I repeat, I didn't really get acquainted with the article as a whole, I had a thought: "If Ilyich is sick and the disease is reflected in the article, and if Ilyich needs to show this article printed, then why not compose special number of *Pravda*?" I expressed this idea. But these were volatile thoughts aloud. I immediately abandoned this thought. I did not repeat it anymore, I did not insist on discussion. (Izv TsK 11, 1989, 188-9)

According to the Secretaries Journal the finished article was handed to Mania Ulyanova, not "through Krupskaya," as Trotsky claimed.

In the plan for the article point 13 gives responsibility for training new members of the WPI to the Secretariat, Stalin's office, as does the completed article.[8] There is no evidence that Lenin

Chapter Seven. Trotsky on the Testament

"demanded" that the article be published immediately or that he "feared" a negative reaction from Stalin. Nor did the article reflect poorly on Stalin's work as commissar of the WPI, since he had left that post nine months earlier, either on April 22 or May 6, 1922.[9] Here Trotsky is lying once more.

The documentary evidence shows that no one in the Politburo opposed the publication of Lenin's article or the changes proposed in it. Trotsky himself drafted, and also signed, the unanimous Politburo letter to reassure the Party that there was no danger of a split.

The word "split" is mentioned four times in the article. The passage that concerned the Politburo is this one:

> I also think that in addition to the political advantages accruing from the fact that the members of the Central Committee and the Central Control Commission will, as a consequence of this reform, be much better informed and better prepared for the meetings of the Political Bureau ... there will also be the advantage that **the influence of purely personal and incidental factors in our Central Committee will diminish, and this will reduce the danger of a split.** (XLV, 387; CW 33, 485)

No "Polemic" of Lenin with Stalin

Trotsky wrote:

> In the autumn of 1922 we were preparing the transformation of the Soviet state into a federated union of national republics ... Stalin, on the other hand, who in his position as People's Commissar for Nationalities directed the preparatory work, was conducting in this sphere a

---

[8] CW 42, pp. 434, 439; 482.
[9] The Russian Wikipedia page on Stalin gives the former date, that on the WPI gives the later date.

policy of bureaucratic centralism. Lenin, convalescing in a village near Moscow, **carried on a polemic with Stalin** in letters addressed to the Political Bureau.

This too is a lie. Trotsky does not say which article of Lenin's he means, but it was probably "On the Establishment of the U.S.S.R." addressed to Kamenev for the Politburo.[10] Lenin says that Stalin "tends to be too hasty," but notes that Stalin has withdrawn his proposal that all the Soviet lands should enter the RSFSR as autonomous republics and instead join with the RSFSR as equal, union republics. That is in fact what happened.

The article is phrased in comradely terms. It was not "polemical." Even Trotsky admits that "In his first remarks on Stalin's project for the federated union, Lenin was extremely gentle and restrained." Where then is the "polemic"?

Trotsky continues:

> Stalin's verbal concessions did not quiet Lenin in the least, but on the contrary sharpened his suspicions. "Stalin will make a rotten compromise," Lenin warned me through his secretary, "in order then to deceive." And that was just Stalin's course.

Trotsky first made this claim in a letter to the members of the C.C. and the C.C.C. on October 23, 1923.[11] But there is no independent evidence that either Lenin's secretary or Lenin himself ever said this.

This letter by Trotsky was intended to counter a letter by the other Politburo members, which read, in part:

> Com. Trotsky in his "letter-platform" speaks more diplomatically. He outwardly polemicizes only against the current majority of the Politburo, while his closest

---

[10] CW 42, pp. 421-3.
[11] Izv TsK KPSS 10, 1990, p. 172.

Chapter Seven. Trotsky on the Testament

> associates are well aware that the same charges that are now being brought against us were brought by com. Trotsky against the majority of the Politburo, headed by com. Lenin, a year ago and earlier. These urgent questions were discussed several times in the Politburo during the period when com. Lenin was working. And none other than com. Lenin, by the end of 1921, introduced to the Politburo a decision on the appointment of com. Trotsky to the Ukraine as plenipotentiary of the People's Commissariat of Food, a decision that was subsequently quashed, but which was caused precisely by the intolerable situation that was created by the constant declarations of com. Trotsky against the majority of the Central Committee. (Izv TsK 7, 1990, 187)

Trotsky goes on to refer to "The Question of Nationalities ..." which we have discussed in a previous chapter. It is clearly not by Lenin.

Did Stalin Try To Isolate Lenin For His Own Purposes?

Trotsky claims:

> Stalin tried to isolate the dangerous supervisor from all information which might give him a weapon against the Secretariat and its allies. This policy of blockade naturally was directed against the people closest to Lenin.

Trotsky is lying. He knew the real situation. We have already pointed out that on December 24, 1922, Stalin was assigned by the Politburo to "isolate" Lenin from political news that might upset him. Trotsky was a Politburo member at that time:

> Assign to com. Stalin personal responsibility for isolating Vladimir Ilyich, both in relation to personal relations with employees and correspondence, (Izv TsK 12, 1989, 191)

On December 24, 1922, doctors Ferster, Kramer, and Kozhevnikov, in consultation with Politburo members Stalin, Kamenev, and Bukharin, issued the following directive:

> "1. Vladimir Ilyich is given the right to dictate daily for 5-10 minutes, but this should not be in the nature of correspondence, and Vladimir Ilyich should not wait for an answer to these notes. Meetings are forbidden.
>
> 2. Neither friends nor family should inform Vladimir Ilyich concerning anything political, so as not to give material for thought and excitement."
>
> Time for dictation to a stenographer was set at five to ten minutes, first once, then twice a day for 10 minutes each. (Izv TsK 6, 1991, 193; XLV, 710)

Did Lenin Try to Create a "Bombshell Against Stalin"?

Trotsky:

> We should remember that at that moment there already lay on Lenin's writing table, besides the testament insisting upon the removal of Stalin, also the documents on the national question which Lenin's secretaries Fotieva and Glyasser, sensitively reflecting the mood of their chief, were describing as "a bombshell against Stalin."

Neither Lenin nor any of his secretaries record this phrase – literally, "a bomb against Stalin." Only Trotsky claims that he heard it. If he did, why did he wait until 1927, in his "Letter to the Bureau of Party History (III)," to make this claim? It would have carried more weight earlier.

> On the national question Vladimir Ilyich was preparing for the Twelfth Party Congress a decisive attack upon Stalin. Of this his secretaries told me in his name and at his direction. The phrase of Lenin that

they repeated oftenest of all was: "Vladimir Ilyich is preparing a bomb against Stalin."

If there was a plan to create a "bombshell against Stalin" it would have been by the Gorbunov-Fotieva-Glyasser "commission." But this commission was unable to find any evidence against Stalin. On the contrary, they uncovered the fact that it was Stalin who suggested the harshest penalty against Ordzhonikidze. We have also studied the evidence that the Letter to Mdivani and Makharadze, like "The Question of Nationalities ..." is not by Lenin.

Was "Better Fewer, But Better" Directed Against Stalin?

Trotsky writes:

> On March 4, 1923, Pravda published an article famous in the history of the party, *Better Less but Better*. This work was written at several different times. Lenin did not like to, and could not dictate. He had a hard time writing the article. On March 2 he finally listened to it with satisfaction: "At last it seems all right." This article included the reform of the guiding party institutions on a broad political perspective, both national and international. Upon this side of the question, however, we cannot pause here. Highly important for our theme, however, is the estimate which Lenin gave of the Workers' and Peasants' Inspection. Here are Lenin's words:
>
>> Let us speak frankly. The People's Commissariat of the WPI[12] does not enjoy at the present moment a shadow of authority. Everybody knows that a worse organized institution than our Commissariat of the WPI does not exist, and that

---

[12] The Workers and Peasants Inspection (WPI).

> in the present circumstances you cannot expect a thing of that Commissariat.
>
> This extraordinarily biting allusion in print by the head of the government to one of the most important state institutions was a direct and unmitigated blow against Stalin as the organizer and head of this Inspection.

Trotsky's statement is false. As we saw above, Stalin had left the post of commissar for the WPI almost eleven months earlier.

Trotsky added:

> In the article *Better Less but Better* Lenin openly pointed out that his proposed reform of the Inspection, at whose head Tsuryupa had not long ago been placed, must inevitably meet the resistance of "all our bureaucracy, both the Soviet and the party bureaucracy." In parenthesis Lenin adds significantly, "We have bureaucratism not only in the Soviet institutions but also in the party." This was a perfectly deliberate blow at Stalin as General Secretary.

Trotsky is lying again. However the problem of bureaucracy is defined, it is the responsibility of all the Party leaders, especially the Politburo and Orgburo, to deal with it. Stalin was one of those Party leaders – but so was Trotsky.

Trotsky's Lie About Radek

Towards the end of his essay Trotsky attempts to discredit Karl Radek.

> Still, where did that fantastic tale come from about how I leapt from my seat during the reading of the testament, or rather of the "six words" which are not in the testament, with the question: "What does it say there?" Of this I can only offer a hypothetical

Chapter Seven. Trotsky on the Testament

explanation. How correct it may be, let the reader judge.

Radek belongs to the tribe of professional wits and storytellers. By this I do not mean that he does not possess other qualities. Suffice it to say that at the Seventh Congress of the party on March 8, 1918, Lenin, who was in general very restrained in personal comments, considered it possible to say:

> I return to Comrade Radek, and here I want to remark that he has accidentally succeeded in uttering a serious remark ...

And once again later on:

> This time it did happen that we got a perfectly serious remark from Radek ...

Once again, Trotsky is lying. Lenin did make these two remarks – but about David B. Ryazanov, not Radek. These exact passages can be found in the transcript of the VII Party Congress,[13] on March 8, 1918, and in Lenin's *Collected Works*.

We know that Trotsky was deliberately lying here, because he quotes the exact words that Lenin spoke. Trotsky must have had the text in front of him as he wrote.

Why would Trotsky do this? Anyone who bothered to check the transcript of the VII Party Congress – and this would not have been hard to do in any large city in the USSR, or even abroad, in a research library with a good Russian collection – could have discovered that Trotsky was not misremembering – he was *deliberately* lying.

---

[13] *Sed'moi ekstrennyi s"ezd RKP/b/. Mart 1918 goda. Stenograficheskii otchet.* Moscow, 1962, p. 109; CW 27, 110. Online at http://www.marx2mao.com/Lenin/ESC18.html (page 110).

After finding many such deliberate lies in Trotsky's writings and exposing them, with evidence in *Trotsky's 'Amalgams'* and *Trotsky's Lies*, we asked the same question: Why would Trotsky take the chance of being exposed as a liar? Evidently, he believed that no one would bother to check.

And as it turned out, Trotsky was correct! It appears that for 80 years no one checked those of Trotsky's statement about Stalin that could have been checked even at that time. The power of anticommunism, and especially anti-Stalinism, is so great that negative statements about Stalin are readily accepted as true without any attempt to verify them.

Trotsky Sums Up

> Thus it would be no exaggeration to say that the last half year of Lenin's political life, between his convalescence and his second illness, was filled with a sharpening struggle against Stalin. Let us recall once more the principal dates. In September 1922 Lenin opened fire against the national policy of Stalin. In the first part of December he attacked Stalin on the question of the monopoly of foreign trade. On December 25 he wrote the first part of his testament. On December 30 he wrote his letter on the national question (the "bombshell"). On January 4, 1923, he added a postscript to his testament on the necessity of removing Stalin from his position as General Secretary. On January 23 he drew up against Stalin a heavy battery: the project of a Control Commission. In an article on March 2 he dealt Stalin a double blow, both as organizer of the Inspection and as General Secretary. On March 5 he wrote me on the subject of his memorandum on the national question: "If you would agree to undertake its defense, I could be at rest." On that same day he for the first time openly joined forces with the irreconcilable Georgian enemies of Stalin, informing them in a special note that he was

backing their cause "with all my heart" and was preparing for them documents against Stalin, Ordzhonikidze and Dzerzhinsky. "With all my heart" – this expression was not a frequent one with Lenin.

This paragraph is the proverbial "tissue of falsehoods."

* Lenin did not "open fire" on Stalin's national policy. By the time Lenin wrote, on September 26, 1922, Stalin had modified his initial "autonomization" plan to the plan of creating the USSR from four equal republics. Lenin *agreed* with hm.

* What "attack" against Stalin "on the question of the monopoly of foreign trade" "in the first part of December [1922]" does Trotsky mean? On December 13, 1922, Lenin dictated by telephone a letter to Stalin on this question, but there is nothing in it hostile towards, or even in the least critical of, Stalin.[14]

* The reference to January 23 is to "How To Re-organize the WPI." We showed above that this is in no way an attack on Stalin, who had not headed the WPI for more than eight months.

* March 2 refers to "Better Fewer But Better." But this article contains no criticism of Stalin.

The other writings to which Trotsky refers here are the "Characteristics" (December 25); "The Question of Nationalities …" (December 30); the "Addition" (January 4), the letters to Trotsky and to Mdivani and Makharadze of March 5 and 6, 1923, and the "ultimatum" letter of March 5. We have examined all of them in previous chapters. The evidence is strong that they are forgeries, that Lenin never wrote them.

Why So Many Lies?

In *Trotsky's 'Amalgams'* and *Trotsky's Lies* we demonstrated that Trotsky lied a great deal. The reader will probably wonder: Why

---

[14] CW 33, 455-459; PSS XLV 333-337.

did Trotsky lie so much? After all, he had the "testament" documents in his favor. Aside from whoever fabricated them, no one at the time thought that they were fakes. It is true that they did not have much effect on the Central Committee or the Party Congresses. The C.C. members appear to have believed that these articles reflected diminished capacity and/or misinformation on Lenin's part due to his illness. But they surely helped to solidify Trotsky's own followers around him both within and outside the Soviet Union.

It quickly became clear that Trotsky's efforts to follow Lenin as Party leader would not succeed. Already by the end of the XII Party Congress Trotsky's chances of gaining the leading position in the Bolshevik Party appeared to be remote.

But the lies of Trotsky's that we have exposed here, along with those we discovered and examine in *Trotsky's 'Amalgams'* and *Trotsky's Lies*, were very useful to Trotsky in building his clandestine, ultimately terrorist, organization inside the Soviet Union and his network of supporters abroad. Even now, more than eighty years after Trotsky's death, they continue to sustain the Trotskyist movement.

They have also proven useful to openly pro-capitalist anticommunist writers. Trotsky did not hesitate to ally himself and his followers with even the most rabid anticommunists, fascists and Nazis included.[15] Today Trotskyists continue to repeat the lies of anticommunist "scholars" insofar as those lies are directed against Stalin.

---

[15] See my books on Trotsky, especially *New Evidence of Trotsky's Conspiracy.* Kettering, OH: Erythrós Press & Media, LLC, 2020 and Furr, Grover, with Vladimir L. Bobrov and Sven-Eric Holmström, *Trotsky and the Military Conspiracy. Soviet and Non-Soviet Evidence with the Complete Transcript of the "Tukhachevsky Affair" Trial.* Kettering, OH: Erythrós Press and Media, LLC, 2021.

Chapter 8. Moshe Lewin

Moshe Lewin's 1968 book *Lenin's Last Struggle* was made possible by the Khrushchev-era attacks on Stalin. These attacks began in Khrushchev's 1956 "Secret Speech." There followed several years during which attacks on Stalin seemed to abate somewhat.

But during the XXII Party Congress in October, 1961, attacks on Stalin, now voiced by other speakers, grew even more ferocious. From that point until his ouster by the Central Committee in October 1964 Khrushchev sponsored a flood of pseudo-historical articles and books attacking Stalin. These works seldom cite primary source evidence to support their allegations of crimes by Stalin. When they do, they distort those sources, usually by significant omission. We know this today because many of these sources have become public. But the striking omission and the falsifications by Khrushchev and his followers continue to be ignored by both Soviet and Western anticommunist scholars.

Khrushchev's speech, and the subsequent flood of anti-Stalin fabrications disguised as history, appeared to vindicate Leon Trotsky. Trotsky had attacked Stalin since the early 1920s, and with increased vigor after his exile in 1929. Indeed, some of the intimations of crimes leveled by Khrushchev and his followers against Stalin, such as raising the suspicion that Stalin had been responsible for the 1934 murder of Sergei M. Kirov, seem to have been copied from Trotsky.

Even though Khrushchev did not "rehabilitate" Trotsky, Soviet history during and after Khrushchev's time seemed to tacitly confirm many of Trotsky's accusations against Stalin. In addition to providing large stores of anti-Stalin accusations for overtly anticommunist writers, Khrushchev's attacks on Stalin breathed new life into the Trotsky movement around the world. David

North, a leading American Trotskyist, writes: "The discrediting of Stalin was, to a great extent, a vindication of Trotsky."[1]

In 1968 Moshe Lewin[2] published *Lenin's Last Struggle* (LLS). It is no exaggeration to call *LLS* a crypto-Trotskyist work. It provides a narrative that weaves Lenin's last writings, and especially the documents of the "testament," into a story that closely follows Trotsky's own dishonest and self-serving narrative by depicting Trotsky as Lenin's choice to be his successor.

Lewin accepted the version of Lenin's "testament" as it is documented in the Khrushchev-era volumes of the fifth Russian edition of Lenin's works, the *Polnoe Sobranie Sochineniy*, or PSS. Sakharov has shown that these volumes were edited in a tendentious, anti-Stalin manner.

Lewin frames his narrative of Lenin's last six months of activity before his final, devastating stroke of March 10, 1923, around Trotsky's account in the 1937 translation of Trotsky's essay collection *The Stalin School of Falsification*. We don't know why Lewin chose to ignore Trotsky's essay "On Lenin's Testament," the work we have examined in a previous chapter.

Like Trotsky, Lewin narrates the story of Lenin's last months chronologically. He does not question the dates on the documents – a crucial point. Lewin also accepts the remarks of the editors of the PSS volumes without reservation.

Lewin goes beyond uncritical acceptance of Trotsky's account of Lenin's last months. He provides narrative links to force the series of documents into a story line. At times Lewin invents meetings or documents in order to fill in blank spots needed for his narrative.

---

[1] David North, *In Defense of Leon Trotsky*. Oak Park, IL: Mehring Books, 2010, p. 28.
[2] Lewin was a mainstream anticommunist historian of the Soviet Union who had been in the Red Army and had worked in a factory and a collective farm. A Zionist, he emigrated to Israel, and later to France.

Chapter Eight. Moshe Lewin

At other points, Lewin simply has recourse to falsehoods that could have been exposed in his day but were not.

All of Lewin's inventions and falsehoods are tendentiously anti-Stalin, as befits his obvious anti-Stalin bias. As a result, some are explicitly pro-Trotsky.

Documents Not Mentioned by Lewin

A number of important documents available to researchers today were not published at the time Lewin wrote.

* Stalin's reply to the "ultimatum" letter of March 7, 1923;

* the "Journal of Doctors on Duty";[3]

* Maria Ulyanova's statement of 1926;

* Lenin's request of March 17, 1923, to Stalin for poison;

* many other documents first published in the Gorbachev-era series *Izvestiia Tsentral'nogo Komiteta KPSS*.

Nor could Lewin study the documents in Soviet archives to which Sakharov had considerable, though far from complete, access.

Lewin's main error is his uncritical acceptance of the Khrushchev-Trotsky version of Lenin's last writings – the "testament" and related documents. In this chapter we will indicate places where Lewin falsifies or invents in order to make his anti-Stalin / pro-Trotsky narrative flow more smoothly.

Lewin's "Chronology of Events" (pages xix – xxiv)

Under May 15 [1922] Lewin writes:

---

[3] In this book we refer to it as 'Doctors Journal.'

> [Lenin's] Letter to Stalin suggesting a decision of the Politburo to reconfirm as inalterable the principle of state monopoly of foreign trade. **Stalin resists.**

Lewin wishes to establish opposition by Stalin to Lenin's ideas. But Lewin is lying here. In reality, Stalin did not "resist" at all. Instead, he agreed with the monopoly of foreign trade, although he believed that it would not be possible to maintain it.

> At this stage **I am not opposed** to the strict prohibition of measures that would lead to the weakening of the monopoly of foreign trade. I think however that such a weakening is becoming inevitable. (LLS 37; XLV 548)[4]

Under October 11 [1922] Lewin states:

> Lenin meets Trotsky. They discuss the monopoly problem and common fight against bureaucracy.

This is a deliberate falsehood – in plain language, a lie. The passage in the chronology in volume XLV of Lenin's Russian works contains no reference to any "common fight against bureaucracy."

> Lenin talks with L. D. Trotsky regarding the discussion at a meeting of the plenum of the Central Committee of the RCP(b) on October 6 of the question of the monopoly of foreign trade and the decision of the plenum on this issue. (XLV 689)

Lewin's statement is not only false – he has invented it. Lewin *invents* a discussion about "bureaucracy," no doubt to "save" Trotsky's account of an (undated) meeting with Lenin to form a "bloc" against "bureaucracy" – that is, against Stalin. But in the text

---

[4] The translation in Lenin's *Collected Works* 4th edition is: "I have no objections to a 'formal ban' on measures to mitigate the foreign trade monopoly at the present stage. All the same, I think that mitigation is becoming indispensable." CW 42, 600, note 476.

of his book (38) Lewin does not repeat his claim that the Lenin-Trotsky "common fight against bureaucracy" was discussed on October 11.

What is going on here? Lewin is trying to make room for a meeting between Trotsky and Lenin during which Lenin proposes a 'bloc" with Trotsky against bureaucracy. Trotsky told this story many times. In "On Lenin's Testament" Trotsky intimated that such a meeting took place in October, 1922:

> In October he [Lenin] returns to the Kremlin and officially takes up his work ... At this time occurred the "conspiratorial" conversation between Lenin and me in regard to a combined struggle against Soviet and party bureaucratism, and his proposal of a "bloc" against the Organization Bureau – the fundamental stronghold of Stalin at that time.

In *The Stalin School of Falsification*, at section 65, Trotsky writes as follows:

> Vladimir Ilyich reflected a moment and — here I quote him verbatim — said: "That is, I propose a struggle with Soviet bureaucratism and you are proposing to include the bureaucratism of the Organization Bureau of the Party." [Stalin as General Secretary was at the head of this Bureau. - L. T.]
>
> "I laughed at the unexpectedness of this, because no such finished formulation of the idea was in my mind.
>
> "I answered: 'I suppose that's it.'
>
> "Then Vladimir Ilyich said: 'Very well, then, I propose a bloc.'
>
> "I said: 'It is a pleasure to form a bloc with a good man.'
>
> "At the end of our conversation, Vladimir Ilyich said that he would propose the creation by the Central

Committee of a commission to fight bureaucratism in general,' and through that we would be able to reach the Organization Bureau of the Central Committee.

Here Trotsky concludes by saying that nothing came of this purported bloc:

> At that we parted. I then waited two weeks for the bell to summon me but Ilyich's health became continually worse and he was soon confined to bed. After that Vladimir Ilyich sent me his letters on the national question through his secretaries. And so that work was never carried through.

Contradicting the account in "On Lenin's Testament" Trotsky here implies a meeting with Lenin later than October, 1922, because Lenin remained active long after the earlier date.

After his exile from the USSR, in his autobiography *My Life*, published in 1930, Trotsky explained that this event was Lenin's way of selecting him, Trotsky, as his successor.

> He planned to create a commission attached to the Central Committee for fighting bureaucracy. We were both to be members. This commission was essentially to be the lever for breaking up the Stalin faction as the backbone of the bureaucracy, and for creating such conditions in the party as would allow me to become Lenin's deputy, and, as he intended, his successor to the post of chairman of the Soviet of People's Commissaries. (377)

By 1932 Trotsky has backed off from this claim and simply insists that this meeting did occur:

> The fact of this conversation as well as its content soon found their reflection in documents, and **they constitute an episode of the party history undeniable and not denied by anyone.**

Chapter Eight. Moshe Lewin

Trotsky is bluffing. This supposed "meeting" was never a part of "the party history." By "undeniable and not denied by anyone," Trotsky appears to mean something like this: "Now that Lenin is dead, and the conversation was just between Lenin and me, no one can disprove it." Trotsky wanted people to believe him, and Lewin does believe him.

> **At the beginning of December** Lenin asked Trotsky to come and see him again. In the course of the conversation he suggested that a "bloc against bureaucracy" should be formed and that Trotsky should join a special committee whose purpose would be to lead such a struggle. Lenin also suggested that Trotsky should become one of his deputies in the government. On this occasion, Trotsky expressed his long-held conviction – it was probably the basis of his previous criticisms of the Workers' and Peasants' Inspection which at the time had so irritated Lenin – that the struggle against bureaucracy should begin with the elimination of the evil from among those most likely to foster it, namely the Party, and more particularly the Party leadership. (LLS 67-8)

Here, Lewin's documentation for these statements is Trotsky alone:

> See Trotsky's account of this conversation in *The Stalin School of Falsification*, pp. 73-74, and Deutscher, *The Prophet Unarmed*, pp. 66, 68-69. Once again Trotsky refused to become Lenin's deputy, but with less conviction than before.

Moreover, Lewin's claim that Lenin suggested a "bloc against bureaucracy" with Trotsky in December 1922 contradicts his own and Trotsky's previous claim that Lenin made this suggestion in October 1922.

Dmitri Volkogonov, an anticommunist Soviet and Russian historian very hostile towards Stalin who during the 1980s and 1990s had full access to all "closed" archives, does not believe Trotsky's claim.

> The dubiousness of Trotsky's version is revealed by what Lenin actually wrote. Lenin had absolutely no need of any sort to form a 'bloc' with Trotsky against Stalin. His authority was indisputable.[5]

Lewin: November (first part):

> Numerous complaints from Georgia to Moscow against Ordzhonikidze.
>
> Tsintsadze's letter reaches Lenin and arouses his suspicions against the Stalin-Ordzhonikidze line in Georgia.

But Lewin does not document any of these claims. The chronology in PSS, XLV that Lewin uses does not mention "numerous complaints from Georgia," or in fact *any* complaints. Lewin never mentions *any* letter by Tsintsadze. Lidia Fotieva does not mention such a letter in her memoir about Lenin, which Lewin often cites.

And what is the "Stalin-Ordzhonikidze line? Lewin later mentions "… 'nationalist deviation,' a charge that Stalin and Ordzhonikidze were constantly leveling at the Georgians." (45) But Lewin does not document Stalin's doing this even one time, much less "constantly." This is the *only* passage where the term "nationalist deviation" is mentioned in Lewin's book. Another lie by Lewin!

For November 24, 1922, Lewin's chronology has:

> Lenin, suspicious, abstains from voting on the composition of the investigation commission on the Georgian affair.

---

[5] *Stalin. Triumph and Tragedy.* (New York: Grove-Weidenfeld, 1991), 89.

Chapter Eight. Moshe Lewin

This is taken from the Secretaries Journal for November 24, which states:

> The question of the composition of the commission in connection with the statement by the C.C. of Georgia was handed to Vladimir Ilyich from the Politbureau for voting. Vladimir Ilyich did not vote. (CW 42, 467)

But this is what Lewin claims:

> We do not know whether he intended in this way to express some doubt as to the impartiality of the commission, whose three members – Dzerzhinsky, Lozovsky and Kapsukas-Mitskevitchius – **had been proposed by Stalin**, but it is clear at least that he had become suspicious of his first informants and was seeking other sources of information on which to base an opinion. (LLS 58)

Here is Sakharov's description of the manner in which the Dzerzhinsky commission was formed:

> The Politburo on November 25 accepted the proposal of the Secretariat of the Central Committee of the RCP(b) to create a commission for "urgent consideration of the application" and "outlining the measures necessary to establish a lasting peace in the Communist Party of Georgia." It included F.E. Dzerzhinsky (chairman), D.Z. Manuilsky [**not** Lozovsky, as Lewin has it][6], and B.C. Mitskevicius-Kapsukas. Lenin was aware of the matter, and if he were against the adopted decision, he could and should have definitely declared his protest. There was time for this, since the results of the "poll" vote by

---

[6] Jeremy Smith confirms that the second member was Manuil'sky. Smith, "The Georgian Affair of 1922. Policy Failure, Personality Clash or Power Struggle?" *Europe-Asia Studies* 50, 3 (1998), 532. Richard Pipes agrees: *The Formation of the Soviet Union* (Harvard U.P. 1997 [1954]), 281.

telephone were subject to approval at the next meeting of the Politburo, and only after that it was formalized in a special protocol. The confirmation took place at a meeting of the Politburo on November 30 in the presence of Bukharin, Zinoviev, Kamenev, Kalinin, Molotov, Stalin, Trotsky. If we take into account that Lenin worked on November 30, and the day before, on November 29, he received the minutes of the meeting of the Secretariat of the Party Central Committee dated November 25 with proposals regarding the goals and composition of the commission, then all grounds for believing that Lenin was against the composition of the commission or that he was bypassed in addressing this issue are dispelled. (252)

What's more, we have evidence that Lenin did approve of the commission's membership. At the XII P.C. (April, 1923) Avel' Enukidze said the following:

> As for the Dzerzhinsky commission, I must say the following. All these complaints and cries that were spoken of here, came here, and then the Central Committee decided to send a commission there. At first it was suggested to me to go there as chairman or member of the commission, but I stated that I had recently returned from Georgia, knew the state of affairs, knew these comrades with whom, by the way, I am connected by friendship and years of previous work, and already had a certain attitude towards these issues. I considered the policy of the deviating comrades to be wrong. I then refused to go there ... **Another commission was chosen, chaired by Comrade Dzerzhinsky. Lenin specially then asked me: "Do you think this commission is suitable?" I answered frankly and now confirm that the commission was very pertinent and reputable. No**

Chapter Eight. Moshe Lewin

serious commission could bring a different solution. (XII P.C., 590)

There is no evidence that Lenin was "suspicious" here. There is not even any evidence that Stalin had "proposed" the members of the Dzerzhinsky commission.

Therefore, Lewin has "made it up" – invented it. Why? The most obvious explanation is that Lewin's narrative requires a Lenin who was steadily growing more and more suspicious of Stalin and thereby justify his, Lewin's, uncritical reliance on Trotsky's writings.

Under December 12 [1922] Lewin states:

> Proposition to Trotsky to defend, at the next CC session, their common opinions on the foreign trade monopoly.

This is false. Lenin wrote about this in a letter *to Stalin* on December 15. Two days earlier he had also dictated a much longer letter, again *to Stalin*, about defending the monopoly of foreign trade. (XLV 333-338; CW 33, 456-459)

For January 24, 1923, Lewin states:

> Lenin asks for the dossiers of the Dzerzhinsky commission findings. The Politburo is reluctant. (xxiii)

But on page 94 Lewin writes:

> On January 24, after finishing and sending off to Pravda his article on the Workers' Inspection, Lenin called Fotieva and asked her for the documents of Dzerzhinsky's commission of inquiry in Georgia. He did not know that this question was about to be discussed at the Politburo. The next day he asked again whether Stalin or Dzerzhinsky had sent him the papers.

Lewin can find no evidence that the Politburo was "reluctant" to send Lenin the materials. He is fabricating – in plain language, lying – yet again.

Fotieva's memoir (1967, reprinted in 1990) states that on January 27 she asked Dzerzhinsky for the materials, and he told her that Stalin had them. Stalin was not in Moscow, but on January 29 Stalin told her by telephone that he would need permission of the Politburo. On January 30 Lenin called her and told her that Stalin had told him he would get him the materials.[7] We should recall that on December 24, the Politburo had put Stalin in charge of keeping political materials away from Lenin because of his illness.

Lewin's Chronology

> January 25, 1923:
>
> The Politburo session endorses the conclusions of the Dzerzhinsky commission on the Georgian affair which whitewashes Ordzhonikidze and condemns Mdivani and the Georgian CC.

In the text Lewin says the same thing:

> Meanwhile, the Politburo approved the conclusions of the commission, condemned the Georgians once again, and whitewashed Ordzhonikidze and Stalin. (LLS, 94)

Ordzhonikidze's slapping Kabakhidze was over a personal insult. It had nothing to do with the issue of Georgian independence. We have discussed this issue thoroughly in a previous chapter.

However, the Khrushchev-era edition of Lenin's works says nothing about this. Evidently, this is why Lewin *assumed* that Ordzhonikidze was trying to force his decisions on the Georgians. But Lewin was wrong. He made this assumption – and dishonestly

---

[7] Fotieva, L.A. "Iz vospominaniia o V.I. Lenine. (Dekabr' 1922 g. – mart 1923 g.), *Vospominaniia o Lenine* (Moscow, 1990), t. 8, 202-3,

Chapter Eight. Moshe Lewin 223

states it not as his assumption but as a fact – to conform to the other elements of his anti-Stalin, pro-Trotsky position.

And what did Stalin have to do with this? We have seen that "The Question of Nationalities …" does indeed blame Stalin but gives no reason, cites no evidence, for doing so. This is one of many details that exposes "The Question of Nationalities …" as a forgery, not authored by Lenin.

Even Fotieva's account does not claim that Dzerzhinsky's report "whitewashed" Stalin. Lewin has fabricated – lied about – this too.

> February 1, 1923:
>
> The Politburo yields to Lenin's demand and turns over to him the commission's papers.

We have just seen that Fotieva's account states that it was *Stalin* who, with the permission of the Politburo, gave Lenin the Dzerzhinsky Commission's materials.

> March 3, 1923:
>
> Lenin's private investigation committee submits to him its findings on the Georgian affair.

This is false. This claim does appear in the chronology in the PSS.[8] But Lewin – who was a historian, and should have known better than to take "authorities" at the word – should have pointed out that there is *no evidence* that this occurred. The Secretaries Journal has no entries for March 3, or for any date between February 14 and March 5. The entry in the Doctors Journal (unavailable to Lewin) makes it clear that on March 3 Lenin received no materials, did no dictation, and received none of the members of the "commission." His sole activity was reading "the corrections of his

---

[8] XLV 714. The English 4th edition of Lenin's works has no corresponding chronology.

new article," but was able to read only two pages before saying that he was too tired to read any more.

So there is no evidence that Lenin saw the findings of this "commission." But there *is* evidence that he *could not* have seen them. Referring to archival materials, Sakharov states that the document of February 1, 1923, in which the Politburo turned the Dzerzhinsky Commission's materials over to Lenin, also says

> postpone the question of a report to com. Lenin until Prof. Ferster's conclusion. (347)

There is no record that Dr. Ferster agreed.

Lewin:

> March 6, 1923:
>
> Kamenev hears from Krupskaya that Lenin intends to crush Stalin politically. (LLS, xxiv)

Here Lewin is not being honest with his readers. In the text he states:

> **There is every reason to believe Trotsky** when he says that one of Lenin's secretaries, probably Glyasser, told him that Vladimir Ilich was preparing a "bomb" against Stalin. (LLS, 103)

Of course, for any honest historian, there is never any reason for "believing" one of his sources, especially such a biased and interested source as Trotsky. Lewin refers here to this passage in Trotsky's *The Stalin School of Falsification*:

> On the national question Vladimir Ilyich was preparing for the Twelfth Party Congress a decisive attack upon Stalin. Of this his secretaries told me in his name and at his direction. The phrase of Lenin that they repeated oftenest of all was: "Vladimir Ilyich is preparing a bomb against Stalin."

Lewin takes Kamenev's involvement from another Trotsky passage, this one in Isaac Deutscher's biography.

> Krupskaya sought advice before making up her mind and, as so often, it was to the amiable Kamenev that she turned. This was how he learned that Vladimir Ilich was planning "to crush Stalin politically." (LLS 103)

Deutscher:

> About the same time Trotsky learned from Kamenev that Lenin had written a letter to Stalin threatening to 'break off all personal relations'. Stalin had behaved in an offensive manner towards Krupskaya **when she was collecting information for Lenin on the Georgian affair**; and when Lenin learned about this, he could hardly contain his indignation. He decided, Krupskaya told Kamenev, 'to crush Stalin politically'.[9]

But why cite Deutscher? He just took this from Trotsky's autobiography *My Life*.[10]

However, this passage is revealing in another way. Trotsky and Deutscher connect the "ultimatum" letter with *Krupskaya* "collecting information for Lenin *on the Georgian affair.*" This suggests at least two things. First, it directly contradicts Krupskaya's letter to Kamenev dated December 23, 1922, where Krupskaya ties Stalin's rebuke to a letter by Lenin to Trotsky of December 21, 1922 *concerning the monopoly of foreign trade*. This is further evidence that Krupskaya predated Stalin's rebuke, as we have discussed in a previous chapter.

Second, we have no other information that Krupskaya was "collecting information for Lenin on the Georgian affair." It was the

---

[9] Deutscher, *The Prophet Unarmed*, p. 75.
[10] Russian edition, Moscow: Panorama, 1991, p. 461. For other editions, see chapter 39, "Lenin's Illness."

Gorbunov-Fotieva-Glyasser "commission" that was doing that. As we pointed out, this was in effect a two-person effort since Gorbunov was not active in this regard. So Trotsky's and Deutscher's implication is that *Krupskaya was guiding the work of this "commission,"* since Fotieva and Glyasser, secretaries in Lenin's secretariat, would not have acted independently from Krupskaya.

In his hostile biography of Stalin Dmitry Volkogonov wrote:

> У меня нет конкретных данных о намерении Ленина "разгромить" генсека.[11]
>
> I have no concrete facts about an intention of Lenin's to "crush" the Gensec.

Lewin accepts as true many fact-claims that are to be found only in Trotsky's works. That might be understandable – though it still would be just a hypothesis, not evidence – if Trotsky could be trusted to tell the truth. But as we have seen in a previous chapter and demonstrated in other books, Trotsky lied a great deal. Nothing that Trotsky says should ever be accepted as truthful. It must always be verified. Doing so often reveals yet another lie by Trotsky.

But Lewin makes no attempt at verification. Trotsky is the *only* source for the stories about "a bomb for Stalin" and for Krupskaya's telling Kamenev that Lenin wanted to "crush Stalin politically."

Moshe Lewin's Fabrications

The statements of Lewin's that I call "fabrications" here can also be reasonably termed "lies." These are statements made either by ignoring evidence to the contrary, or invented – fabricated – to abet Lewin's anti-Stalin thesis, which is also Trotsky's, and similar to Khrushchev's as well.

---

[11] *Stalin. Politicheskii portret. T. 1. Vozhdi* Moscow: Novosti, 1998, p. 144.

There is not enough space here to identify and confute all Lewin's fabrications, so here I have selected some important and typical examples.

> As Lenin was losing his capacity for work and the conduct of affairs was slipping increasingly from his hands, Stalin was gaining in ease and assurance, **often in opposition to Lenin.** (LLS, 35)

Lewin gives no example to support this claim. As far as we can determine, no such evidence exists – nothing of the kind occurred. Again, Lewin is deliberately lying.

Throughout his book Lewin tries to show that Stalin was opposing Lenin. He can do so only when he draws upon the contested documents of the "testament" as evidence. When Lewin makes this claim elsewhere he is forced to do so without any evidence.

Lenin: "I Propose"; Lewin: Lenin "Demands"

Concerning Lenin's insistence on maintaining the state monopoly on foreign trade, Lewin writes:

> Lenin was most annoyed and wrote to Stalin **demanding** that the monopoly principle be reaffirmed and that all projects of a contrary nature be dropped at once. (35)

But *was* Lenin "most annoyed"? Lewin's source is a letter to Stalin of May 15, 1922. It begins with these words:

> т. Сталин! Предлагаю, ввиду сего опросом членов Политбюро провести директиву ...
>
> Com. Stalin! I propose, in view of this, to get a directive passed by the Politburo by poll ...[12] ...

---

[12] PSS, XLV 188; CW, 42, 418. *Opros* means that the members could be polled, e.g. by phone, so no actual meeting was necessary. This method was used in between scheduled meetings, or when one or more members were not in Moscow.

Lenin's language here shows no sign of annoyance. The official English translation uses the word "please" instead of "I propose," which is what Lenin actually wrote. Lewin is trying to create – fraudulently – the appearance of a quarrel between Lenin and Stalin where there was none. Throughout this book Lewin does this kind of thing – fabricates "facts" to conform to his bias.

Lewin continues:

> It was perhaps on this occasion that Lenin discovered that the Gensek was not at all in agreement with him and was asserting his own point of view with increasing assurance. (LLS 37)

Here Lewin's anti-Stalin bias shows up very clearly. *All* the Politburo members "asserted their own points of view." Lenin was not surrounded by a bunch of yes-men. And Lenin disagreed with Trotsky more than with anyone else. "No one had given him more grief" than Trotsky. (Kotkin 414)

Lewin:

> Between December 12 and 15 the two men [Lenin and Trotsky] corresponded with each other at great length ... (39)

This is a lie. In reality, on December 13, Lenin wrote Trotsky, along with others. On that same day, December 13, Lenin wrote to Stalin on the question of the monopoly of foreign trade. *This* letter could perhaps be described as "at great length" since it occupies 4½ pages in the PSS. On December 14 and 15, Lenin wrote to Trotsky *and* to Stalin. The very chronology that Lewin expressly cites elsewhere records this. (XLV, 708)

It is clear that Lewin is striving – once again, dishonestly – to give a false impression of some kind of special bond or "bloc" between Lenin and Trotsky, and does so by lying to his readers.

Lewin:

Chapter Eight. Moshe Lewin

> Now, even before his plans for autonomization had been discussed, Stalin **appears** to have sent a telegram to Mdivani on August 29, 1922, informing him that henceforth the decisions of the highest governing bodies of the RSFSR (VTSIK, Sovnarkom and STO - the Council of Labor and Defense) were binding on all the Republics. (LLS 48)

"Appears to have"? Lewin cites no evidence for such a telegram. In fact, Lewin copied this passage almost word for word from Richard Pipes, *The Formation of the Soviet Union*.[13] He should have acknowledged this. But Pipes has no definite evidence of such a telegram either.

Lewin concludes:

> For his part, Stalin was sincere in claiming that the new version of the project of union differed only in certain details from his own original project, which as he said was also "correct in principle and absolutely acceptable." **He was convinced, in fact, that in the course of events the real interests of the state would gain the upper hand and that the Union would function in any case as he had expected it to. In these circumstances he saw no reason why he should not give in to Lenin completely, on paper.** (LLS, 62-3)

The first sentence is correct enough – Lewin cites the Orgburo document from which he quoted on page 53. (PSS XLV, 559-60; CW 42, 602-605)

But the rest, in boldface here, is just Lewin allowing his anti-Stalin bias free rein. Lewin, of course, had no idea what Stalin was thinking. He just *assumed* that Stalin was being devious in some

---

[13] Cambridge, MA: Harvard University Press, 1990 [1954], 271.

way, in conformity to Khrushchev-era, Trotskyist, and his own anti-Stalinism.

More Anti-Stalin Bias, Without Evidence

> Stalin was perfectly well aware that relations between Lenin and Trotsky had recently become increasingly close ... (LLS, 71)

This is false. Lewin cites no evidence for this statement, and we have none today. In reality, Lenin and Trotsky were *not* "becoming closer." Trotsky *claimed* that they were, and Lewin "believes" Trotsky.

> It is hardly surprising then that **Stalin, more concerned than anybody with the problem of the succession, should have exploded with indignation** on learning of this new mark of esteem conferred on Trotsky by Lenin, especially as he was beginning to fear that the rapprochement between the two men would be accompanied by a positive campaign against himself. (LLS, 72)

No evidence whatever is cited to support these statements. How does Lewin know that Stalin "exploded with indignation," "was more concerned than anybody" with who would succeed Lenin, or feared a "campaign against himself"? It is pure anti-Stalin bias on Lewin's part.

Lewin:

> Apart from the notes, these ideas are developed in five articles written in January and February 1923, **although a majority of the Politburo had made attempts to prevent or delay their appearance**. (LLS, 74)

Lewin identifies the articles in a footnote. But he has *no* evidence for the statement in boldface above – that *anyone* in the Politburo had tried to "prevent or delay" the publication of *any* of Lenin's articles. Nor is there any evidence to support it today, when a great many more primary sources from this period of Lenin's life have been published.

Evidently, Lewin invented this. In plain language, he is lying yet again.

Of Rykov's eye-witness account of Ordzhonikidze slapping Kabakhidze – whom Lewin carelessly misnames "Kabanidze"[14] – Lewin first says this:

> Rykov returned at last from Georgia and reported back to Lenin on December 9, 1922. The "Journal" merely mentions this meeting, and **we do not know what Rykov said**. (LLS, 68)

However, some pages later, Lewin contradicts himself:

> Without going into too much detail, one might well question Rykov's objectivity. On December 9, 1922, when he submitted his report to Lenin, **he had not breathed a word about the incident. Lenin learned of it only three days later, from Dzerzhinsky himself**. (LLS, 97)

Which is it? How does Lewin know that Rykov did *not* mention the "slap" incident? Does Lewin know what Rykov told Lenin on December 9, 1922, or doesn't he? This is yet another lie by Lewin.

It is convenient for the notion that Lenin was very upset (in Fotieva's words) about Dzerzhinsky's report. That story would lead nicely into his writing "The Question of Nationalities..." and the attacks on Stalin and Ordzhonikidze in it.

But if Lenin really were interested in what was going on with the Georgians he would have asked Rykov, an eye-witness, for his

---

[14] The 2005 re-edition of Lewin's book by University of Michigan Press fails to correct this error.

account. In a previous chapter we reproduced Rykov's account as he wrote it down in February, 1923. It vindicates Ordzhonikidze, as do Rtveladze's account and Dzerzhinsky's report.

Lewin:

> [On March 6] Trotsky, who had received the memorandum of December 30 and other papers by Lenin on Georgia, suggested that they should be shown to Kamenev so that he might begin to take certain measures on the spot. Fotieva went off to ask Lenin and came back to Trotsky with a categorical negative: "It is entirely out of the question. Vladimir Ilich says that Kamenev would show the letters to Stalin and Stalin would make a rotten compromise in order then to deceive." (LLS, 101-2)

What's Lewin's source for this story? Once again, Trotsky, and only Trotsky! Even Fotieva, whose 1967 "Reminiscences of Lenin" are full of falsifications (as we shall see), does not record this story. But Lewin urges us to take Trotsky's word for it when he states "we may take him [Trotsky] as a reliable witness in this case." (102, n.18) Again, on the adjacent page, Lewin tells us:

> There is every reason to believe Trotsky when he says that one of Lenin's secretaries, probably Glyasser, told him that Vladimir Ilich was preparing a "bomb" against Stalin. (103)

On the contrary! There is *no* reason to believe *any* of this. Responsible historians do not "believe or "disbelieve" their sources – they check them against other primary source evidence. If Lewin had done this in Trotsky's case, as we have done in *Trotsky's 'Amalgams'* and *Trotsky's Lies*, using sources that were available in Lewin's day, he could have discovered that Trotsky lied very often.

Lewin Defends Trotsky's Racism

On page 107 Lewin writes:

Chapter Eight. Moshe Lewin

> An explanation of the Stalinist phenomenon has sometimes been sought in terms of an Oriental heritage: **this interpretation is quite Leninist**.

Lewin does not say so, but he is probably referring to this infamous passage at the beginning of Trotsky's biography of Stalin.

> The late Leonid Krassin ... was the first, if I am not mistaken, to call Stalin an "Asiatic." In saying that, he had in mind no problematical racial attributes, but rather that blending of grit, shrewdness, craftiness and cruelty which has been considered characteristic of the statesmen of Asia.

And a few pages further,

> The national character of the Georgians is usually represented as trusting, impressionable, quick-tempered, while at the same time devoid of energy and initiative. Above all, Reclus noted their gaiety, sociability and forthrightness. Stalin's character has few of these attributes, which, indeed, are the most immediately noticeable in personal intercourse with Georgians. Georgian emigres in Paris assured Souvarine, the author of Stalin's French biography, that Joseph Djugashvili's mother was not a Georgian but an Osetin and that there is an admixture of Mongolian blood in his veins. **But a certain Iremashvili, whom we shall have occasion to meet again in the future, asserts that Stalin's mother was a pure-blooded Georgian, whereas his father was an Osetin, "a coarse, uncouth person, like all the Osetins, who live in the high Caucasian mountains."**

"No problematical racial attributes" indeed! *Then* Trotsky identifies his source:

> Most profuse in details are the reminiscences of the aforementioned [Joseph] Iremashvili, published in

> 1932 in the German language at Berlin, under the title, "Stalin und die Tragödie Georgiens." Since their author is **a former Menshevik who subsequently became something in the nature of a National Socialist**, his political record as such does not inspire great confidence. **It is, nevertheless, impossible to ignore his essay.**

Trotsky takes his racialist characterization of Stalin from an anticommunist who "subsequently" became "something of" a Nazi. And this is indeed a racist – Nazi-like – statement. Naturally, Lewin does not tell us how this stuff is "quite Leninist" – that is another lie. Lewin should have said that this racist statement is "quite Trotskyist" – and also quite Nazi-like.

Lewin Is Confused

Lewin writes:

> Trotsky had begun to attack the RKI[15] at the beginning of 1922. At that time Lenin still defended the commissariat, and therefore indirectly its head, but in his last writings he depicted it as a haven of ineptitude, a "hopeless affair": "None of the commissariats is worse organized than the RKI, and it is utterly devoid of authority." These barbs, directed at Stalin through the commissariat for which he had been responsible ... (LLS, 120)

Lewin is just copying Trotsky here. In an earlier chapter we showed that Trotsky claimed that this article of Lenin's was an attack on Stalin. But Lenin's article of January, 1923, "How Should We Reform the WPI" [i.e. the RKI, Rabkrin] could not have been "directed at Stalin," since Stalin had not been the commissar of the WPI/RKI since April, 1922, almost nine months earlier.

---

[15] The initials, in Russian, for the Workers and Peasants Inspectorate (WPI), whose Russian acronym is "Rabkrin."

Chapter Eight. Moshe Lewin

Lewin continues:

> These barbs, directed at Stalin through the commissariat for which he had been responsible, were probably the reason why the article "Better Fewer, But Better," which had been finished on February 10, did not appear in Pravda until March 4.

The footnote to this passage reads:

> According to Deutscher, *The Prophet Unarmed*, pp. 88-90, a majority of the [Polit]bureau was against publication; Kuibyshev had even suggested printing a special copy of *Pravda*, for Lenin's use, that would contain the article in question.

Lewin suggests that Stalin and his allies in the Politburo held back publication of Lenin's article for more than three weeks! However, he makes a number of false statements.

* There is no evidence that Lenin "finished" the article "Better Fewer, But Better" on February 10. The Secretaries Journal – here it is Fotieva – for February 10, 1923, simply states this:

> Called me in a little past 6. Asked that the article "Better Fewer, But Better" be given to Tsuryupa to read, if possible within 2 days. (CW 42, 492)

Fotieva is more specific in her "Reminiscences" which Lewin cites many times, though not here:

> 2 м а р т а Владимир Ильич последний раз просмотрел свою статью «Лучше меньше, да лучше» и отправил в печать. Она была опубликована в «Правде» 4 марта 1923 года. (1990 ed., 211)

> March 2: Vladimir Ilyich looked at his article "Better Less, Better" for the last time and sent it to be printed. It was published in Pravda on March 4, 1923.

How could Lewin have "just forgotten" to consult Fotieva's book, which he cites many times? And why cite Deutscher, when Deutscher too gives no evidence to support his assertion? It is hard to avoid concluding that once again Lewin is deliberately lying here.

As for Kuibyshev's fleeting suggestion that a special copy be printed for Lenin, it was made in January, and concerned Lenin's article "How Should We Reform the WPI," not "Better Fewer, But Better." Moreover, Kiubyshev was not a Politburo member. We have discussed this in a previous chapter. Lewin's readers, of course, would not know this.

* * * * *

In his final chapter Lewin muses about "what might have been" – how the history of the USSR might have been different had Lenin lived or had Trotsky become his successor. He bases these thoughts on two false assumptions. First, that the "testament" documents are genuine; second, that Trotsky and, secondarily, Fotieva in her "Reminiscences," told the truth.

But these assumptions are wrong. Trotsky and Fotieva lied many times. And the "testament" documents are falsified.

Lewin does not know what to make of the essay "The Question of Nationalities or 'Autonomization.'" He admits that it, plus the letter (which Lewin also believes genuine) to Mdivani and Makharadze of March 6, 1923, show that "Lenin had arrived at diametrically opposite conclusions" from those he had expressed in his exasperated letter to the Georgians of October 21, 1922.[16] (102)

Did Lewin really believe that during the months of his most serious illness Lenin's thinking had become *clearer* than it had been when he was healthy? In any case, Sakharov, Kotkin, and Stalin and the speakers at the XII Party Congress in April, 1923, all

---

[16] PSS LIV 299-300; CW 45, 582.

believe that this essay was either the product of Lenin's failing powers or a forgery.

Lewin also ends on a note surprisingly friendly to the then-current Soviet leadership, Khrushchev and Brezhnev. He recognizes what they did not wish to admit: that accepting "Lenin's testament" as genuine involves a *de facto* "rehabilitation" of Trotsky. Indeed, Trotsky's widow had recognized this as soon as she heard about Khrushchev's "Secret Speech."[17]

Conclusion

Lewin's lies and fabrications seriously distort historical truth. But there is an important logic behind them. Lewin is trying to concoct an account of Lenin's last months that will explain the sudden estrangement from and emerging opposition to Stalin and equally uncharacteristic closeness with Trotsky that are implied in the "testament."

Without some such account Lenin's last writings appear to reflect mental deterioration due to his illness. But Sakharov has argued, and we agree with him, that a number of Lenin's last writings do not show any signs of mental deterioration.

Through guesses, invention, and even lies, Lewin has fabricated a false narration in order to make sense of the sudden *volte-face* in Lenin's "testament." All the evidence available today strongly suggests that the "testament" is a fabrication.

---

[17] Aimermakher, K., et al., *Doklad N.S. Khrushcheva o kul'te lichnosti Stalina na XX S"ezde KPSS. Dokumenty.* Moscow: ROSSPEN, 2002, 545. A letter from Natalia Sedova, Trotsky's widow, to the Presidium of the XX Party Congress referring to the attacks on Stalin and requesting that her late husband and son be rehabilitated, is on p. 610.

Chapter 9. Lidia Fotieva's Memoir

Early in *Lenin's Last Struggle* Lewin notes his most important sources:

> Among the documents from which our source material has been taken, three are of exceptional importance: first, the latest edition of Lenin's Works—the fifth edition—not only more complete than previous ones but accompanied by an important body of notes and commentary; **second, the memoirs of Fotieva, one of Lenin's personal secretaries**; and third, the "Journal of Lenin's Secretaries," working notes made between November 21, 1922, and March 6, 1923 ... (LLS, x)

There are problems with each of these sources. Lewin does not mention them. Perhaps he did not know about the problems with the fifth edition of Lenin's works, the *Polnoe sobranie sochineniy* (PSS), or with the Secretaries Journal. But the problems with Fotieva's memoirs should have been clear to him. We'll discuss some of them here.

At one point Lewin seems to be suspicious of Fotieva's memory, after the passage of forty years:

> However, Fotieva mentions in *Iz Vospominaniy* some notes taken down on January 10 (p. 70) and February 16 (p. 75). But they do not appear in the "Journal." (LLS, 98, n. 9)

Was Fotieva, then, keeping *two* journals, and these and other details missing from the Secretaries Journal were in that *second* journal? Hardly! It seems clear that Fotieva was being coached, in conformity with the Khrushchev-era attacks on Stalin. Her supposed memoir may actually have been ghostwritten by other persons who strove to make it congruent with Khrushchev's anti-Stalin campaign.

Fotieva's "memoirs" – real title, *Iz vospominaniy o Lenine* " [Selections] From Reminiscences about Lenin" – was published in 1964, 40 years after Lenin's death. It clearly reflects the Khrushchev-era anti-Stalin campaign that had been inaugurated with Khrushchev's "Secret Speech" at the XX Party Congress on February 25, 1956. We know now that every allegation in that infamous speech of crime or misdeed by Stalin (or by Lavrentii Beria, a secondary target of Khrushchev's accusations) is false, and that most of them are deliberate lies by Khrushchev.[1]

Thereafter, Khrushchev sponsored a flood of lies about Stalin, the Moscow Trials and Military conspiracy of the 1930s, and the persons executed during Stalin's tenure. Marshal Zhukov lied about the Military Conspiracy at the Central Committee Plenum of February, 1957. The XXII Party Congress of October, 1961, witnessed an even greater outpouring of falsehoods about Stalin.

After the XXII Party Congress Khrushchev sponsored hundreds of articles and books by journalists and historians in which yet more falsehoods about Stalin were invented and spread abroad as the truth. This spate of falsifications went on until a year or so after Khrushchev was ousted in October, 1964.

None of these works drew upon primary-source documents. Khrushchev, of course, had access to all the archives and could have made them available to anyone he pleased. But he refused to do so.

Primary source documents from the archives were never published and not used. At a conference of Party historians – historians who specialized in the history of the CPSU – in December 1962 Presidium member and Party historian Piotr Pospelov answered a question from the audience in this way.

---

[1] For the evidence see Furr, *Khrushchev Lied* (2011).

> Later in this same note it says: "Students are asking whether Bukharin and the rest were spies for foreign governments, and what you advise us to read."
>
> I can declare that it is sufficient to study carefully the documents of the 22nd Congress of the CPSU to say that neither Bukharin, nor Rykov, of course, were spies or terrorists.
>
> The following note reads: "Why can't you create normal conditions for work in the Central Party archive? They do not let us see the materials on the activity of the CPSU." I have already given the answer. [2]

Pospelov was using "weasel words" here. Bukharin and Rykov were not accused of themselves being spies for foreign governments, and were not convicted of those charges. But he will not permit even Party historians to consult the archives.

Of course he didn't! The documents in the Party archive would have shown that Khrushchev and his minions were lying about everything concerning Stalin and the crimes they were blaming him for. We know this today because since the end of the Soviet Union in 1991 a great many documents from former Soviet archives have been published. These documents provide primary-source evidence that proves that Khrushchev and his men, then Gorbachev and *his* men, plus the Trotskyists, Social-Democrats, and overtly pro-capitalist anticommunist historians and writers in every country, have been lying and continue to do so.

This is the atmosphere that gave rise to all of the sources that Lewin cites. In the case of Fotieva's memoirs we can compare them to the Secretaries Journal of forty years earlier. There is no reason to believe that the details that Fotieva added in her 1964 memoir

---

[2] *Vsesoiuznoe soveshchanie o merakh uluchsheniia podgotovki nauchnopedagogicheskik kadrov po istoricheskim naukam, 18-21 dekabria 1962 g.* Moscow: Nauka, 1962, 298.

Chapter Nine. Lidia Fotieva's Memoir 241

are more accurate than her notes in the Secretaries Journal, which is itself falsified, as we have seen.

We'll note issues in her memoirs that are relevant to our present inquiry. Abbreviations: FM = Fotieva's Memoirs; SJ = Secretaries Journal.

Under December 12, 1922: FM claims that Lenin was "very upset" at Dzerzhinsky's report about the Georgian incident. SJ (XLV, 478) merely says "Dzerzhinsky from 6 to 6.45."

It was important to Khrushchev that the anti-Stalin "testament" portray Lenin as "very upset" about the Georgian matter, in order to lead to other documents: the Gorbunov-Fotieva-Glyasser "commission" of January – March, 1923, the letter to Mdivani and Makharadze, and the article "The Question of Nationalities ...," all of which are part of the attack on Stalin, as we have discussed in previous chapters.

In the fabricated part of SJ we do find the following statement under the entry for January 30 but written in as "January 24":

> He said: "Just before I got ill Dzerzhinsky told me about the work of the commission and about the 'incident,' and this had a very painful effect upon me." (SJ 484)

Lenin could not have been pained by Dzerzhinsky's report, which explained Ordzhonikidze's slap to Kabakhidze as a personal, not a political matter, and this was confirmed by Rtveladze and Rykov. In addition, if Lenin had really been upset by all these reports he surely would not have waited *six weeks* – from December 12, 1922 until the end of January, 1923 – to react to the Georgian situation. But in 1964, when Fotieva's "memoir" was published, her readers could not have known this.

Discussing events of February 3, 1923, Lewin writes:

> Without supplying further details as to her sources, Fotieva reports a meeting of the bureau:

> Kamenev: "Since Vladimir Ilich insists, I think it would be even worse to refuse."
>
> Stalin: "I don't know. Let him do as he likes."
>
> But this was obviously not what he wanted, for he demanded to be freed from his responsibility for Lenin's medical supervision. This request was not granted and the bureau gave its permission for Lenin to see the papers, without really knowing what he intended to do with them. (LLS, 95)

Lewin is in error here. Fotieva places this event under February 1, not February 3. What's more, she admits that she does remember this, but takes it from some source that she does not name.

> 1 ф е в р а л я на заседании Политбюро было разрешено выдать нам материалы по «грузинскому вопросу». Вероятно, именно на этом заседании Политбюро произошел следующий обмен записками между Сталиным и Каменевым.
>
> Каменев Сталину: «Думаю, раз Владимир Ильич настаивает, хуже будет сопротивляться».
>
> Сталин Каменеву: «Не знаю. Пусть делает по своему усмотрению».[3]
>
> On February 1, at a meeting of the Politburo, it was permitted to issue us materials on the "Georgian question". Probably exactly at this meeting of the Politburo, the following exchange of notes took place between Stalin and Kamenev.
>
> Kamenev to Stalin: "I think that since Vladimir Ilyich insists, it will be worse to resist."

---

[3] L.A. Fotieva, "Iz vospominaniia o V.I. Lenine (Dekabr' 1922 g. – mart 1923 g.)." *Vospominaniia o Vladimire Il'iche Lenine v 10 tomakh. Tom 8.* (Moscow: Politizdat, 1989), 203.

> Stalin to Kamenev: "I don't know. Let him do it at his own discretion."

Fotieva was lying. Her source is now available.[4] The note in question was not published until 1989. It was an exchange between Kamenev and Stalin at a Politburo session on *September 28, 1922*. Fotieva quotes it under *early February 1923*, in the context of Lenin's request for the materials of the Dzerzhinsky Commission. (FM 203) Fotieva's readers could not have known this.

This is more evidence that Fotieva was being coached, and her "coach" was lying to her. Perhaps she did not write these memoirs at all! Or perhaps she played only a secondary role, while Khrushchev-era editors or ghostwriters supplied material convenient to Khrushchev and hostile to Stalin for insertion into her text.

Fotieva says that Stalin requested at this time to be relieved of the responsibility for seeing that Lenin was not disturbed by political matters, a task that had been laid upon him on December 24, 1922. In her memoir Fotieva is explicit that Stalin made this request, because she says that he grilled her about how Lenin could be so up to date on political matters (FM 202-3). *None* of this is in the Secretaries Journal. (SJ 483-6) Conclusion: Fotieva, or her ghostwriter, has invented it.

On page 98, Lewin writes:

> On February 14, additional instructions were given to the commission that reveal a good deal about Lenin's state of mind and his determination to leave no stone unturned:
>
> "Three elements: (1) it is not permitted to strike someone; (2) concessions are indispensable; (3) one cannot compare a small state with a large one.

---

[4] Izv TsK 9, 1989, 208-9.

"Did Stalin know (of the incident)? Why didn't he do something about it?"

Lewin gives the reference to this note as PSS XLV, 607, where it is attributed to Fotieva, but without any indication of where in her writing this note is to be found. It is not in SJ. In FM (210) Fotieva says that Lenin gave this note to her on February 14, to give to A.A. Sol'ts, Chair of the Central Control Commission (TSKK).

For some reason Lewin omits the last sentence of this note – that the "great power chauvinists" themselves show a Menshevik deviation. This sentence is quoted by Fotieva in FM. Why does Lewin omit it? Perhaps because no one – other than Trotsky – had, or could, ever accused Stalin of Menshevism, as we have discussed in a previous chapter.

The Letters of March 5

The Secretaries Journal reads:

> March 5 (entry by M. A. Volodicheva).
>
> Vladimir Ilyich did not send for me until round about 12. Asked me to take down two letters: one to Trotsky, the other to Stalin; the first letter to be telephoned personally to Trotsky and the answer given to him as soon as possible. (SJ 493)

But Lewin states this:

> Lenin managed to conceal from his doctors the deep emotional stress that he felt when he took these decisions, and told them, Fotieva reports, that he was merely dictating a few business letters. (LLS, 99)

Lewin doesn't cite any source, but he must have had this passage is from FM in mind:

> В разговоре с доктором Кожевниковым Владимир Ильич не хотел признаться, как он был

взволнован, и сказал, что письма, продиктованные им, были чисто деловые. (211)

In a conversation with Dr. Kozhevnikov, Vladimir Ilyich did not want to admit how excited he was, and said that the letters dictated by him were purely business.

But this cannot be true. For how could Fotieva know what Leinin said? She was not even present! The final two entries in SJ, for March 5 and 6, are by Volodicheva. But Volodicheva does not mention this. Fotieva and/or her ghostwriter is lying again.

In a previous chapter we saw that the Doctors Journal stated that Lenin told the doctors that these were purely business letters that did not upset him. It appears that whoever was coaching Fotieva felt the need to get rid of this contradiction. Perhaps there was some talk that the Doctors Journal might be published at that time, in the 1960s. In fact, the Doctors Journal was not published until 1990.

In March 1967 Soviet writer Aleksandr Bek interviewed both Volodicheva and Fotieva about the last period of Lenin's life and his "testament." Fotieva concluded her remarks by revealing that she had altered the upcoming edition of her memoir according to the editor's wishes.

> Вы должны понять: Сталин был для нас авторитет. Мы Сталина любили. Это большой человек. Он же не раз говорил: я только ученик Ленина. Он был генеральный секретарь. Кто же мог помочь, если не он. И шли к нему. А мы: гений, гений. Двадцатый съезд был для нас душевной катастрофой. И теперь еще у меня борются два чувства: возмущение им и любовь к нему. Но сейчас (1967 год) опять изменяется отношение к Сталину. Изменяется к лучшему. В этом году выйдет новое издание моей книги, дополненное. (Имеется в виду книга Фотиевой «Из жизни В. И.

> Ленина»}. Вообще самое полное издание было в 1964 году. Вы его достаньте. А теперь я по сравнению с тем изданием по-другому пишу о Сталине. Редакция от меня потребовала других слов. Это и вы должны иметь в виду, если будете писать о Сталине.
>
> You must understand: Stalin was an authority for us. We loved Stalin. He was a great man. He said more than once: I am only a student of Lenin. He was the general secretary. Who could help if not he? And they went to him. And we thought – a genius, a genius. The Twentieth Congress was a spiritual disaster for us. And now I still have two feelings warring within me: indignation at him and love for him. But now (1967) the attitude towards Stalin is changing again. Changing for the better. This year there will be a new edition of my book, with additional material. (This refers to the book by Fotieva "From the Life of V. I. Lenin.") In general, the most complete edition was in 1964. You should obtain it. And now, compared to that edition, I have written about Stalin in a different way. The editors demanded different words from me. You must bear this in mind if you write about Stalin.

Though made in 1967, this interview was not published until 1989. It reflects the fact that, after Khrushchev's abrupt dismissal from the post of First Secretary in October, 1964, by the Central Committee, his anti-Stalin campaign was toned down under Leonid Brezhnev.

According to Fotieva here, she was instructed to revise her memoirs in order to moderate her anti-Stalin comments. We have already seen that those "memoirs" were falsified. Fotieva had no problem in further altering her "memoirs" to fit the new political atmosphere. This, along with the forty-plus years since the events of Lenin's last months of activity invalidates Fotieva's memoir as a reliable historical source.

Chapter 10. The Diary of the Secretaries

"The Diary of Duty Secretaries" or Secretaries Journal is widely believed to be one of the most important sources of information about Lenin's work on the texts of the "testament" and about his political mood and views during the last period of his active life. A version was published in the PSS, the Russian-language 5th edition of Lenin's works, and also in the 4th English edition.

However, Sakharov has had access to the archival originals. They make it clear that after the entry for December 18, 1922, the "Diary" is not what it purports to be. The evidence now available strongly suggests that these latter sections of the "Diary" are a fabrication, some of it probably done during the 1920s, some of it perhaps done after Nikita Khrushchev's "Secret Speech" in 1956. In the present chapter we'll discuss Sakharov's evidence and analysis, with some remarks of our own.

The "Diary" begins on November 21, 1922, in Lenin's secretariat. Until the end of the entry of December 18, 1922, it appears to be genuine. It reads like a diary should read – a documentation of Lenin's activities for record-keeping purposes, with daily entries in real time – that is, each day.

But thereafter, the "Diary" is virtually a different work. This is not acknowledged in any way in the PSS edition or in the English edition based upon it.

> There are no entries for December 19-21. However, on the pages of the book are dates written in the hand of N.S. Alliluyeva[1] with a small space between them (4-5 lines): "19 / XII", "20 / XII", "21 / XII", "23 / XII" ... The last working note in the diary made in real time is the record of the date "23 / XII". **All subsequent**

---

[1] N.S. Alliluyeva was Stalin's wife.

entries were made later than the dates indicated in the diary. (Sakharov, 70)

The next entry after December 18 is one for December 23. The date, as we noted, was written by Nadezhda Alliluyeva, Stalin's wife and a member of Lenin's secretariat. But the entry is by a different secretary, M.A. Volodicheva. It contains "memoir" material – Lenin's concern for her, why she looked pale, why wasn't she at the Congress, his regret at taking up her time.[2] This is personal stuff that had not been recorded in previous "Diary" entries. It has no record-keeping value. It could have been inserted at any later time.

The entry for December 24 begins "the next day." This means that it was not written on December 24, but sometime later. Likewise, "next day" implies that the entry for December 23 was also written later, as we might suspect given its memoir-like contents.

A new document has begun! This is not the "old" and genuine "Diary" but something else – a different document, produced for different reasons, with entries not written down in real time, i.e. on the given dates, but written down later, either from memory or by invention. Sakharov notes at this point:

> The handwriting of Volodicheva in the notes after December 18 is somewhat different from before. The change in the frequency of its use of various forms of individual letters is striking. This is most noticeable in relation to the capital letter "d", which it uses in three different forms.

That is, it is Volodicheva's handwriting, but with a difference. That is consistent with the passage of time – perhaps of years or even of decades.

Sakharov continues:

---

[2] XLV 474; CW 42, 481, under entry for December 23.

Chapter Ten. The Diary of the Secretaries

> From this point on the nature of the records changes markedly. If before they were purely clerical, now many of them acquire a frankly "memoir" character, recording events "retroactively". These include the important notes for our topic of December 23 and 24, 1922, as well as for January 24-30 and March 5-6, 1923. Some postscripts were made in the margins in a different handwriting, the evidence of later reworking of the finished text. "Lyrical" inserts appear that do not concern the essence of the matter, but fix the reader's attention on the care that Lenin showed in relation to Fotieva and Volodicheva, on Lenin's state of health, or on mitigating the negative impression of the recognition of Lenin's weakening memory ... These notes suggest that they were not intended for "memory", not for a working report, not for a change in the person on duty, but for an outside reader. For History. (71)

The entries increasingly take on an anti-Stalin character as well.

> In content they are directly or indirectly related to the characterization of relations between Lenin and Stalin and always highlight them negatively.

At the same time, there are no more entries by Stalin's wife, N.S. Alliluyeva, although we know that she continued to work in Lenin's secretariat.[3] If there were more such entries by Allilueva they have not been preserved and other entries have been substituted. Sakharov, with access to the archival originals, notes details that were omitted by the editors of the PSS.

> The later fabrication of diary entries after December 23 is indicated by a series of omissions in the entries

---

[3] Sakharov (page 680, note 9) cites an archival document by Volodicheva that records Alliluyeva's continued presence in Lenin's secretariat..

> and traces of later attempts to make up for them. On a blank sheet there are someone's notes made in pencil: "V. 26 / XII", "L.F. 28 / XII", "L.F. 4/1", "L.F. 9-10 / 1", "L.F. 24/1 ". Considering all that is known to us about this "Diary", we have the right to assume that these pencil marks indicate the days for which Volodicheva and Fotieva were supposed to make notes. **When publishing the "Diary", these markings were not reproduced. Their presence is not even mentioned in the editors' notes.** (72)

Omissions such as these are clear evidence that the PSS was edited in a tendentious manner by its Khrushchev-Brezhnev era editors.

> There are other hidden traces that indicate later work on the "Diary" …

Sakharov notes "a deliberate distortion of the dating of the very important record of December 24th." This is the date when the first part of the document that later comes to be called the "Letter to the Congress" is supposed to have been dictated by Lenin.

> In the published version this record, which is usually referred to as Lenin's work on "Characteristics," is dated December ("December 24"), in the original of the so-called "Diary" it is actually dated November and looks like this: "24 / XI"! It is followed by the text: "The next day …" … it cannot be ruled out that the appearance of this date is somehow related to the time when Volodicheva made this entry. It clearly has the characters of a memoir rather than a diary. (72)

This further undermines any confidence in the editors of the PSS.

> In any case, the correction of this "mistake" without reservation by "conscientious" and vigilant editors suggests that they tried to remove from the "Diary" anything that could cast doubt on its authenticity and to present to the scientific community an impeccable source that could become one of the main foundations

Chapter Ten. The Diary of the Secretaries

of the "Khrushchev version" of Lenin's "testament". (72)

On December 24, a day that is called "the next day" in the "Diary", nothing is said about what Lenin dictated, only that it is "strictly confidential," "categorically secret," and that "everything" he dictated should be kept especially secure. But nothing about the crucial "Letter to the Congress," and particularly nothing about the "Characteristics." (CW 42, 482) The end result is that

> there is a political, or rather, historical-political sense — informing the public that on these days Lenin dictated something super secret, that can be disclosed only by secretaries, who in this case will be able to tell anything they want. To challenge their "testimony" will be either impossible or extremely difficult. (73)

After the entry for December 24 (actually, for November 24 – see above; another "silent correction" by the PSS editors) the next entry is for December 29. Yet the chronology of Lenin's life and activities shows that during these very days Lenin is supposed to have dictated many important documents: completion of the dictation of the "Characteristics" on December 25; texts on the State Planning Commission (Gosplan) on the 27th and 28th; more on Gosplan and on adding members to the Central Committee on December 29. But there is nothing about any dictation in the "Diary" for December 29. (CW 42, 482)

The "Diary" records the beginning of the dictation of the "Letter to the Congress" on December 24. But it does so with a note that is *not* a diary entry but has been inserted later and made to resemble a diary entry: "Next day (December 24) ..." Completion of work on the "Letter to the Congress" on December 25, and work on the all-important "Addition" to it of January 4 – the strongest anti-Stalin text of Lenin's "testament" – are not recorded at all. Nor is any work recorded on "The Question of Nationalities or 'Autonomization'", another important piece of the "testament" that is sharply critical of Stalin.

The article "Pages from a Diary" is supposed to have been dictated on January 1-2, 1923, then "On Cooperation" on January 5-6. The only entries are a few lines on December 29 and a single sentence for January 5. Neither mentions any dictation work by Lenin. This means that the "Diary of Duty Secretaries" is useless in determining Lenin's authorship of these crucial documents.

The entry for December 24 does not mention *what* was dictated. Neither does that of December 29 or that of January 5. There are no entries between January 5 and January 17 at all. During these days the secretariat is operating and Lenin is dictating. But nothing is recorded in the "Diary." How is this possible if the "Diary" really is a record-keeping document composed in real time?

Once the "Diary" format no longer exists, there is no reason to trust anything in it. Clearly, its purpose has changed. If important materials are omitted, fictitious materials can also be entered. Sakharov, who has studied the archival documents, notes that the records of early January, 1923 show that the "Diary" has been falsified.

> The record of January 5 is followed by a blank sheet with pencil marks, which were mentioned above and which can be understood as traces of planning work on the fabrication of "diary" notes. On the next sheet there is a record for January 17, made by Volodicheva. In the archival version of the "Diary" you can see what is hidden in the published version. To Volodicheva's text, which establishes Lenin's bad memory, the word "jokingly" [*шутливо*] is inserted in the margin. This indicates that someone has edited the text. (74)

The entries for the dates from January 24 to January 30, made by Fotieva, were all written down after the fact and out of order. Once again, this is clearly not a "diary." Supposedly writing on January 30, Fotieva notes the sequence is as follows: January 24, then the 25th, then the 27th ("Saturday"), then the 29th ("Yesterday"), then "today," the 30th; then back to the 24th, followed by the 26th, and back again to January 30th ("Today"). (CW 42, 484-5)

Chapter Ten. The Diary of the Secretaries

> These records, obviously not of a record-keeping nature, resemble, rather, the draft of a memoir. This is indicated, for example, by the fact that Fotieva, who is believed to have made them, is mentioned in the third person:

Some examples:

> January 29: (Entry by L.A. Fotieva)
>
> On January 24 Vladimir Ilich sent for Fotieva ... This assignment was given to Fotieva, Glyasser and Gorbunov. (CW 42, 484)

We have seen that Sakharov recognized that Volodicheva's handwriting changed after the December 18, 1922 entry. Here Sakharov has discerned a change in Fotieva's handwriting too, consistent with the passages of time, perhaps of many years:

> The handwriting is similar to Fotieva's handwriting, but the style of individual letters differs from her notes made in mid-December 1922. (75)

Sakharov also found a third handwriting at work.

> We should add that these texts were edited by someone. In a note dated January 29[4], part of the words attributed to Lenin ("For instance, his article about the W.P.I. showed that certain circumstances were known to him.") were inserted into the main text later in a handwriting somewhat different from the handwriting of the main record. (75)

Sakharov also notes that the paper of the archival version changes at the January 30 entry:

> Starting from this day, the recordings are made on sheets of paper markedly different in color (gray

---

[4] But written down under the entry of January 30, 1923. See CW 42, 484.

> instead of white) and quality from the previous ones. (74, note)

The archival original also contains a remark by Lenin of a "memoir" nature having nothing to do with the record-keeping of the secretariat.

> The February 1 entry has another editorial edit, an insertion in the margin. And what an insertion! The text reads: "V.I. said: if I were free (I misspoke at first, and then repeated, laughing: if I were free), then I would easily have done all this myself."

This has been removed from the published version – yet another sign that the editors of the PSS "cleaned up" the "Diary" or attempted to do so, no doubt to make it appear more "diary-like." These volumes were prepared for publication during and shortly after Khrushchev's anti-Stalin campaign.

Another serious defect in the "Diary" entries occurs in the records of February 7 to Februray 12, 1923.

> In the archival version the "diary" entries follow this order: February 10, morning of February 7, morning of the 9th, followed by the second time on February 10. After that, February 7 (evening) returns again, then the "second coming" of February 9 (morning, evening) follows. February 9th is followed by the 12th ... (75)

Unlike the earlier defect, however, this one is not recorded accurately in the printed version. Some editor has straightened it out.

> Compared to January, the February defect in the calendar is much more graphic evidence that the "Diary of Duty Secretaries" is actually a later fabrication. Perhaps this is why its publishers had to assume the role of editor and correct the "defect" left by its authors, hiding not only the confusion of

Chapter Ten. The Diary of the Secretaries

calendar dates, but also the very fact of later historical and political work.

After the records for February 12 and 14 the rest of the sheet is left blank. Why? To anticipate being filled in later? Because there are *no entries at all* between February 14 and March 5. (XLV 485-6; CW 42, 493)

> On the next sheet are the last two entries of the "Diary" for March 5 and 6, 1923, telling the story of the creation and the sending of letters to Trotsky, Mdivani and others, as well as the ultimatum letter to Stalin.

We have studied these letters in the present book. The evidence strongly points to their being fabrications. The fact that the "Diary" resumes only for these dates suggests that these entries may have been made for the purpose of "legitimating" these letters.

The archival version of the "Diary" contains more evidence of Khrushchev-era reworking.

> In the record for March 6, most of the text, starting with the words "Nadezhda Konstantinovna asked" to the end, was executed by Volodicheva in cipher. It was transcribed on June 14, 1956, exactly when the political need arose. (76)

This is recorded in the notes to the "Diary," where we read:

> The text beginning with the words: "Nadezhda Konstantinovna asked…" is written in the Journal in shorthand; this was deciphered by Volodicheva on July 14, 1956. (CW 42, 622 n. 618)

Naturally, this means that the entry for March 6 has no value as evidence, since Volodicheva could have written anything in 1956.

Working from the archival originals Sakharov notes this:

> It is interesting that the authors of the notes in the PSS changed the date of Volodicheva's transcription from June 14 to July 14, i.e. to a time after the adoption of the decree of the Central Committee of the CPSU "On overcoming the cult of personality and its consequences". (76)[5]

This resolution was passed on June 30, 1956.[6]

After the entry of December 18, 1922, the "Diary of Duty Secretaries" is no longer a record-keeping or clerical document that reflects the events in real time – that is, on the same day that they occurred. On the contrary, its character changes markedly after that date. Therefore, it is not free from the effects of the political situations that followed. The texts entered in violation of the chronology or having a memoir character (entry made later than the specified date) add up to approximately 4.7 pages out of 12.7 pages of entries, or 37% of the whole "Diary."

> All this allows us to assert that its creators pursued certain political goals. Therefore, the "Diary" is a document of political struggle, created to be able to use Lenin's authority in the interest of someone. It does not give us any serious information about Lenin's work on the texts of the "testament." (76)

Even if one accepts this part of the "Diary" as a "memoir" it is still the case that this "memoir" does not contain definite indications of Lenin's dictation of a number of the most important texts of the "testament" — the "Letter to the Congress," the notes "On the Question of Nationalities or 'Autonomization'," and other important documents.

The Secretaries Diary does appear to support Lenin's authorship of the letters dated March 5 and 6, 1923. But we shall see that this

---

[5] See illustration #5. The date of June 14, 1956 – not July 14 – in Volodicheva's handwriting is clearly visible.
[6] For the resolution and date see https://ria.ru/20160630/1454189888.html

is contradicted by the account in the "Diary of Duty Doctors." We shall also see that, during the Khrushchev era, Fotieva – or whoever worked with her, coauthored, or perhaps even created her "Reminiscences" of Lenin's last days – recognized this contradiction and tried to cover it up. Perhaps this was done in view of an anticipated publication of the Doctors Diary. As it happened, the Doctors Diary was not published until 1991.

> Thus, everything that we know about the entries in the "Diary" beginning with December 23, 1922, speaks against the recognition of this document as a valuable source on the history of Lenin's work on the latest letters and articles. **Instead, it is valuable and important as a source on the history of the falsification of Lenin's "testament."** (76)

The "Diary of Duty Doctors"

Unlike the secretaries' "Diary" Sakharov was unable to study the archival version of the Doctors Diary or Doctors Journal. He says that he found evidence that it was being prepared for publication as early as the 1920s. Fotieva or her ghostwriter certainly knew it during the 1950s, so it is likely that its publication was being considered at that time also.

Why wasn't it published then? Possibly because it contradicts the secretaries' "Diary" on many points. Its publication could have opened the door at that time, as it does now, to doubts not just about the secretaries' "Diary" but about those critical documents of Lenin's supposed "testament" that have a strongly anti-Stalin orientation.

The Doctors Diary does not describe the contents of the dictations by Lenin to his secretaries, so it can't be used to verify facts stated in the secretaries' "Diary" or in the chronology of Lenin's last months contained in the PSS. It too may have been reworked in places – we can't know for certain, because the originals are not accessible, but this can't be ruled out. It would be surprising if there had been no attempt to bring it into line, wherever possible, with the secretaries' accounts. After all, publication of the Doctors' Diary was being contemplated in the 1920s (Sakharov), then probably in the Khrushchev era, as we can tell from Fotieva's memoirs, and possibly earlier in the Gorbachev era, when active falsification of evidence against Stalin was still proceeding.[7]

So the original, archival version will be of great interest, should it ever be made available. Meanwhile the "Diary of Duty Doctors" is the only source now available that gives systematic information recorded in real time about Lenin's work and about his health and ability to work after December 18, 1922.

A number of the doctors' notes challenge the account of Lenin's work that we find in the secretaries' "Diary" and the chronologies. For example, the doctors' account has no record of any work by Lenin on January 6, 1923, though this is elsewhere said to be the day when he dictated the second part of his article "On Cooperation." Likewise on January 9, when Lenin supposedly worked on the article "What Should We Do with the W.P.I.?" (VI KPSS 9, 1991, 47-8; PSS, XLV 711).

And the doctors virtually deny Lenin's work on the crucial documents supposedly dictated on March 5 and 6, 1923.

> ... the "Diary of doctors on duty" is most valuable in that it makes it possible to determine the reliability of other sources, especially the "Diary of Duty Secretaries." Comparison of information on the work of Lenin contained in the "Diary of Doctors" with the "Diary of Secretaries" yields striking results. Matches are sorted into four groups: December 24, 1922; third week of January (17-19, 22 and 23); the first week of February (3, 4, 6, 7) and March 5, 6, 1923. That's all for two and a half months - one day in December, five in January, four in February and two in March. For 73

---

[7] It was finally published in the last half of 1991 during the final months of the existence of the USSR.

Chapter Ten. The Diary of the Secretaries

diary entries of doctors (December 24 - March 6) and 30 entries of secretaries there are only thirteen matches! This cannot but be surprising — if the "Secretaries Diary" is indeed a diary. (77)

The "Diary of Secretaries" is silent about work with Lenin (including due to lack of notes), while the "Diary of Doctors" reports such work on these dates: December 25, 29-31, January 1-4, 10, 13, 16, 19, January , 18-20, February 25-27, March 2, 3. Twenty days of disagreement out of 73 calendar days! To this we should add an additional 6 days when, according to the doctors, Lenin did not work with the secretaries, yet the secretaries talk about their working with Lenin: January 24, 25, 26, and February 9, 10, and 12.

Sakharov adds it up:

> So, there are inconsistencies in 26 cases out of 73 and records in agreement are recorded only for 13 days. But for the "Diary of Secretaries" even these coincidences are no better than contradictions. More than three quarters of them (10 out of 13 diary entries) are saturated with large and small contradictions ... (78)

These two documents, the "Diary of Duty Secretaries" and "Diary of Duty Doctors," are our main source of evidence about Lenin's activity and dictation during the period of December 23, 1922, to March 6, 1923 – the period when the "testament" was supposedly composed.

*****

We know that Fotieva was willing to take an active part in falsifying the Secretaries Journal because of a note that Sakharov found in an archive. In 1971, Fotieva offered to insert entry about "Addition" into the Journal.

> Пятьдесят лет спустя Фотиева в письме в ИМЛ при ЦК КПСС от 15 мая 1971 г. попыталась восполнить

этот пробел и предложила включить в текст «дневника» недостающую информацию: «4/1. Добавление к "Письму к съезду"»

(РГАСПИ Ф. 5. Оп. 1. Д. 12. Л. 1)[8].

Fifty years later, Fotieva, in a letter to the IML [Institute of Marxism-Leninism] attached to the Central Committee of the CPSU of May 15, 1971, tried to fill this gap and suggested including the missing information in the text of the "diary": "4/1. Addendum to the "Letter to the Congress" »

(RGASPI F. 5. Op. 1. D. 12. L. 1).

We have seen that Fotieva's memoir has been tendentiously edited, filled out with details to make the anti-Stalin tendency of the Secretaries Journal and the "testament" fit together better.[8]

---

[8] Sakharov 350, note.

Chapter 11. Ulyanova's statements

Lenin's sister Maria Il'inichna Ulyanova spent a great deal of time with Lenin during the period of his illness. On July 26, 1926, Ulyanova presented a statement about Lenin's relationship with Stalin to the Joint Plenum of the Central Committee and the Central Control Committee.

Sometime later Ulyanova wrote a second statement about the Lenin-Stalin relationship. We do not know when Ulyanova composed this second statement. She might have written it around April, 1929, when she sent a letter to the Joint Plenum of the Central Committee and the Central Control Commission in defense of Rykov, Bukharin, and Tomsky. That letter is attached to this chapter as an appendix.

This second statement is handwritten. There is no indication that Ulyanova showed it to anyone. It was not published until December, 1989, though Ulyanova had died in 1937. Ulyanova's second statement differs in important respects from her first statement. In this chapter we will study both statements to see what they can reveal about "Lenin's testament."[1]

Ulyanova's First Statement – Her Letter to the Joint Plenum of the CC and CCC, July 26, 1926

Ulyanova's first statement consists of three paragraphs plus a few concluding sentences. We will examine it one paragraph at a time.

> During the recent period the oppositional minority in the CC has carried out systematic attacks on Comrade Stalin not even stopping at affirming a supposed break by Lenin with Stalin in the last months of V.I.'s life.

---

[1] I have put both statements, in the original Russian and in my own translation, online at https://msuweb.montclair.edu/~furrg/research/ulianova.html

> With the objective of re-establishing the truth I consider it my obligation to inform comrades briefly about the relations of Lenin towards Stalin in the period of the illness of V.I. (I am not here concerned with the period prior to his illness about which I have considerable evidence of the most touching attitude of V.I. towards Stalin of which CC members know no less than I) when I was continually present with him and carried out a number of tasks for him.

Ulyanova asserts that Lenin had a very close relationship with Stalin both before and during his illness, but she will only comment on the latter period, when she was in Lenin's presence regularly.

> Vladimir Il'ich valued Stalin very highly. For example, in the spring of 1922 when V. Il'ich had his first attack, and also at the time of his second attack in December 1922, he invited Stalin and turned to him with the most intimate tasks. The type of tasks with which one can address only to a person on whom one has total faith, whom you know as a dedicated revolutionist, and as an intimate comrade. Moreover Il'ich insisted that he wanted to talk only with Stalin and nobody else.

Here Ulyanova is probably referring to Lenin's turning to Stalin for poison and making Stalin promise to give it to him when he demanded it. As we have seen, these requests are well documented.

> In general, during the entire period of his illness, while he had the opportunity to associate with his comrades, he invited comrade Stalin most often. And during the most serious period of the illness, he generally did not invite any of the members of the C.C. except Stalin.

Chapter Eleven. Ulyanova's statements

Here Ulyanova claims that Lenin was closer to Stalin than to anyone else in the Party, either inviting Stalin more often than others or, when Lenin was very sick, exclusively.

> There was an incident between Lenin and Stalin which comrade Zinoviev mentioned in his speech and which took place not long before Il'ich lost his power of speech (March, 1923) but it was completely personal and had nothing to do with politics. Comrade Zinoviev knows this very well and to refer to it was absolutely unnecessary. This incident took place because on the demand of the doctors the Central Committee gave Stalin the charge of keeping a watch so that no political news reached Lenin during this period of serious illness. This was done so as not to upset him and so that his condition did not deteriorate ...

Here Ulyanova is referring to the doctors' order of December 24, 1922, taken in consultation with Stalin, Bukharin, and Kamenev, and charging Stalin with keeping political discussion away from Lenin. This later order refers to "political life" – the order of December 18, 1922, does not.

From this point on Ulyanova's account of the origin of the "ultimatum letter" is very different from the official version.

> ... he (Stalin) even scolded his [Lenin's] family for conveying this type of information. Il'ich, who accidentally came to know about this and who was also always upset by such a strong regime of protection, in turn scolded Stalin. Stalin apologized and with this the incident was settled. It goes without saying that if Lenin had not been so seriously ill during this period, as I had indicated, then he would have reacted to the incident differently.

Let us sum up. Ulyanova claims:

* that Stalin scolded not Krupskaya alone, but Lenin's family. In addition to Krupskaya, this evidently included Ulyanova herself

who, she claims, "was continually present with him." The editors of this document in Izv TsK KPSS No. 12, 1989, say that they do not know who else in Lenin's family Ulyanova meant.

This version contradicts the "official" version contained in Krupskaya's letter to Kamenev, in which Krupskaya says only that Stalin had been rude to her and says nothing about Stalin "scolding" Lenin's family.

* Lenin found out about this "accidentally." Ulyanova does not say who told him. The official version says that Krupskaya told him.

* Lenin "scolded" Stalin. If by this Ulyanova meant the "ultimatum letter" she does not say so, and "scolded" is a poor description of that letter. It seems that she may have meant a different event or a different document.

> "Stalin apologized ..."

* The official version mentions Stalin's note to Lenin, dictated to Volodicheva but not given to Lenin or read to him but given, shown, or read to Kamenev, who described it in a letter to Zinoviev. In fact Stalin's note does not contain any apology, although Stalin's agreeing to "take back" his words to Krupskaya might be interpreted as an apology of sorts. We do not know what those words were, other than Stalin's brief reference to them in his reply.

> "... and with this the incident was settled."

* According to the official version, no "settlement" – resolution or conclusion – of the incident took place. Ulyanova claims that it *was* "settled" with an apology by Stalin to Lenin.

> "It goes without saying that if Lenin had not been so seriously ill during this period, as I had indicated, then he would have reacted to the incident differently."

* Here Ulyanova appears to lay much of the blame for the incident not on Stalin but on Lenin himself, whose reaction, due to his

illness, was "different" – perhaps sharper – than it should have been.

> "There are documents regarding this incident and on the first request from the Central Committee I can present them."

* Could the documents Ulyanova mentions be Lenin's "ultimatum letter" to Stalin and Stalin's reply? We can't rule this out. But the "ultimatum letter" had already been shown to the XV Party Congress and reprinted in an appendix to its transcript. So Ulyanova would seem to be referring to different documents. Perhaps she meant her own copy of Stalin's reply to Lenin? We just don't know.

The Soviet editors passed over this remark in silence. Evidently they had no idea what documents Ulyanova was referring to, and we do not know today.

Analysis of Ulyanova's First Statement

Ulyanova claims that the whole incident took place in a very different manner than described by other members of the Central Committee, including Zinoviev and Trotsky. Ulyanova's statement goes a long way towards vindicating Stalin. She tacitly denies that Lenin ever threatened to break off relations with Stalin. She states that "the incident" was "settled" by an apology by Stalin to Lenin.

Ulyanova fails to mention the dramatic "ultimatum letter" at all, even though the members of the C.C. and the C.C.C. would certainly have been aware of it. She does not mention Krupskaya. But she implicitly rejects Krupskaya's claim that Stalin was rude to her alone rather than to his "family." Ulyanova also claims that Stalin apologized to Lenin. This too contradicts the official version, according to which Lenin never received Stalin's reply to Lenin's "ultimatum letter."

Taken as a whole, Ulyanova's statement about the circumstances of Stalin's "rudeness" and Lenin's reaction to it is very supportive of Stalin, to the point of being mildly critical of Lenin himself. It is very different from the version outlined by Krupskaya.

Ulyanova's Second Statement on Relations between Lenin and Stalin

At some later point Ulyanova wrote another statement about Lenin's relationship with Stalin. This statement was first published in the December 1989, issue of the Gorbachev-era journal *Izvestiia TsK KPSS*. The editors state that it was found among her personal papers after her death, which occurred on June 12, 1937. We do not know when or why Ulyanova wrote it. In some respects it presents a different account of Lenin's relations with Stalin. In other respects it echoes her first statement. As it bears directly on the question of the official version of the "ultimatum letter" we must examine it carefully.

> In my statement to the Central Committee plenum I wrote that V.I. valued Stalin. This is of course true. Stalin is an outstanding worker and a good organizer. But it is also without doubt, that in this statement I did not say the whole truth about Lenin's attitude towards Stalin. The purpose of the statement, which was written at the request of Bukharin and Stalin, was to protect him a little from the attacks of the opposition by referring to Il'ich's relation towards him. The opposition was speculating on the last letter of V. I.'s to Stalin where the question of breaking off relations with him was posed. The immediate reason for this was a personal incident – V. I.'s outrage that Stalin allowed himself to be rude towards N. K. At that time it seemed to me that Zinoviev, Kamenev and others were using this strictly personal matter for political purposes, for factional purposes. But after further considering this fact with a number of V.I.'s statements, with his political testament and also with Stalin's behavior during the period since Lenin's death, his "political" line, I more and more began to

Chapter Eleven. Ulyanova's statements

> clarify to myself Il'ich's real attitude towards Stalin during the last period of his life. I consider that it is my duty to talk about this, if only briefly.

Ulyanova states that Bukharin and Stalin had asked her to write the first statement, and that she had agreed to do so. She does not say that she falsified it in any way, only that she "did not say the whole truth about Lenin's attitude towards Stalin."

Ulyanova states:

> The opposition was speculating on the last letter of V. I. to Stalin where the question of breaking off relations with him was posed.

Here Ulyanova specifically refers to the "ultimatum letter," which she had not mentioned directly in her first statement.

She continues:

> The immediate reason for this was a personal incident – V. I.'s outrage that Stalin allowed himself to be rude towards N. K. At that time it seemed to me that Zinoviev, Kamenev and others were using this strictly personal matter for political purposes, for factional purposes.

In her first statement Ulyanova had said that Stalin had "scolded" Lenin's family. Here she says only that he had been "rude" to Krupskaya – the same word Krupskaya had used in her letter to Kamenev. She repeats her view that Lenin's anger at Stalin was not political but personal.

> But after further considering this fact with a number of V.I.'s statements, with his political testament and also with Stalin's behavior during the period since Lenin's death, his "political" line, I more and more began to clarify to myself Il'ich's actual attitude towards Stalin during the last period of his life.

Ulyanova mentions four matters that she intends to take into account in this statement.

* "A number of V.I.'s statements." However, she discusses only *one* statement: her claim that Lenin said Stalin "is not at all intelligent."

* "His political testament." Ulyanova refers briefly to some of these documents.

* "Stalin's behavior during the period since Lenin's death, his 'political' line …" Ulyanova says nothing at all about this.

* "I more and more began to clarify to myself Il'ich's actual attitude towards Stalin during the last period of his life." Does "actual" mean that her description of Lenin's attitude towards Stalin, which she had described in unequivocally positive terms, was not accurate? Or does she perhaps simply mean that it was more complicated?

Ulyanova continues:

> V.I. had a lot of self-control. He knew very well how to conceal, how not to show his attitude towards persons when he thought that to be most expedient for whatever reason. I remember how he hid himself in his room and closed the door behind him when a worker from the All-Russian Central Executive Committee whom he could not tolerate, came to our flat. He was indeed afraid to meet him, **afraid that he would not be able to control himself**, and that his real attitude towards this person would reveal itself in a harsh manner.

This is confusing. First Ulyanova says that Lenin "had a lot of self-control." Then she appears to contradict herself by relating an incident where Lenin was so "afraid to meet" a high-ranking Party member whom he did not like that he avoided meeting him altogether for fear that he would *not* be able to control himself, would *lose* his self-control.

Chapter Eleven. Ulyanova's statements

She then claims that, in the interest of keeping Trotsky because of his abilities, Lenin set aside with difficulty – "What this cost him – that's another question" – his negative attitude towards Trotsky, for whom "he never had any sympathy ... – this person had too many characteristics which made collective work with him extremely difficult."

Here she makes it clear that, in her view, Lenin did not like or support Trotsky. This is consistent with her first statement, where she says that Stalin was Lenin's favorite, but here it is more pointedly anti-Trotsky. If she did compose this second statement for the April 1929 Joint Plenum, then it was after Trotsky had been expelled from the Party and exiled from the Soviet Union.

Stalin's Attitude Towards Helping Martov

Ulyanova claims that Lenin was "very upset" (*ochen' rasstroen*) and "very angry with Stalin" (*ochen' rasserzhen na St[alina]*) because Stalin called the Menshevik Martov an enemy of the working class and refused to transfer money to him when Lenin wanted to help Martov. Lenin and Martov had worked together for many years, beginning before the Bolshevik-Menshevik split of 1903. It was understandable that Lenin viewed his relationship with Martov as, in part, a personal one, whereas Stalin, who had never worked with Martov, saw only the latter's political errors.

So for Lenin helping Martov was a "personal" matter. This is a second example where Lenin was unable to keep the personal separate from the political.

Ulyanova then makes a curious and inexplicable statement:

> Were there other reasons also for dissatisfaction with him [Stalin] on the part of V.I.? Evidently there were. Shklovski told about a letter from V.I. to him in Berlin, when Sh[klovsky] was there. According to this letter it was clear that somebody was undermining V.I. Who and how – that remains a mystery.

The editors of this document identify and reprint a letter from Lenin to Shklovsky. This letter cannot be about Stalin, since in it Lenin complains about "new" Party members who do not trust "the old [members]," and concludes that "we struggle, to win the *new* youth to our side." (Izv TsK KPSS 12, 1989, p. 201, n. 32)

What could this have to do with Stalin? The editors have no idea. More to the point: Ulyanova herself had no idea either! Why, then, does she mention it? It looks as though she may have wanted to cite another reason for Lenin to have been dissatisfied with Stalin, but could not think of one. We don't know.

Lenin, Stalin, and Lenin's Request for Poison

Ulyanova then devotes three paragraphs to a more detailed discussion of Lenin's request to Stalin for poison, and how Stalin handled it. This part of her letter shows Stalin in a very positive light. She spends an additional two paragraphs describing how Lenin "was with Stalin against Trotsky," how Stalin "visited [Lenin] more often than others" during Lenin's illness, how Lenin "met him amicably, joked, smiled, and demanded that I play the hostess to Stalin, bring wine and so on." These passages suggest that Lenin's relationship with Stalin was an excellent one.

Ulyanova then writes:

> V.I. was most dissatisfied with Stalin concerning the national question in the Caucasus. His correspondence with Trotsky regarding this matter is well known. **Evidently** V.I. was terribly troubled with Stalin, Orjonikidze and Dzerzhinsky. This question tormented him strongly during the rest of his illness.

Here Ulyanova clearly refers to (1) Lenin's letter to Trotsky of March 5, 1923[2], and possibly to his letter to Mdivani and Makharadze.[3] Her use of the word "evidently" – *vidimo* –suggests

---

[2] LIV 329; CW 45, 607.

Chapter Eleven. Ulyanova's statements

that she had no *independent* knowledge of Lenin's dissatisfaction with Stalin concerning this issue but was taking it from another source.

This is significant, because Ulyanova was with her brother virtually every day. Yet she did not know *at first hand, from Lenin himself*, that he was "troubled with Stalin, Ordzhonikidze, and Dzerzhinsky." Where could she have learned about this? Only from Krupskaya, the members of Lenin's secretariat, and/or from the documents of the "testament."

She continues:

> To this was united the conflict that led to V.I's letter to Stalin of 5.3.23, which I will quote below. It was like this. The doctors insisted that no one should speak to V.I. about anything concerning work. **It was necessary to fear more than anything else that N.K. should tell something to V.I. She was so used to sharing everything with him that sometimes, completely unintentionally and without wishing to do so, she might blurt things out.** The PB assigned Stalin to make sure that this prohibition of the doctors was not violated. And so once, **evidently**, having learned about some conversation between N.K. and V.I., Stalin called her to the telephone and in a rather sharp manner, thinking, **evidently**, that this would not reach V.I., began to instruct her that she should not discuss work with V.I. or, he said, he would take her before the Central Control Commission ...

Ulyanova does not date these events. Krupskaya said that they occurred on December 22 and 23, 1922. (LIV 674-5) This is the official version. Stalin stated that they occurred at the end of January or beginning of February, 1923. Ulyanova makes it clear

---

[3] LIV 330; CW 45, 608.

that she does not have first-hand knowledge of a phone call by Stalin to Krupskaya – she twice says "evidently" (*ochevidno*).

Ulyanova also reveals something else: that the "prohibition of the doctors" was aimed at Krupskaya especially ("more than anything else"). The fact that the December 24, 1922 prohibition was aimed mainly at controlling Krupskaya appears to mitigate Stalin's action in criticizing Krupskaya.

Ulyanova continues:

> This discussion upset N.K. exceedingly: she completely lost control of herself, she sobbed and rolled on the floor. But she told Kamenev and Zinoviev that Stalin had shouted at her on the phone and, it seems, also mentioned the Caucasus business.

Ulyanova's statement here contradicts the official version. She says that Krupskaya "also mentioned the Caucasus business." But Krupskaya said nothing about "the Caucasus business" in her December 23, 1922, letter to Kamenev. There she claimed that it was a letter to Trotsky that she had taken in dictation from Lenin that caused Stalin's "rudeness" to her.

Stalin's version, that the incident between Krupskaya and himself occurred at the end of January or beginning of February, is consistent with Ulyanova's claim that Krupskaya mentioned "the Caucasus business," which was under discussion at that time.

We do not know where Ulyanova got the notion that "the Caucasus business" played a role in Stalin's upbraiding of Krupskaya. Ulyanova makes it clear that shoe does not know this for a fact ("it seems"). Where, then, did she learn of it?

Once again, Ulyanova's version of events does not agree with Krupskaya's. Krupskaya said nothing about "losing control, sobbing, rolling on the floor." Ulyanova may well have been present to witness this. It is new information. It does reinforce Krupskaya's claim to Kamenev that she really was upset.

Chapter Eleven. Ulyanova's statements

> After a few days she told V.I. about this incident and added that she and Stalin had already reconciled. Stalin had actually called her before this and obviously tried to smooth over the negative reaction his reprimand and threat had produced on her.

These details completely contradict the official version and Krupskaya's account.

* According to the official version, Lenin wrote the "ultimatum letter" to Stalin on March 5, 1923, almost two and a half months *after* Krupskaya claimed that Stalin had been rude to her over the phone. Here, Ulyanova claims that Krupskaya told Lenin about this incident "a few days" afterwards.

* Ulyanova claims that Krupskaya told Lenin "that she and Stalin had already reconciled" and that Stalin had phoned her to "smooth over" upsetting her. If "smooth over" means "apologize for," then Stalin had already apologized by the time he received the "ultimatum letter." And if he had already apologized, that would explain why Stalin's reply to the "ultimatum letter" expresses confusion but contains no apology – he had *already* apologized.

In the first paragraph about Lenin's request to Stalin for poison Ulyanova wrote:

> Why did he appeal to St[alin] with this request? Because he knew him to be a firm, steely man devoid of any sentimentality. He had no one else but Stalin to approach with this type of request.

But later she tells a story about Stalin that contradicts the description of him that she had already given – that Stalin had no "sentimentality":

> Once in the morning Stalin invited me to V.I.'s office. He looked very upset and afflicted. "Today I did not sleep the whole night," he said to me. "Who does Il'ich think I am, how he behaves towards me! As towards some kind of traitor. But I love him with all my heart.

> Tell him this somehow." I felt sorry for Stalin. It seemed to me that he was sincerely distressed.

This is odd. First Ulyanova claimed that Lenin "had a lot of self-control" and then proceeds to give an example where Lenin did not trust his self-control. Here, having described Stalin as "devoid of any sentimentality" she relates a story in which Stalin exhibits precisely a sentimental side. ` We have no idea when this occurred or what interactions with Lenin Stalin was referring to. No other source reports it.

She then tells the story of Lenin calling Stalin "not intelligent":

> Il'ich called me for something and I told him by the way that the comrades were sending him regards. "Ah" – objected V.I. "And Stalin asked me to give you his warmest greetings, and to tell you that he loves you very much". Il'ich smiled and remained silent. "What then," I asked, "should I convey your greetings to him?" "Yes." answered Il'ich quite coldly. "But Volodia," I continued, "he is still the intelligent Stalin." "He is not at all intelligent," answered Il'ich resolutely, wrinkling his brow.

Ulyanova says that this event occurred shortly after Stalin's lament to her. It is worth noting that she says that Lenin was not in the least upset. According to Ulyanova, Lenin said these words calmly:

> But howsoever irritated Lenin was with Stalin there is one thing I can say with complete conviction. His words that Stalin was "not at all intelligent" were said by V.I. **absolutely without any irritation**. This was his opinion about him – definite and concise, that he told me.

Whatever Stalin had done to annoy Lenin and provoke this remark, it must have been a small matter if Lenin was not in the least irritated.

Then comes the story of the "ultimatum letter:"

Chapter Eleven. Ulyanova's statements

> I did not continue the discussion and a few days later V.I. came to know that Stalin had behaved rudely to N.K. and that K[amenev] and Z[inoviev] knew about it, and in the morning, very distressed, he asked for the stenographer to be sent to him, first asking whether N.K. had already left for Narkompros [People's Commissariat of Education- GF] to which he received a positive answer. When Volodicheva came V.I. dictated the following letter to Stalin...

Ulyanova describes the following sequence of events:

(1) Stalin complains to Ulyanova that Lenin is treating him badly and asks her to tell Lenin that he, Stalin, "loves him with all his [my] heart."

(2) Shortly after this Ulyanova tells Lenin "Stalin asked me to give you his warmest greetings, and to tell you that he loves you very much."

(3) Lenin says that Stalin is "not at all intelligent."

(4) "A few days later" Lenin "came to know that Stalin had behaved rudely to N.K." This must have been on March 5, 1923.

(5) "In the next morning" – that is, March 6 – Lenin dictated the "ultimatum letter."

Ulyanova then reproduces the text of the "ultimatum letter," saying that

> V.I. asked Volodicheva to send it to Stalin without telling N.K. about it and to give me a copy in a sealed envelope.

There are a number of problems with Ulyanova's account here.

When was it that, in Stalin's estimation (according to Ulyanova), Lenin had treated Stalin badly? It cannot be Lenin's purported letter to Mdivani and Makharadze, which is dated March 6, 1923, the same day as the "ultimatum letter." Likewise, the purported

Lenin letter to Trotsky about the Georgian affair is dated March 5, 1923, one day before the "ultimatum letter," so it can't be this one either.

The other documents supposedly by Lenin that contain criticisms of Stalin are the "Characteristics" and the "Addition." They are dated December 25, 1922 and January 4, 1923 respectively. However, neither Stalin nor anyone else knew about them in March – undoubtedly because, as we know now, they did not yet exist. They were not put into circulation until sometime after the XII Party Congress, which closed on April 25, 1923.

We have no evidence that Lenin had treated Stalin badly or had written anything negative about him before March 5, 1923. Of course, we would not expect Stalin to mention such an event to others. But Trotsky, Zinoviev, and Kamenev surely would have mentioned it, to use against Stalin in their various factional struggles. Yet they did not. Therefore, it appears safe to say that they were unaware of any such incident. Therefore, assuming that Ulyanova did not simply invent this incident – and she would have had no reason to do that – it must have been a very minor matter since there is no other mention of it by anyone..

Ulyanova's description of this incident – Stalin's upbraiding of Krupskaya, Lenin's learning about this, and Lenin's "ultimatum letter" to Stalin – contradicts her own account of 1926. It also contradicts Krupskaya's own version in several important ways:

* Ulyanova claims that Lenin learned about Stalin's "rudeness" to Krupskaya "a few days" after Ulyanova reported to Lenin Stalin's message that he "loves you very much" and Lenin replied that Stalin was "not at all intelligent."

* Ulyanova writes as follows:

> After returning home and seeing V.I. distressed N.K. understood that something was wrong. And she asked Volodicheva not to send the letter. She said that she would personally talk to Stalin and ask him to apologize. **That is what N.K. is saying now, but I**

Chapter Eleven. Ulyanova's statements 277

> **think that she did not see this letter** and it was sent to Stalin as V.I. had wanted. Stalin's reply was delayed somewhat, and then they decided (probably the doctors and N.K.) not to give it to V.I. as his condition had worsened. And so V.I. did not know about his reply, in which Stalin apologized.

Volodicheva's account in the Secretaries Journal does not say how Krupskaya learned about Lenin's draft letter to Stalin. Ulyanova does not tell us either. Ulyanova says that Krupskaya said that "she would personally talk to Stalin and ask him to apologize." This is not in the Secretaries Journal.

Ulyanova then says:

> That is what N.K. is saying now, but I think that she did not see this letter and it was sent to Stalin as V.I. had wanted.

Volodicheva's entry in the Secretaries Journal does not say whether Krupskaya read the letter or not. It only states that Krupskaya asked Volodicheva not to send the letter to Stalin, as a result of which it was not sent until the next day, March 7. Ulyanova states that Lenin instructed Volodicheva *not* to show the letter to Krupskaya. This important detail is missing entirely from the account in SJ.

Ulyanova says that she does not believe Krupskaya's account ("This is what N.I. is saying now, but I think ..."). Evidently, this means that Ulyanova thought that Krupskaya did not see the "ultimatum letter" at all. And *that* means that Ulyanova is accusing Krupskaya of not telling the truth. She does not trust Krupskaya's word about this important matter. We are left to wonder: How much did Ulyanova know, or suspect, about Krupskaya's falsifications?

* Ulyanova says "Stalin's reply was delayed somewhat." This directly contradicts Volodicheva's statement in the Secretaries Journal, according to which there was no delay:

> **Stalin's answer was received immediately on receipt of Vladimir Ilyich's letter** (the letter was handed to Stalin personally by me and his answer to Vladimir Ilyich dictated to me). (CW 42, 494)

The final paragraph of this undated statement by Ulyanova begins by briefly reassuring the reader that, though Lenin did personally tell her that Stalin was "not at all intelligent," he did so "absolutely without any irritation." She also repeats that Lenin personally told her this: "This was his opinion about him – definite and concise, that he told me."

> This opinion does not contradict the fact that V.I. valued Stalin as a practical worker, but he considered it absolutely essential that there should be some restraining authority over some of his manners and peculiarities, by virtue of which V.I. considered that Stalin should be removed from the post of general secretary. **He spoke about this very decisively in his political testament, in the characteristics of a number of comrades which he gave before his death and which thus did not reach the party.** But about this some other time.

First-hand and Second-hand Knowledge

Ulyanova's direct reference to the "political testament" and the "characteristics" in her last paragraph reveals that she claimed no independent knowledge of any desire by Lenin to remove Stalin as Gensec. Rather, she has taken this version of events from these documents. Ulyanova's direct quotation of the text of the "ultimatum letter" shows that it too is taken from the "political testament."

Nor does she claim personal knowledge of Krupskaya's telling Volodicheva not to send the "ultimatum letter" to Stalin on March 6; that she would personally ask Stalin to apologize; that Stalin's reply was "delayed somewhat" – Volodicheva wrote in the Secretaries Journal that this is incorrect – and that the doctors and

Chapter Eleven. Ulyanova's statements

Krupskaya "probably" decided not to give Stalin's reply to Lenin. We know this because Ulyanova tells us directly: "that is what N.K. is saying now."

Other details in this statement of Ulyanova's that she is repeating at second hand are:

* Trotsky calling Lenin a "hooligan" in a Politburo meeting and Lenin's restrained response to him.

* The story about Lenin's request for money for Martov and Stalin's refusal. Ulyanova says "I was told that ..."

* Her suggestion that Lenin's letter to Shklovsky in Berlin refers somehow to Stalin. She must have heard this at second or third hand, and it was incorrect. Whoever is meant by this cryptic letter, it cannot be Stalin.

* Ulyanova's statement that Krupskaya "told Kamenev and Zinoviev that Stalin had shouted at her on the phone and, it seems, also mentioned the Caucasus business." By the phrase "it seems" Ulyanova makes it clear that she did not know any of this at first hand.

Krupskaya's own account does not mention the Caucasus issue. But this phrase is revealing anyway, since it was the monopoly of foreign trade, not the Caucasian issue, that was in the foreground in the fourth week of December, 1922, when Krupskaya claimed that Stalin had upbraided her. That is the subject of Lenin's supposed letter to Trotsky of December 21, 1922, which Krupskaya claimed was the occasion for Stalin to upbraid her.

After meeting with Rykov on December 9, 1922, and with Dzerzhinsky on December 12, 1922, Lenin did not take up the Caucasus issue again until late January, 1923. This is precisely the time period that, in his reply to Lenin's "ultimatum letter," Stalin said the incident with Krupskaya had taken place. So on this point Ulyanova's account confirms Stalin's version of events and calls Krupskaya's version into question.

* Concerning Ulyanova's reference to Lenin's supposed dissatisfaction with Stalin, Ordzhonikidze, and Dzerzhinsky, she says that Lenin's "correspondence with Trotsky regarding this matter is well known" – a reference to Lenin's supposed letter to Trotsky of March 5, 1923 (CW 45, 607; LIV, 329). She claims no first-hand knowledge of Lenin's supposed dissatisfaction.

What does Ulyanova claim to know at first-hand?

* That Lenin never had any sympathy for Trotsky.

* That she believed Lenin did not like Zinoviev.

* That Lenin sought out Stalin as the person who could be relied upon to obtain poison and give it to him when he, Lenin, asked him to.

* That during Lenin's illness Stalin visited Lenin more than others.

* That during the autumn of 1922 Lenin met frequently with Kamenev, Zinoviev, and Stalin.

* That a few days after Stalin had criticized Krupskaya for discussing politics with Lenin, Krupskaya told Lenin about this and said that she and Stalin had already reconciled.

* That Stalin had told her, in Lenin's office, that Lenin was treating him with hostility, that he, Stalin, loved Lenin "with all my heart," and asked Ulyanova to tell Lenin so.

* That she felt sorry for Stalin because of this.

* That Lenin had told her that Stalin "is not at all intelligent."

None of the fact-claims that Ulyanova says she knows *at first hand* contradicts her statement of July 26, 1926. She does *not* contradict her story about the Stalin-Krupskaya-Lenin incident that she gave in her first statement. We have reproduced it above and do so again here for the convenience of the readers:

Chapter Eleven. Ulyanova's statements

> ... he (Stalin) even scolded his family for conveying this type of information. Il'ich, who accidentally came to know about this and who was also always upset by such a strong regime of protection, in turn scolded Stalin. Stalin apologized and with this the incident was settled. It goes without saying that if Lenin had not been so seriously ill during this period, as I had indicated, then he would have reacted to the incident differently.

Stalin scolded Lenin's "family." Lenin scolded Stalin. Stalin apologized. End of incident. Lenin overreacted. This is Ulyanova's account. It sharply contradicts the official version, which is put together from Volodicheva's entries in the Secretaries Journal and Krupskaya's letter to Kamenev.

Ulyanova's account makes sense of the text of Stalin's reply to the "ultimatum letter" of March 7, 1923, which Stalin certainly believed to be genuine, i.e. from Lenin. In it Stalin agrees to "take back" what he said to Krupskaya, but insists that he does not know what the problem is, wherein he is at fault, and what is expected of him. As Sakharov notes, Stalin did *not* apologize.

Stalin says that the incident between Krupskaya and him occurred about five weeks beforehand – that is, at the end of January or beginning of February, 1923. That directly contradicts the "official" version, which is based on Krupskaya's claim and the "Letter to the Congress." In an earlier chapter we have shown that these documents are fabrications.

Ulyanova's account also makes sense of Lenin's request to Stalin, less than two weeks later, to get him poison. Lenin had obviously not "broken relations" with Stalin, as the "ultimatum letter" said that he would do unless Stalin apologized.

But Stalin had not apologized and Lenin had not seen the letter that Stalin had dictated to Volodicheva. Lenin simply acted as though he had never made this threat to break relations.

Our own study and that of Valentin Sakharov, outlined in previous chapters, have concluded that Lenin did not dictate the "ultimatum letter." If Lenin had actually dictated the "ultimatum letter" to Stalin, then surely he was entitled to have Stalin's reply read to him despite his illness.

But if Lenin did *not* dictate the "ultimatum letter," then of course Krupskaya and the secretaries who were her accomplices could not allow Lenin to see Stalin's reply. That would have exposed their falsification.

Conclusions

* Ulyanova tells a very different version of the dispute between Stalin, Krupskaya, and Lenin.

* Her version is consistent with Stalin's version as reflected in his reply to the "ultimatum letter."

* It is *not* consistent with Krupskaya's version, which is the "official" version.

* Ulyanova affirms Krupskaya's version only at second hand. She does not claim any independent knowledge of it.

* Ulyanova has a very positive attitude about Stalin.

* She tries to come up with some independent account of Lenin's being dissatisfied with Stalin, but ultimately she could not.

* Ulyanova thinks Krupskaya is not telling the truth concerning at least one important aspect of the Lenin-Stalin issue.

Why Did Ulyanova Draft This Document?

We do not know why Ulyanova composed this document. We do not have the original. The editors tell us that it is handwritten by Ulyanova herself (*avtograf*). We don't know whether there are any other drafts, notes, or corrections, or other documents in her archive that might shed light on her reasons.

Chapter Eleven. Ulyanova's statements

It is far too positive towards Stalin to have been useful to the opposition groups. For the same reason it can hardly be a forgery during the Khrushchev or Gorbachev eras.

Could Ulyanova have written it as a concession to Krupskaya? We do not know how close they were to each other, but these are the two women who were closest to Lenin. Ulyanova's statement to the Joint Plenum of July 26, 1926, must have hurt Krupskaya, since it contradicted her own story.

It appears that Krupskaya did have something to do with Ulyanova's second statement. Ulyanova wrote:

> That is what N.K. is saying now, but I think that she did not see this letter and it was sent to Stalin as V.I. had wanted.

This must mean that Krupskaya had spoken to Ulyanova concerning the circumstances of the "ultimatum letter" some time after Ulyanova's statement to the July 1926 Joint Plenum. It appears that Ulyanova did not believe Krupskaya's claim that she, Krupskaya, had asked Volodicheva not to send the letter to Stalin and that she would personally talk to Stalin and ask him to apologize. U'lianova suggests that she believes this to be false – that Kurpskaya did not see the letter. That is, Ulyanova thinks that Krupskaya did not talk to Stalin and ask him to apologize.

Ulyanova does say: "Stalin's reply was delayed somewhat." But Volodicheva's account in the Secretaries Journal say that this is not true. So who told Ulyanova this? Presumably it was Krupskaya herself. Why might Krupskaya have done this? Perhaps in order to provide an excuse for not showing Stalin's reply to Lenin?

Why might Krupskaya want such an excuse? Perhaps because she could not give Stalin's response to Lenin – because Lenin had not dictated the "ultimatum letter."

In his response, Stalin said that he had had "explanations with N.K." some weeks before. There is no reason to doubt Stalin's dating of this whole story as "about five weeks" earlier, later

January or early February, 1923. But that means that Krupskaya lied to Ulyanova when she, Krupskaya, said that she would talk to Stalin – because she and Stalin had *already* talked weeks earlier. This is similar to what Ulyanova had told the Joint Plenum in her first statement.

Ulyanova's second statement does not contradict her 1926 statement. Ulyanova affirms Krupskaya's story only as a version she knows from documents, not from first hand.

Therefore, whatever the reason was that she composed it, Ulyanova's first-hand account still contradicts Krupskaya's "official" version while being consistent with Stalin's account in his reply to the "ultimatum letter." That is, Ulyanova's account is consistent with our contention that Krupskaya's account is yet another of her falsehoods.

* * * * *

Ulyanova's second statement was not published or – as far as we can tell – given to anyone else. Although we would like to know more about why Ulyanova came to write it, we can understand why she never did anything with it. Sakharov writes:

> Он предположительно был создан в конце 20-х - начале 30-х годов, когда она, активно выступая в защиту Н.И. Бухарина и его сторонников, использовала «Завещание» Ленина, например, в письме в адрес апрельского (1929) объединенного Пленума ЦК и ЦКК ВКП(б), чтобы оказать политическую поддержку лидерам «правого уклона»[35] (80)

> It was presumably created in the late 20s - early 30s, when she, actively speaking in defense of N.I. Bukharin and his supporters, used Lenin's "Testament," for example in a letter to the April (1929) joint Plenum of the Central Committee and Central Control Commission of the All-Union Communist Party (Bolsheviks) to provide political

Chapter Eleven. Ulyanova's statements 285

support to the leaders of the "right deviation"[35] (Sakharov's footnote is to an archival document.)

The full transcript of the April Joint Plenum has not been published, but Ulyanova's letter to the Plenum was published in Izv TsK KPSS 1 (1989), 126-127.[4] In it she does refer to the "Lenin testament" but says nothing about the Krupskaya-Stalin-Lenin issue, the "Letter to the Congress," or Lenin's supposed desire to remove Stalin as Gensec.

Ulyanova does state that she had missed attending the Joint Plenum due to illness. It's possible that her second statement was a draft that she was considering for presentation there. Or perhaps she wrote it at the request of Bukharin, who along with Stalin had urged her to write her first statement.

It would not have pleased Krupskaya, because Ulyanova suggests that Krupskaya did not tell the truth, and because her own account in her first statement contradicts Krupskaya's version. Ulyanova closes her second statement by affirming Krupskaya's version, but she does not resolve the contradiction between it and her own.

The document is far too positive towards Stalin to serve the purposes of the demonizers of Stalin like Khrushchev and Gorbachev, or to help the opposition groups of the '20s and '30s, all of which were strongly anti-Stalin. It is far too negative towards Trotsky to have been of any use to the Trotskyists. In repeating the "official" or Krupskaya version of the "testament" it is *less* positive about Stalin than her first statement, so Stalin and his supporters would have had no reason to like it. Because it affirms two contradictory versions of the supposed argument between Stalin, Krupskaya, and Lenin, it would not even have served the purpose of self-clarification.

---

[4] See the Appendix to this chapter for Ul'ianova's letter.

Chapter 12. Krupskaya

We now have a great deal of evidence that Krupskaya was conducting some kind of conspiracy against Stalin by creating false documents and then christening them the "testament of Lenin."

* The falsification of the article "How Should We Reorganize the Workers and Peasants Inspection" came out of Lenin's secretariat. Lenin's secretaries would not have dared do this by themselves. Krupskaya had to be a party to it. It was almost certainly, therefore, done by Krupskaya herself or at her direction.

*Krupskaya predated her quarrel with Stalin. No one but she claims that this incident occurred on or about December 22, 1922. All other accounts date it to about five weeks later.

* In her letter to Kamenev dated December 23, 1922, Krupskaya claims that Stalin was upset by her writing down at Lenin's dictation a letter to Trotsky dated December 21, 1922. Our analysis of the subject matter and signatures of this letter argue that it is a forgery. Krupskaya must have forged it in an effort to justify the letter to Kamenev complaining about Stalin's "rudeness" to her.

It was "leaked" to and published in the Menshevik paper *Sotsialisticheskii Vestnik* in 1923. (387) Either Krupskaya smuggled this letter to the Mensheviks abroad, or she gave it to someone who did so. This leak could serve only the opposition, of which Trotsky was the leading figure, and which Krupskaya herself supported during the first half of the 1920s.

Chapter Twelve. Krupskaya

* According to Trotsky, Krupskaya was in a conspiracy with the Georgian leaders.

> Через Крупскую Ленин вступил с вождями грузинской оппозиции (Мдивани, Махарадзе и др.) в негласную связь против фракции Сталина, Орджоникдзе и Дзержинского.[1]

> Through Krupskaya, Lenin entered into a secret relationship with the leaders of the Georgian opposition (Mdivani, Makharadze, etc.) against the faction of Stalin, Ordzhonikidze and Dzerzhinsky.

* For this and other reasons it is reasonable to conclude that it was probably Krupskaya who composed the letter to Mdivani and Makharadze on March 7 or 8, predating it to March 6.

Trotsky must have been a party to this conspiracy too. Aside from Krupskaya and the secretaries, he was the first person to be given a copy of "The Question of Nationalities or 'Autonomization'."

* Krupskaya probably wrote "The Question of Nationalities ...", perhaps with the help of the ousted Georgian party leaders and perhaps with that of other oppositionists as well. In any case, this document could not have come out of Lenin's secretariat without Krupskaya being a party to it.

> Trotsky might also have been complicit by this point. Controversy ensued over his claim that he had received Lenin's "Notes on the Question of Nationalities" before the Central Committee had—and,

---

[1] Trotsky, *Portrety revoliutsionerov*. Ed. Fel'shtinsky, M. 1991. At http://lib.ru/TROCKIJ/Trotsky.PortretyRev.txt (Also at https://www.gumer.info/bibliotek_Buks/History/trozk/04.php)

supposedly, before Lenin's third stroke—but had inexplicably held on to them. Lenin's purported dictation happened to dovetail with views Trotsky published in *Pravda* (March 20, 1923). Even more telling, Lenin's secretaries had kept working on the counterdossier on Georgia, for a report by Lenin to a future Party Congress, even after he had his third massive stroke and permanently lost his ability to speak ... In fact, their counter-Dzierzynski Commission dossier reads like a first draft of the "Notes on the Question of Nationalities." (Kotkin 494)

On the basis of his study of the documents (still in an archive), Sakharov that the "counter-Dzerzhinsky" report of the "commission" of Gorbunov – Fotieva – Glyasser looks like a draft of "The Question of Nationalities or 'Autonomization'". We know that Gorbunov did little or no work on the "commission," so it was done by its other two members, Fotieva and Glyasser They were both members of Lenin's secretariat. They would not have acted without Krupskaya's guidance and instructions. Krupskaya herself probably had a hand in writing the report.

* Krupskaya released the "Letter to the Congress" (L2C) after the XII Party Congress. We know Krupskaya was lying and that this document is a fabrication. Part I, the document dated December 23, 1922, is not a "letter to the congress." It is a letter to an individual, almost certainly to Stalin, so it could be a letter *for* – in preparation for – a congress. Trotsky's copy has no title. Later Krupskaya added the various parts, including "Characteristics," and "Addition" and added the title.

* Krupskaya also lied in claiming that Lenin's wish was to have it released after his death. She gave it to Zinoviev while Lenin though incapacitated was still alive. Krupskaya

Chapter Twelve. Krupskaya

changed her story as she went along in order to lend Lenin's authority to the L2C.

* Krupskaya either wrote or was a party to the composition of "Characteristics." As Sakharov has argued from its textual problems, this document seems to have been first intended for discussion within some opposition faction. When Krupskaya introduced it, sometime in late May or early June, 1923, the first part and the "Addition" were not yet attached to it

> It is important to note that at that time neither Krupskaya, nor any of the members of the Politburo of the Central Committee and the Presidium of the Central Committee of the RCP(b) regarded "Characteristics," which she had submitted, as a "letter to the congress" or as an appeal to the Politburo of the Central Committee or Central Committee of the RCP(b).[2]

Zinoviev and Bukharin received copies of the "Addition" – at that time evidently known as "Il'ich's letter about the secretary" (at least that is how Stalin referred to it) – sometime before July 10, 1923. By May, 1924, the Addition," though not Part I, has been included in the L2C.

* Krupskaya smuggled the "testament," via some member of the opposition, to anti-Stalin oppositionist and later vehemently anticommunist publisher Boris Souvarine in Paris. Souvarine then gave it to Max Eastman, who got it published in the *New York Times*.

> According to Eastman's own account, the text published in 1926 "was copied from the original

---

Sakharov, Na Rasput'e, page 150 in print edition; page 99 in the digital (pdf) edition.

retained by Krupskaya herself when she turned the document over to the party, and was brought to France by an emissary of the opposition and delivered to Boris Souvarine."[3]

In 1956, in a letter to Trotsky biographer Isaac Deutscher, Eastman revealed the details of the clandestine smuggling of the "testament."

> Earlier in the year an emissary of the Opposition had indeed brought the text of Lenin's will to Paris and handed it to Souvarine who prompted Eastman to publish it. 'I think it was not only Souvarine's decision,' Eastman writes, 'but the idea of the Opposition as a whole that I should be the one to publish it, one reason being that I had already got much publicity as a friend of Trotsky, another that a good many consciences in Moscow were troubled by Trotsky's disavowal of my book.'[4,5]

* In July 1925 Krupskaya wrote her letter to the "Sunday Worker," also published in *Bol'shevik*. In it she repudiated Max Eastman's book *Since Lenin Died* and the whole idea of the "testament" of Lenin. Trotsky also published his repudiation of Eastman's book in the same issue.

Kotkin notes:

---

[3] Carr and Davies, *Foundations of a Planned Economy, II*: 16, n2

[4] Isaac Deutscher, *Trotsky: The Prophet Unarmed* (London and New York: Oxford University Press, 1959) 247, and see n. 19, p. 419: "Quoted from Eastman's letter to the author."

[5] See also Christoph Irmscher, *Max Eastman: A Life*. New Haven: Yale University Press, 2017, 391, n. 117: "Lenin Testament at Last Revealed," *New York Times*, October 18, 1926; see also ME to EE, October 9, 1926, EEM; ME to Trotsky's biographer Isaac Deutscher, April 20, 1956, EM." EM = Eastman Mss., Lily Library, Indiana University Bloomington

Chapter Twelve. Krupskaya

Her repudiation raised the question of whether she had been involved in the Eastman incident, and was perhaps linked to Trotsky.[6]

Yet in July 1926, speaking to the joint plenum of the Central Committee and the Central Control Commission, Krupskaya said:

> «То, что называется "завещанием" Владимира Ильича, Ильич хотел, чтобы было доведено до сведения партии. В какой форме доведено, я с ним не говорила... Так как первая статья была озаглавлена "Съезду партии" (судя по тексту, имеется в виду статья "Как нам реорганизовать Рабкрин", имевшая подзаголовок «Предложение XII съезду партии». – В.С.), то я сочла необходимым обратиться к Центральному Комитету, чтобы Центральный Комитет нашёл форму доведения до сведения партии тех статей (статей! Это и о «характеристиках». – В.С.), которые носят название «завещания»

> What is called the "testament" of Vladimir Ilyich, Ilyich wanted it to be brought to the attention of the party. In what form it was to be communicated, I did not speak to him about that ... Since the first article was entitled "To the Party Congress,"[7] I considered it necessary to appeal to the Central Committee so that the Central Committee could find a form to bring to the attention of the party **those articles that bear the title "the testament**." (Sakharov, Na Rasput'e 165 n.33; 108 n.33)

This, of course, is a lie. No collection of articles bore the title "the testament." This title was invented either by Krupskaya

---

[6] Kotkin, note 282 to page 573.
[7] Sakharov suggests that this is the article "How Shall We Reorganize the W/P.I.?"

herself or by the opposition that she supported. We should also note Krupskaya's carelessness – or perhaps temerity – in using the term "testament" in July, 1926, when just a year before she had publicly denied in her article in *Bol'shevik* that Lenin left any testament.

In the same document Krupskaya tried to limit the damage done by a letter of hers to Trotsky. Apparently it was the following letter:

> 29 января 1924 г.
>
> Дорогой Лев Давыдович,
>
> Я пишу, чтобы рассказать Вам, что приблизительно за месяц до смерти, просматривая Вашу книжку, Владимир Ильич остановился на том месте, где Вы даете характеристику Маркса и Ленина, и просил меня перечесть это место, слушал очень внимательно, потом еще раз просматривал сам.
>
> И еще вот что хочу сказать: то отношение, которое сложилось у В.И. к Вам тогда, когда Вы приехали к нам в Лондон из Сибири, не изменилось у него до самой смерти.
>
> Я желаю Вам, Лев Давыдович, сил и здоровья и крепко обнимаю.[8]
>
> January 29, 1924
>
> Dear Lev Davydovich,
>
> I am writing to tell you that about a month before his death, looking through your book, Vladimir Ilyich

---

[8] *Kommunisticheskaia oppozitsiia v SSSR 1923 – 1927. t.1* p. 54 of 168 (online text edition), p. 89 of the print edition (Moscow: Terra, 1990)

stopped at the place where you characterize Marx and Lenin, and asked me to reread this passage, listened very attentively, and then looked it over himself.

And one more thing I want to say: the attitude that V.I. to you when you came to us in London from Siberia, it did not change with him until his death.

I wish you, Lev Davydovich, strength and health and hug you tightly.

Was this even possible? A month before Lenin's death would be December, 1923. According to all accounts Lenin had lost the power of speech in March, 1923. It is certain that he dictated nothing after March 7, 1923, at the latest. It is doubtful that he could have expressed anything at all.

Dmitri Volkogonov quotes from some of the bulletins on Lenin's health issued on March 14 and March 17, 1923. According to these bulletins Lenin did retain at least some of the ability to speak after his attack on March 10, 1923:

"Бюллетень №1

О состоянии здоровья Влцимира Ильича.

Затруднение речи, слабость правой руки и правой ноги в том же положении. Общее состояние здоровья лучше, температура 37,0, пульс 90 в минуту, ровный и хорошего наполнения.

14 марта, 2 часа дня 1923 г. Проф. Минковски, проф. Ферстер, проф. Крамер, прив. доцент Кожевников, наркомздрав Семашко".

"Бюллетень No 6

Вместе с продолжающимся улучшением со стороны речи и движений правой руки наступило

> заметное улучшение и в движениях правой ноги. Общее состояние здоровья продолжает быть хорошим. 17 марта, 1 час дня 1923 года"[9]

> From the published bulletins, it was impossible to guess Lenin's real condition. On 14 March 1923 **it was reported that he was having difficulty speaking** and moving his right arm and leg, but also that 'his general health is improved, his temperature is 37.0, his pulse 90, steady and full'. On 17 March, 'along with the continuing improvement in speech function and movement of the right arm, there is a noticeable improvement in the movement of the right leg. His general health continues to be good.'[10]

But Lenin dictated nothing after March 7, and perhaps after March 4, as Volodicheva told Alexander Bek. So it is doubted that he could utter more than a word or two – if that. It appears that the Party leadership did not wish to reveal to the world that Lenin had lost the power of speech. But whatever the case, this letter demonstrates that Krupskaya was very well disposed towards Trotsky before and at least up to the time of Lenin's death.

In her letter to the 'Sunday Worker' Krupskaya tried to mitigate the extent to which this letter suggested that Trotsky was close to Lenin.

> In the face of the confidence that the working class displayed in their party and its Central Committee at a difficult moment, the old Bolsheviks doubly felt the responsibility that fell upon them after Lenin's death.

---

[9] Dmitri Volkogonov. *Lenin. Kniga II. Vozhdi.* Moscow: Novosti, 1998, 348.
[10] *Lenin. A New Biography.* NY and London: The Free Press, 1994, p. 329 of 403 of the digital edition. The English edition is abbreviated in places.

Everyone felt somehow even more united, ready to carry out his work to the end.

Under the influence of such a mood, I then wrote a personal letter to Trotsky, who at that time was not in Moscow. This letter, however, can in no way be interpreted as M. Eastman interprets it. Vladimir Ilyich considered Comrade Trotsky as a talented worker, devoted to the cause of the revolution, to the cause of the working class, who could be very useful for the party. This is how V.I. appraised Trotsky in the first days of their meeting in 1902, and this is how he appraised him in the most recent period. Such an assessment carries responsibility. I was thinking about it when I wrote to Comrade Trotsky. The letter was written not to M. Eastman, but to Trotsky. Trotsky, of course, could not deduce from it the conclusion that V.I. considered him his deputy or thought that Comrade Trotsky understands his views most correctly. I couldn't write anything like that. In the same way, I did not write that V.I. was always in solidarity with Comrade Trotsky. Every member of the RCP (b) knows that until 1917 Trotsky was not a Bolshevik, that the party and V.I. often disagreed with him on the most fundamental issues, that V.I. more than once sharply spoke out against Trotsky, that even after Trotsky entered the ranks of the party, V. I. had disagreements with him. Comrade Trotsky now knows exactly how Lenin treated him when he met in 1902, from Lenin's letter about him to Plekhanov,[11] published in *Leninskii sbornik III*, and how Lenin treated him recently, from Lenin's letters to the party congress.[12]

---

[11] This seems to be Lenin's letter to Plekhanov of March 2, 1903, in which Lenin recommends "Pero" ("the pen", i.e. Trotsky) to the editorial board of *Iskra*. If it is this letter, it was first published in *Leninskii sbornik IV*.

[12] "N. Krupskaya: to the editorial office of the Sunday Worker." *Bolshevik* 16

* In the light of her prior actions we should suspect that Krupskaya also wrote the "ultimatum letter." This letter puzzled Stalin, who expressed his frustration and refused to apologize for whatever it was he had said to Krupskaya. Ten days after it was supposedly written, Lenin managed somehow to ask Stalin for poison – or, at least, Krupskaya told Stalin that Lenin had done so. In this tense situation all of them – Lenin, Stalin, and Krupskaya – acted as though the "ultimatum letter" did not exist.

* Krupskaya did not allow Lenin to see Stalin's reply. Why? The excuse was that Lenin "had fallen ill." (CW 42, 494; XLV 486) But this carries the implication that it would be shown to him once he was better. In fact, Lenin lived for more than 10 more months. Whether Lenin could speak or not, he could read and be read to. Yet as far as we know Stalin's reply was *never* shown to him.

Why not? If Lenin had really dictated the "ultimatum letter" he would have been anxious to receive Stalin's reply to it. But if Lenin had *not* dictated the "ultimatum letter" Krupskaya could not have allowed him to see or hear Stalin's response.

Stalin and Krupskaya

Molotov – and perhaps Stalin, to whom Molotov was very close – linked Krupskaya to Trotsky, and then to other oppositionists like Zinoviev.

> Она становится соратником Троцкого, переходит на троцкистские рельсы ... После смерти Ленина она некоторое время фактически выступала против Ленина [13]...

(1925) pp. 71-73 (my translation – GF)
[13] Feliks Chuev. *Molotov. Poluderzhavniy Vlastelin.* Moscow: Olma-Press, 2000,

Chapter Twelve. Krupskaya

Krupskaya was becoming Trotsky's comrade-in-arms; she was switching to Trotskyist rails ... For some time after Lenin's death she in fact opposed Lenin.[14]

Stalin distrusted Krupskaya for her political waverings towards the opposition. On September 16, 1926, he wrote the following in a letter to Molotov:

> 5) Переговоры с Крупской не только не уместны теперь, но и политически вредны. Крупская — раскольница (см. ее речь о «Стокгольме» на XIV съезде). Ее и надо бить, как раскольницу, если хотим сохранить единство партии. Нельзя строить в одно и то же время две, противоположные установки, и на борьбу с раскольниками, и на мир с ними. Это не диалектика, а бессмыслица и беспомощность. Не исключено, что завтра Зиновьев выступит с заявлением о «беспринципности» Молотова и Бухарина, о том, что Молотов и Бухарин «предлагали» Зиновьеву (через Крупскую) «блок», а он, Зиновьев, «с негодованием отверг это недопустимое заигрывание» и пр. и пр.[15]

> 5) Negotiations with Krupskaia are not only ill timed now, they are politically harmful. Krupskaia is a splitter (see her speech about "Stockholm" at the XIV Congress). She has to be beaten, as a splitter, if we want to preserve the unity of the party. We cannot have two contradictory lines, fighting splitters and making peace with them. That's not dialectics, that's nonsense and helplessness. It's possible that

---

270. Hereafter "PV".
[14] *Molotov Remembers. Conversations with Felix Chuev.* Chicago: Dee, 1993, 132. Hereafter "MR".
[15] *Pis'ma I.V. Stalina V.M. Molotovu. 1925-1938 gg. Sbornik dokumentov.* M. "Rossia Molodaia, 1995, p. 90.

tomorrow Zinoviev will come out with a statement on Molotov's and Bukharin's "lack of principle," [saying] that Molotov and Bukharin "offered" Zinoviev (through Krupskaia) a "bloc" and that he, Zinoviev, "rejected this intolerable flirtation with disdain," and so forth and so on.[16]

We do not know of any other statement by Stalin himself about Krupskaya during this period of time. Perhaps we can learn a little more by examining some of Molotov's statements to Felix Chuev.

> ... Я к Крупской относился, в общем, положительно, более или менее - личные отношения. А Сталин косился.
>
> - У него были основания. На XIV съезде партии она неважно себя показала.
>
> - Очень плохо. Она оказалась плохой коммунисткой,ни черта не понимала, что делала. (PV 271)

> ... My attitude toward Krupskaya was more or less positive in our personal relations. But Stalin regarded her unfavorably.
>
> He had reasons. She made a poor showing at the XIVth Party Congress. Very bad. She turned out to be a bad communist. She didn't understand what she was doing at all. (MR 132).

> - В чем все-таки причина конфликта Сталина и Крупской?

---

[16] Stalin to Molotov Sept. 16, 1926. *Stalin's Letters to Molotov 1925-1936*, ed. Lars Lih, Oleg Naumov, Oleg V. Khlevniuk. New Haven: Yale University, Press, 1995, p. 127.

> - Крупская же плохо вела себя после смерти Ленина. Она поддерживала Зиновьева. Явно путаную линию Зиновьева. Да не только она. Были члены Политбюро, которые путались в этом вопросе. Фактически отходили от Ленина. Хотя думали, что это и есть Ленин. (PV 274)

Anyway, what caused the conflict between Stalin and Krupskaya?

> Krupskaya acted badly after Lenin's death. She supported Zinoviev and obviously was confused by Zinoviev's line. (MR 133)

Stalin Suspected Krupskaya Was Behind the "Testament of Lenin"

According to Molotov Stalin suspected that Krupskaya was behind the attacks on him in some of the documents of "Lenin's testament."

> Крупская была обижена очень на Сталина. Но и он на Крупскую был обижен, потому что подпись Ленина под завещанием под влиянием Крупской. Да, так считал. В какой-то мере, может быть, да. [17]

> Krupskaya had a big grudge against Stalin. But he had a grudge against her, too, because Lenin's signature to his testament was supposedly affixed under Krupskaya's influence. Yes, he thought that. To some extent, perhaps – yes.[18] (MR 135)

---

[17] *Molotov. Poluderzhavniy Vlastelin.* 274.
[18] *Molotov Remembers*, 135. The English translation the last two sentences as "Or so Stalin believed. Perhaps it's true to some extent."

In fact Lenin did not sign *any* of the documents in the "testament." Lenin never even verbally acknowledged any of the documents that have an anti-Stalin orientation. Molotov had either forgotten or possibly never knew these facts.

If Stalin had asked to see the original documents he would have discovered that there *were no* "originals," and no Lenin signatures on the "copies" either. Stalin could also have learned the contents of the Secretaries Journal, either at first hand or from his wife Nadezhda, who as we have seen was a member of Lenin's secretariat. Nadya must have sensed among the other secretaries and Krupskaya the hostility towards her husband and friendlier attitude towards Trotsky. She must have informed Stalin.

Stalin was correct to suspect Krupskaya was behind the hostile remarks about him in the "testament." Thanks to the research of Valentin Sakharov, we have the evidence today.

Chapter 13. Conclusion

All of the evidence points unequivocally to the conclusion that there was, and is, no such thing as "Lenin's testament."

Lenin did not leave any "testament." Lenin was not the author of those articles dated between December 1922 and March 1923 that are critical of Stalin. Those articles, which we have examined in detail in the present book, were written by Nadezhda Krupskaya, probably with the help of other persons including Leon Trotsky.

These documents are evidence of a clandestine conspiracy among prominent Bolsheviks who would later openly form opposition groups within the party, and later still would renounce opposition but continue their secret conspiracies against Stalin and the Bolshevik leadership. Some of these people were already in secret oppositional conspiracies before Lenin's death. At the time the false "Lenin testament" documents were composed this secret group included Krupskaya, Trotsky, and some of Trotsky's followers. We know that Trotsky was already leading a secret opposition conspiracy by 1921.[1]

There is no evidence that Lenin knew anything about the anti-Stalin documents. Lenin never mentioned removing Stalin from the post of Gensec after January 5, 1923, the date of the "Addition" document that calls for Stalin to be removed. Lenin asked Stalin for poison repeatedly, most

---

[1] At the Third Moscow Trial of March 1928 defendants Krestinsky and Sharangovich testified that Trotsky's conspiracy had begun as early as 1921. For the evidence that the defendants' confession statements are accurate see Furr, *Trotsky's 'Amalgams'* and Furr, *The Moscow Trials As Evidence*.

significantly in March, 1923. Stalin's reply to Lenin's purported letter of March 7, 1923, threatening to cut off relations, was never shown to Lenin.

It appears that Krupskaya had decided to conspire against Stalin by the end of December 1922. The document dated December 23, 1922, attributed to Lenin and much later said to be the first document of the "Letter to the Congress" was clearly addressed to an individual. The handwritten version is addressed to Stalin. In 1963 Volodicheva claimed that Fotieva told her to show this letter to Stalin. It appears, therefore, that no steps in the conspiracy had been taken as of December 23, 1923.

On December 29, 1922, Fotieva wrote to Kamenev claiming that Lenin wanted the December 23 letter to be kept secret and not given to anyone until after his death. (As we have seen, Krupskaya gave this document to others well before Lenin died.) We have examined the problems of this document in Chapter 2. On the surface, this letter makes no sense. There is no reason that the contents of the letter should have been secret. But it does make sense if it was the first act of the plan to concoct anti-Stalin materials and attribute them to Lenin. This plan unfolded swiftly during the last months of Lenin's life.

The anti-Stalin documents in the "Lenin testament" did not accomplish what the oppositionists wanted. Stalin was not voted out of the position of General Secretary. On the contrary, Stalin was able to point out that although the "testament" called him, Stalin, "rude", it imputed errors of principle to all the other Bolsheviks mentioned in it.

After Stalin's victory over the oppositionists at the XV Party Congress in December 1927, the "testament" was never mentioned again in Party Congresses or Conferences until

Khrushchev's day. All of the oppositionists who had been expelled from the Party for factional activity, including all of the prominent ones, who applied for readmission were indeed readmitted. The last time "Lenin's testament" was used against Stalin is in the so-called "Riutin Platform" of the united opposition groups in 1932.[2]

Khrushchev, Gorbachev, and Beyond

The "Lenin testament" was resurrected by Nikita Khrushchev. Early in his "Secret Speech" to the XX Party Congress of the CPSU on February 25, 1956, Khrushchev invoked the "testament" and quoted liberally from the supposed Lenin document of December 24, 1923: the "Addition" dated January 4, 1923, Krupskaya's letter to Kamenev with the inserted date of December 23, 1922, and the "ultimatum letter" to Stalin dated March 5, 1923.

There followed, during Khrushchev's tenure as First Secretary of the CPSU and for some time after that, the omissions and changes in the texts of the "testament" documents in the fifth Russian edition of Lenin's works, the PSS, and in the fourth English edition, the Collected Works. The PSS was tendentiously edited to support anti-Stalin fabrications, to insert dates, delete sections of documents, and make other changes without documentary legitimation and without acknowledging these changes to its readers.

Official anti-Stalinism was reduced during the Brezhnev period, although there was no acknowledgment, let alone correction, of the falsifications of the Khrushchev era. On March 11, 1985, Mikhail S. Gorbachev became General

---

[2] The "Riutin Platform" was actually composed by the leaders of the clandestine Rightist conspiracy Bukharin, Rykov, Tomsky, and Uglanov. See Furr, *Trotsky's 'Amalgams'*, Chapter 15, and Furr, *Trotsky's Lies*, Chapter 4.

Secretary of the CPSU. Within about a year Gorbachev launched an attack on Stalin with an avalanche of falsifications equaling or even surpassing that under Khrushchev.

Gorbachev's evident motive was to discredit centralized planning of the economy and the collectivist initiatives of the Stalin period in order to "rehabilitate" market mechanisms by describing them as a return to the New Economic Policy endorsed by Lenin and the Party in 1921, which had been virtually, though not explicitly, abandoned in 1928 during the period of Stalin's leadership.

During Gorbachev's tenure an enormous number of books and articles were published in which Stalin and his associates were accused of a great many crimes. This torrent of accusations in print continued after the end of the Soviet Union in December 1991, and continues to this day.

The Soviet Archives

After the end of the Soviet Union documents from former Soviet archives began to be published. This process of opening archives to researchers and publishing archival documents in articles, books, and important document compilations, has accelerated over time. This primary source material provides evidence that disproves the version of Soviet history of the Stalin period that has been canonical since Khrushchev's time.

Valentin A. Sakharov's research in the Lenin archives is a striking example of this. His work, on which the present book is based, confirms that since Khrushchev's day Soviet history, including many crucial events of the Stalin period, has been based on lies and fabrications.

Chapter Thirteen. Conclusion

The most immediate result of exposing the "Lenin testament" and the anti-Stalin documents as fabrications is that it dismantles the Trotsky cult. Trotsky's claim to be Lenin's choice to succeed him as Party leader has always been based on the anti-Stalin documents purportedly dictated by Lenin and included in the "testament."

Documents from former Soviet archives have already made it possible to prove the validity of the accusations against Trotsky leveled by the Soviet prosecution during the Moscow Trials. These include conspiracy to assassinate Soviet leaders, collaboration with the Nazis and the Japanese fascists, and working with his Soviet-based followers to sabotage the Soviet economy in collusion with Nazi agents and Soviet fascists – to name just the most prominent of Trotsky's conspiracies.

Along with the fact, now established, that the "Lenin testament" documents are also fabrications, these crimes – for which we now have good, primary-source evidence – will in the long run doom the Trotsky cult. We can hardly expect that Trotsky cultists will accept the evidence and abandon their allegiance to their perfidious guru. However, many others will be open to an objective assessment of the evidence and will draw the inevitable conclusion.

The canonical version of Soviet history of the Stalin period has been exploded by the flood of primary-source evidence from former Soviet archives. Those researchers who are dedicated to discovering the truth about this period in all its heroism and tragedy must patiently set about studying these documents and rewriting that history on the basis of the voluminous evidence now available. The present book, along with my other works on Soviet history, represent a modest effort toward fulfilling this essential task.

Appendix: Ulyanova's letter to the Joint Plenum of the CC and the CCC, April, 1929

From Izv TsK KPSS 1, 1989, 125-6.

М. И. Ульянова в письме Пленуму ЦК и ЦКК так характеризовала создавшуюся обстановку:

«Не имея возможности присутствовать на Пленуме ЦК и ЦКК, ввиду болезни (лежу в постели уже около месяца), прошу огласить следующее мое заявление. С точки зрения дальнейшей истории партии настоящий Пленум имеет, по моему мнению, огромное значение. Вопросы о внутрипартийном положении и составе Политбюро, обсуждаемые на Пленуме, стоят в прямой связи с завещанием Владимира Ильича. Перед своей, смертью Владимир Ильич тревожился за судьбу нашей революции и в завещании, давая характеристику отдельных вождей, предупреждал партию, что не одна из личностей, а только коллегиальная работа может обеспечить правильное руководство и единство партии.

Вывод из Политбюро трех крупнейших работников партии — Рыкова, Бухарина, Томского или дальнейшая «проработка» и дискредитация их, которая приведет к тому же несколько раньше или позднее, является угрозой этому коллективному руководству. В момент, когда перед партией стоят крупнейшие задачи, разрешение которых сопряжено с большими трудностями, вывод этих товарищей из Политбюро, «проработка» их, которая не дает им возможности работать и ведется вместе с тем при отсутствии принципиальных ошибок и антипартийной работы с их стороны, противоречит тому, что завещал нам Ленин, будет по вред пролетарской революции. С подобным отсечением или дискредитацией троих членов ПБ в партии неизбежно сократятся возможности для проявления критической мысли: слишком легко всякая самокритика и критика партийных органов и должностных лиц превращается в «уклоны».

Надо помнить и о том, что говорил Владимир Ильич о возможностях раскола сверху, когда он утверждал, что сверху начатая трещина может разломать классовое основание советского строя и привести к расколу между рабочим классом и крестьянством. Величайшей заслугой партии является то, что ей удалось поднять большие массы на дело перестройки страны на социалистический лад.

Но этому подъему и энтузиазму рабочих но способствует однобокая информация, которая проводится в прессе и в докладах. За последнее время получаются все более тревожные письма, свидетельствующие о больших колебаниях в деревне (в связи с чрезвычайными мерами, голодом в потребляющих губерниях, нарушением революционной законности) и известных колебаниях в городе (в связи с обостряющимся продовольственным положением).

Я считаю заслугой т.т. Рыкова, Томского и Бухарина, что они ставят перед партией эти большие вопросы, а не замалчивают их. Я считаю, что иная точка зрения, точка зрения, замалчивающая или затушевывающая трудности и опасности, а также чрезмерные восторги перед достижениями будут проявлением ограниченного самодовольства и комчванства. Поэтому, протестуя против самой постановки вопроса о выводе троих товарищей из Политбюро и против недопустимой и вредной для партии дискредитации их, я прошу довести до сведения Пленума, что я голосую против вывода этих троих товарищей или кого- либо из них порознь из Политбюро, против их осуждения и дискредитации. С ком. приветом М. Ульянова 22.IV-29 г.»1

Translation:

M.I. Ulyanova, in a letter to the Plenum of the Central Committee and the Central Control Commission, described the situation as follows:

"Not being able to attend the Plenum of the Central Committee and the Central Control Commission, due to illness (I have been in bed for about a month), I ask you to read out the attached statement of mine. From the point of view of the further history of the party, this Plenum is, in my opinion, of great importance. Questions about the internal party position and the composition of the Politburo, discussed at the Plenum, have a direct connection with the testament of Vladimir Ilyich. Before his death, Vladimir Ilyich was worried about the fate of our revolution and in his testament, giving a characterization of individual leaders, he warned the party that no individual person, but only collegial work, can ensure the correct leadership and unity of the party.

The withdrawal from the Politburo of three important party workers - Rykov, Bukharin, Tomsky, or their further "working over" and discreditation, which will lead to the same a little earlier or later, is a threat to this collective leadership. At a time when the party is faced with major tasks, the solution of which is fraught with great difficulties, the withdrawal of these comrades from the Politburo, a "working over" of them, which does not give them the opportunity to work and is carried out at the same time in the absence of fundamental mistakes and anti-party work on their part, contradicts what Lenin bequeathed to us, will harm the proletarian revolution. With such a cutting-off or discreditation of three PB members in the party, the opportunities for the manifestation of critical thought will inevitably be reduced. Any self-criticism and criticism of party bodies and officials are turned too easily into "deviations."

We must also remember what Vladimir Ilyich said about the possibility of a split from above, when he argued that a split started from above could break the class foundation of the Soviet system and lead to a split between the working class and the peasantry. The greatest merit of the Party is that it succeeded in rousing large masses to the cause of restructuring the country on a socialist basis.

But this upsurge and enthusiasm of workers is not promoted by the one-sided information that is carried in the press and in reports. Recently, more and more alarming letters have been received, testifying to large fluctuations in the countryside (in connection with emergency measures, famine in producing provinces, violation of revolutionary legality) and known fluctuations in the city (in connection with the aggravating food situation).

I consider it a merit of Comrades Rykov, Tomsky and Bukharin, that they pose these big questions to the Party, and do not hush them up. I believe that a different point of view, a point of view that silences or glosses over difficulties and dangers, as well as excessive enthusiasm for achievements, will be somewhat of a manifestation of self-righteousness and self-satisfaction. Therefore, protesting against the very posing of the question of the withdrawal of three comrades from the Politburo and against their discreditation as inadmissible and harmful to the party, I ask you to inform the Plenum that I vote against the withdrawal of these three comrades or any of them separately from the Politburo and against condemning and discrediting them. With com. greetings M. Ulyanov 22.IV-29

Bibliography and Illustrations

The bibliography for this book can be downloaded here:

http://msuweb.montclair.edu/~furrg/research/lentestbibl.html

I have placed reproductions of some of the important texts discussed in this book on line at this link:

https://msuwcb.montclair.edu/~furrg/lenin/lentestimages.html

Here is a list of the document reproductions:

---

1. Handwritten and typewritten versions of "Pis'mo k s"ezdu" / "Letter to the / a Congress"

Handwritten version of the letter to V.I. Lenin's "Letter to the Congress" of December 23, 1922, written by N.S. Alliluyeva, and typewritten version of this letter, which is part of the block of texts of the "Testament" that was created later than the date shown.

1a. A full view of the handwritten version of "Letter to the / a Congress."

2. "Characteristics" (dictation of December 24-25, 1922.) A sheet of the "Diary" of the secretaries on duty. The contradiction of the dates in the records is visible. A fragment of the text dated "24 / Xll", when published in the Complete Works of V. I. Lenin, was included without reservation in the text dated "24 / XI", and the combined text was dated as follows: "December 24".

3. "Addition" to "Characteristics" (dictation of January 4, 1923) and a sheet of the "Diary" of the secretaries on duty with traces of later work on filling out the "Diary" (the initials ("M.V." and "L. A.") before the dates are not visible.).

3a. A fuller view of the "Addition."

4. Pages of the typewritten text of the article "How to reorganize Rabkrin", prepared for reading by V.I. Lenin, as well as a galley sheet, in the text of which there is no indication of any danger posed by the General Secretary of the Central Committee of the RCP (b).

A fragment of the text of this article, found in 1949 during analysis of copies, on which there is a handwritten insertion indicating this danger. The author of the insertion and the time and circumstances of its insertion are unknown.

5. A sheet of the "Diary" of the secretaries on duty with a fragment of the text written by M.V. Volodicheva with stenographic marks, and the manuscript of M.V. Volodicheva with its decoding. In the Complete Works of V.I. Lenin's the note is dated inaccurately - July 14, 1956.

6. a. The letter to Mdivani, Makharadze, et al.

b. The letter to Trotsky.

c. Two variants of the letter to Stalin.

7 Letter of J.V. Stalin to V.I. Lenin dated March 7, 1923. Envelope of the Secretariat of the Central Committee of the RCP (b), in which it is believed that Stalin's letter was received, and the envelope in which it was kept in Lenin's secretariat This is the version of Stalin's reply to the "ultimatum letter" that is in Stalin's even, readable handwriting.

7a. Another version of Stalin's reply to "ultimatum letter", March 7, 1923. Three pages in Volodicheva's "scrawl." Why are there two versions?

8. Sheets of the "Diary" of the secretaries on duty with traces of editing of the text.

9. The article "On Cooperation" exists in two variants of dictated notes, the work on which was not completed.

10. Stalin's note to the Politburo of March 17, 1923 about Lenin's desire for poison, with signatures and comments from Politburo members, in handwritten and typed copies. From Volkogonov, Stalin, vol. 2.

https://msuweb.montclair.edu/~furrg/research/stalinleninpoison23.pdf

11. Genrikh Volkov, "Stenografistka Il'icha." *Soveteskaya Kul'tura*, January 21, 1989, page 3.

Index

Because they occur dozens of times I have not indexted the names of Stalin, Trotsky, and Krupskaya, except in certain crucial places.

"Addition", writing attributed to Lenin..19, 41, 64, 80, 191, 288

"Characteristics", writing attributed to Lenin19, 64, 191, 288

"Characteristics", writing attributed to Lenin".................36

"Letter to the Congress", wriiing attributed to Lenin..................19

"Letter to the Congress", writing attributed to Lenin52, 67, 84, 288

"Ultimatum Letter," letter attributed to Lenin....142, 161

Allilueva, Nadezhda S., secretary to Lenin, wife of Joseph Stalin 22

Bazhanov, Boris, Stalin secretary, defector...............159

Bek, Aleksandr, interviewed Lenin's secretaries.......91, 173

Bukharin, Nikolai, Politburo member..............28, 64, 77, 120

Deutscher, Isaac, biographer of Trotsky.................113, 225, 290

Dzerzhinsky commission..........97

Eastman, Max, American writer 20, 289

Enukidze, Avel' S., prominent Bolshevik.......................138, 220

Fotieva, Lidia A., secretary to Lenin.........25, 29, 98, 105, 114

Fotieva's Letter to Kamenev ...26

Furr, Grover C..................................2

Glyasser, Maria I., secretary to Lenin 98, 120

Glyasser's Note..........................102

Hudson, Arthur, Inter-Library Loan Librarian, Sprague Library, Montclair State University 4

Joseph V. Stalin, Bolshevik leader 114

Kabakhidze, Akakii, Georgian Bolshevik...................................109

Kamenev, Lev B., member of the Politburo 28, 76, 89, 114

Kamenev's letter to Fotieva dated April 16, 1923...........111

Index 315

Kamenev's letter to Fotieva of April 16, 1923..........................180

Kamenev's Letter to Zinoviev of March 7, 1923..........................176

Kotkin, Stephen, American historian..................................9, 98

Krupskaya, letter to Trotsky January 29, 1924....................292

Krupskaya, Nadezhda Konstantinovna, Lenin's wife 36, 63, 113, 200, 286

Krupskaya's Note to Kamenev of December 23, 1922153, 286

Kuibyshev, Valerian, Bolshevik Party official...............................39

Lenin letter to Tsintsadze and Kavtaradze. October 21, 1922 123

Lenin, "How Should We Reorganize the WPI?"............12

Lenin's Difficulty with Dictation 45

Lenin's Last Writings 6

Lenin's request to Stalin for poison 270

Lenin's Request to Stalin for Poison, March 17, 1923.....182

Letter to Mdivani and Makharidze, work attributed to Lenin...................88, 109, 192

Letter to Trotsky of March 5, 1923, work attributed to Lenin..109

Lewin, Moshe, historian of the USSR 211

Lidia Fotieva's Memoir 238

Makharadze, Fillip I., Georgian Bolshevik..........................92, 116

McCarthy, Siobhan, Inter-Library Loan Librarian, Sprague Library, Montclair State University..........................4

Mdivani, Budu (Policarp), Georgian Bolshevik 63, 92

Mikoyan, Anastas I., Bolshevik leader 128

Molotov, Vyacheslav M., prominent Bolshevik172, 296

Moshe Lewin's fabrications ..226

On the Suppressed Testament of Lenin..188

Ordzhonikidze, Sergo, Bolshevik Party official....................28, 109

Post of General Secretary, The 67

Prendergast, Kevin, Inter-Library Loan Librarian, Sprague Library, Montclair State University..........................4

Pyatakov, Georgii L., leading Bolshevik......................................78

Radek, Karl, a leading Bolshevik 64, 188, 206

Rykov, Aleksei, leading Bolshevik...........................95, 126

Sakharov, Valentin A., Russian historian 6

Sosnovsky, Lev S., prominent Bolshevik..64

Special Letter denying danger of a split, January 1927...............50

Stalin and Trotsky.........................71

Stalin's reply to Lenin, March 7, 1923..165

The Doctor's Journal 11, 105, 114, 257

The Doctors Journal.....................22

The Gensec passage 12

The Gorbunov-Fotieva-Glyasser "Commission" 10, 98, 108, 120, 181, 288

The Question of Nationalities or 'Autonomization', article attributed to Lenin 94, 114, 191

The Secretaries Journal 11, 114, 200, 247

To Trotsky, March 5, 1923, letter alleged by Lenin........191

Trotsky, Leon, member of the Politburo..28

Trotsky's racism 232

Ulyanova, Maria Ilinichna, Lenin's sister 17, 154, 173, 200, 261

Ulyanova's second statement 265

Ulyanova's first statement.....261

Volkogonov, Dmitry A., Soviet general and historian 113, 162

Volkov, Genrikh, Soviet journalist......................................25

Volodicheva, Maria A., secretary to Lenin 17, 20, 91

XII Party Congress 56

XIV Party Congress, December 18-31, 1925................................87

Zinoviev, Grigory, member of the Politburo..............................76

Libns -
1) Stalin. Waiting For Hitler, 1924-1941. (2017)

Made in United States
Orlando, FL
16 March 2025

59521963R00174